John S. Hatcher

The Body of God

A Reader's Guide

to Bahá'u'lláh's Súrih of the Temple

ABS ASSOCIATION for
BAHÁ'Í STUDIES
NORTH AMERICA

The Body of God: A Reader's Guide to Bahá'u'lláh Súrih of the Temple
/ John S. Hatcher, author

1/6/2023 *study*
Robs study
group

© 2022 by Association for Bahá'í Studies
34 Copernicus Street
Ottawa, ON
K1N 7K4 Canada
https://www.bahaistudies.ca

Cover image: Martina Misar-Tummeltshammer
Cover design, book design, and typeset: Nilufar Gordon

The Body of God

A Reader's Guide

to Bahá'u'lláh's Súrih of the Temple

For the Day of God is none other but His own Self,
Who hath appeared with the power of truth.
This is the Day that shall not be followed by night,
nor shall it be bounded by any praise,
would that ye might understand!

Bahá'u'lláh, Súriy-i-Haykal

Contents

TABLE OF ILLUSTRATIONS

Preface

Like many other new Bahá'ís, I sought to immerse myself in the primary literature of the Faith as much as possible. Around that time, I first encountered the work of John Hatcher upon reading his insightful and stimulating article, "The Metaphorical Nature of Physical Reality." The article left an indelible lesson on me, essential for any Bahá'í: no matter what you think you understand about the Bahá'í Revelation, there is always more to know, and Bahá'ís as a community are collectively engaged in this never-ending exploration. Beyond its specific content, the article was an invitation into a profound global conversation among Bahá'ís about the meaning of the Word and its implications for action.

Among the oldest and most challenging questions human beings face are those concerning issues of self, meaning, and purpose: *Who am I and what should I be doing? Who are we and what should be the relationship among ourselves?* With assuring answers to these questions, it is possible to determine how to live a life that is rich and fulfilling and contribute to a healthy and prospering society. Today, however, because we cannot satisfactorily find answers to such questions, we witness our societies struggling within a failing world order, one that, although adequate for a prior adolescent stage of human social development, is completely inadequate in relation to the needs of a world society struggling to be born. The process of the disintegration of that old order has, for more than a century, increasingly fostered a sense of rootlessness and uncertainty, to which humanity has responded with retreat into contending ideologies and social forms. Collectively, humanity does not know where to turn to determine what is true, what is right, what is good and beautiful. And this consternation has cast the peoples of the world into endless forms of contest over fundamental questions of truth and belief, identity and morality, honor and prejudice.

In response to this fundamental disorientation, Bahá'u'lláh's answer is clear. The Word of God is the true guide for human understanding and action. He states: "Blessed the man who hath sought enlightenment from the Day-Star of My Word."[1] He also explains, "O ye that dwell on earth! The distinguishing feature that marketh the preeminent character of this Supreme Revelation consisteth in that We have, on the one hand, blotted out from the pages of God's holy Book whatsoever hath been the cause of strife, of malice and mischief amongst the children of men, and have, on the other, laid down the essential prerequisites of concord, of understanding, of complete and enduring unity."[2]

Within the Word of God revealed by Bahá'u'lláh are truths about reality and human nature. But the revelation of these verities is in no way a call to fundamentalism or the surrender of choice so often mistakenly associated with the real purpose of Revelation and religion. The best parallel is, instead, the capacity of science to explore and offer insights into material reality in order to propel human progress. Exploration of the inexhaustible meaning of the Word of God provides insight into human social and spiritual reality that is essential for the progress of civilization.

The nature of truths about reality is that they are true, whether or not we understand or believe them. Like the truths of reality explicated by science, the truths brought forth from the ocean of Bahá'u'lláh's Revelation are also empirical and are to be tested and manifested through practical expression in reality and action. Countless parents worldwide, for example, witnessing the almost magical transformative effects of Bahá'u'lláh's teachings on the character and behavior of their children after participation in children's classes and junior youth groups, have reached a conviction no doubter can undermine.

As I write this, millions of people are gathering in conferences large and small, from the local to the international level, to engage in an exploration of the meaning of Bahá'u'lláh's teachings and its implications for personal and social progress. The entry for many into this process is facilitated by the network of training institutes established by Bahá'ís around the world over the past twenty-five years. While, so many years ago, the world's rulers and religious leaders largely ignored Bahá'u'lláh's appeal for the reordering and betterment of the world, today peoples of diverse nations and regions are striving to uncover essential insights from His teachings and to raise their capacity to translate them into effective action.

This work, as the Universal House of Justice has recently emphasized once more, is just the start of a generational process of individual and collective study of the Word through various means that should continually shape the lives of ever-growing numbers of people. Here it is possible to appreciate the value of John's contribution in this work— and indeed his entire body of work over a lifetime—at this propitious moment when Bahá'ís seek to release in greater measure the society-building power of Bahá'u'lláh's teachings.[3] This book is an invaluable contribution to—and for newcomers, an invitation to participation in—a global conversation that will continue for generations.

Some years ago, I likened the efforts of a learned Bahá'í to those of a scout whose understanding and foresight can offer support and assistance to the community as it advances on its long journey of transformation to the ultimate attainment of its intended destination. In this book, John fulfills that role well, offering insights into the nature of reality and the method of learning essential for translating Bahá'u'lláh's teachings into action, before guiding the reader into a deep exploration of one of the central tablets of Bahá'u'lláh. And as is the case with the best scholarship, the aim is discovery and not the imposition of meaning. Those who are veteran Bahá'ís will find many insights to complement previous conceptions and provoke new understandings for future progress, especially through the connections to existing Bahá'í efforts and contemporary challenges. For those who are new to this type of work—welcome to the conversation.

—PAUL LAMPLE

It is clear and evident to thee that all the Prophets are the Temples of the Cause of God, Who have appeared clothed in divers attire.

—Bahá'u'lláh, The Kitáb-i-Íqán

(T)he dissolution of the tabernacle wherein the soul of the Manifestation of God had chosen temporarily to abide signalized its release from the restrictions which an earthly life had, of necessity, imposed upon it. Its influence no longer circumscribed by any physical limitations, its radiance no longer beclouded by its human temple, that soul could henceforth energize the whole world to a degree unapproached at any stage in the course of its existence on this planet.

—'Abdu'l-Bahá quoted in Shoghi Effendi, *God Passes By*

Introduction

Before we begin our attempt to assess the meaning, contemporary relevance, and strategic importance of the Súriy-i-Haykal (the Súrih of the
Temple), it would be helpful for the reader to understand a few salient
points about this work. We can begin with the fact that, while the tablet
was first revealed around 1867, prior to Bahá'u'lláh's final exile to the
prison city of 'Akká in 1868, the version we will study is His final rendering of the work, completed around 1869.

One of the most obvious changes in this final version of the tablet
is its appearance—Bahá'u'lláh had the work rendered calligraphically
into the shape of a pentacle, or five-pointed star. As we will discuss,
the pentacle has various symbolic meanings in different religious and
cultural traditions, but in the context of the Bahá'í writings, it represents
the human body. This is a most fitting symbolic arrangement, given the
various levels of meaning of the word *Temple* in the work's title. On a
literal level, the Temple is a physical place of worship, a place of qui-
etude, reflection, and prayer where spiritual access to God is attained.
On a second level of meaning, the Temple—expressed symbolically by
the pentacle to represent the body of man—is the bodily edifice with
which our soul associates during the physical stage of our life's journey and, therefore, the means by which we first learn about God and
exercise that learning in action. On a third level of meaning—and the
most prominent usage of the term in this work—the Temple represents
the Holy Spirit made manifest through the physical appearance of the
Manifestation in human form, the principal means by which that Spirit
communicates with and guides humankind. At a still a more expansive
level, the Temple can be understood as physical reality itself—or, symbolically, the Body of God, since the Temple of physical reality that
gives tangible expression to Godliness is the counterpart to the spiritual
reality, the realm where the spiritual attributes and powers of God are
expressed directly and unveiled.

The second change is Bahá'u'lláh's inclusion in the tablet of five representative letters from among those He sent to secular and religious leaders, letters announcing His station as the fulfilment of Christian and Islamic eschatological prophecies about the "Day of Days," advising them about the most urgent need for them to construct a collective security pact to avoid further conflicts, and providing each of them with specific guidance about how best to fulfill the weighty tasks of governance by employing the principles of justice and through the example of their own spiritual comportment.

Regarding the five epistles chosen, Shoghi Effendi, Guardian of the Bahá'í Faith, observes, "The most important of these Tablets"—the letters to the kings and rulers proclaiming His station and mission—"together with the celebrated Súriy-i-Haykal (the Súrih of the Temple), He, moreover, ordered to be written in the shape of a pentacle, symbolizing the temple of man, and which He identified, when addressing the followers of the Gospel in one of His Tablets, with the 'Temple' mentioned by the Prophet Zechariah, and designated as '*the resplendent dawning-place of the All-Merciful*,' and which '*the hands of the power of Him Who is the Causer of Causes*' had built."[4]

The relevance of this second change is twofold. Throughout Bahá'u'lláh's four-year exile in Adrianople (1864–1868), He had begun to reveal numerous epistles to world leaders indicating that the long-awaited transformation of human polity foreshadowed in prophecies from the Old Testament, the New Testament, and the Qur'án was now at hand, and that it was His duty as God's Vicegerent to advise them how best to usher in and facilitate this radical re-ordering of the nations of the world into a single global commonwealth. In one sense, then, the inclusion of five of the most important of these epistles in the Súriy-i-Haykal represents the culmination of this declaration to the world. However, it also importantly relates to the Súrih's central theme regarding how God has delegated authority and guidance to humankind—first to the intermediary of the Manifestations of God and, subsequently, from the Manifestations to the rulers and governmental bodies of every nation, territory, and religion.

Even if we are keenly aware of this overall structure and central purpose of the work, our understanding of the Súriy-i-Haykal and how it conveys these themes will necessarily always remain incomplete, for it is an extremely abstruse work, allegorical in structure, replete with symbolic allusions, and, according to Shoghi Effendi, "one of the most challenging works of Bahá'u'lláh."[5]

In the final analysis, then, what I hope this study will provide the reader—most especially in light of current global conflicts and crises—is an appreciation of the profound relevance of Bahá'u'lláh's advice to world leaders today, who face challenges unimagined by the peoples He addressed in 1869. Indeed, so crucial is this tablet that it was among the first works that Bahá'u'lláh Himself had published and circulated. As will be seen, the reaction of the leaders to whom Bahá'u'lláh offered this guidance ranged from ambivalence to outright rejection. The masses of humanity are still suffering from the effects of this rejection today; and yet, as I will suggest in this study, those same masses are beginning to respond to the call that their leaders have yet to heed. For while the five epistles incorporated into the Súriy-i-Haykal were addressed to specific historical figures, the Súrih as a whole, as the revealed Word of God, has a far broader audience. It speaks to us today, and the themes it contains continue to inform painstaking work at the grassroots to build communities, nations, and a global commonwealth of peace and justice. It is my sincere hope that this work might contribute to inspiring those undertaking this noble enterprise.

He introduces us in a unique way

Chapter I

Some Tools Necessary for a Study of the Súriy-i-Haykal

Prior to addressing the ultimate objectives of this attempt to assay the various levels of meaning of the Súriy-i-Haykal and its crucial relevance to contemporary world affairs, it would be helpful—indeed, for those unfamiliar with Bahá'í studies, quite essential—to establish at the outset the perspective, point of view, or lens we will employ in analyzing this work. For as we will note, certain explanations from the perspective of secular materialist historical scholarship regarding some of the events we will discuss are distinct from, and even contrary to, how the Bahá'í academic might view and explain these same events. But even more important for the reader is to appreciate that, from a Bahá'í viewpoint, the unfolding of human history, together with the evolution and increasing complexity of human civilization and social systems, is driven by, and thus inseparable from, the influence and guidance derived from the spiritual realm via the successive appearance of Prophets of God, what Bahá'u'lláh refers to as "Manifestations."[6]

This does not mean that the reader is obliged to assume the Bahá'í perspective, but it does mean that the reader needs from the beginning to understand and appreciate the foundational assumptions that viewing history in general, and the unfolding of the dispensation and Writings of Bahá'u'lláh specifically, from such a perspective require and impose. Otherwise, some or most of the inferences we will draw from examining this complex work might seem farfetched or baseless. For it is only this lens that allows us to appreciate the purpose of the Súriy-i-Haykal, by revealing how the text, while making various theological assumptions, is simultaneously thoroughly grounded in a political context illuminated in some detail, both in the history that has occurred since its revelation and, perhaps more importantly, in its foreshadowing of the events that characterize our present difficulties, and posits forthrightly the solutions that constitute our sole hope for remedying contemporary challenges that threaten the very future of humankind on planet Earth.

Of course, it goes without saying that one obvious objective of our study is to come to some conclusions as to why Bahá'u'lláh felt this tablet was so important that He revised it, included in the final version a selection of five of the various letters He penned to religious and political leaders of His day, had the work arranged calligraphically into the form of a five-pointed star, and published it that it might be disseminated during His own lifetime.

SOME FOUNDATIONAL ASSUMPTIONS
INCORPORATED IN A BAHÁ'Í PERSPECTIVE

To articulate more plainly this crucial point about the necessity of understanding the Bahá'í perspective as we examine this work, let us first establish what are the most fundamental elements of the Bahá'í point of view regarding the essential nature of reality, its purpose, and how that purpose informs the Bahá'í view of secular and religious history. Of course, there is no need here to go into extensive detail about these foundational matters, which are set forth simply and clearly online and in numerous introductory books on the Bahá'í Faith and its teachings.[7]

THE RATIONALE FOR PHYSICAL CREATION

First and foremost, the Bahá'í teachings assert belief in a single deity, a God Who is beyond any complete understanding yet is aware of our existence and has devised creation precisely because He is a loving and personal Being Who desires that we should benefit from becoming aware of Him and thereby partaking of that love.[8]

Related to this view of the Creator is the Bahá'í belief that God has created a unified, organic, and coherent reality consisting of two complementary and reciprocal dimensions—the metaphysical realm and the physical realm. Therefore, according to this belief, these two dimensions are not separate existences; the primary aspect of reality is the metaphysical or spiritual dimension, whereas the physical realm is the metaphorical expression of that reality.[9] Put succinctly, each dimension is, according to 'Abdu'l-Bahá, the "exact counterpart" of the other.[10]

Essential to appreciating the divine logic underlying the need for twin expressions of reality—both of which are precisely designed for the enlightenment and progress of human souls—is understanding that the Creator's purpose in the totality of creation is to bestow His love upon a being capable of understanding this abstract relationship, freely accepting participation in that relationship, and then advancing by degrees by expressing that relationship in increasingly expansive modes of action, whether in the initial physical phase of our existence or, subsequently, in the continuation of our existence in the spiritual realm.

From this axiom derives the Bahá'í belief that we human beings learn how to initiate this journey of the soul in the spiritually endowed classroom that is physical reality. And essential to this progressive experience are the human intellectual capacity to recognize the spiritual attributes inherent in physical reality and the free will to choose to translate this knowledge into creative patterns of social action, all the while realizing and acknowledging that the source of this design for human advancement is God's unrelenting love for us. Indeed, recognition of God's love becomes our individual impetus for participation in this process, including through our reciprocation of that love. For the fact is that a relationship which is not freely chosen and bilateral cannot logically be said to be an authentic love relationship, as suggested by Bahá'u'lláh's statement that His love reaching us is contingent on our active response: "O Son of Being! Love Me, that I may love thee. If thou lovest Me not, My love can in no wise reach thee. Know this, O servant."[11]

It is in this context that the Bahá'í writings assert that the Creator has endowed the totality of physical creation with His signs and attributes, an endowment that permeates both the physical and the metaphysical realms. In this regard, Bahá'u'lláh states: "Know thou that every created thing is a sign of the revelation of God. Each, according to its capacity, is, and will ever remain, a token of the Almighty." [12] He concludes by asserting, "So pervasive and general is this revelation that nothing whatsoever in the whole universe can be discovered that doth not reflect His splendor."[13]

the necessity of our knowledge

The Essential Reality of Human Nature

The question then arises as to why, if it is the intention of the Creator that humans become spiritual beings, He has devised such an indirect process for our education. Allied to this enigma is the query as to why the inherently spiritual nature of physical reality, including the identity of the spiritual Teachers for this classroom—the Manifestations of God—is concealed or veiled.

The answer to this important concern is twofold. First, if it were easy to recognize the essentially spiritual nature of physical reality or the divinely ordained Educators God has created to manifest perfectly His nature and guide us in our progress, then not much would be required of us in striving to understand our purpose—all would be readily apparent. And as any capable teacher knows, true education occurs when the educator provides tools whereby the student is required to participate in the learning, to become curious and active in striving to learn, rather than merely being a repository of the teacher's facts and theories.

Second, there are many individuals who are trying to convince us of their beliefs about reality and to enlist us in promulgating their views, ideologies, or objectives—quite often with ulterior motives of personal aggrandizement or of attaining recognition and power over others. But for us to recognize the "intended" Teacher, the One sent by God to advance civilization itself, the One Who is selfless, self-sacrificing, and altruistic, we must become aware of how to recognize those qualities when they are manifest by that Being. This recognition requires that we know precisely what we are looking for so that we freely choose our path rather than having it imposed on us.

The Need for Educators

spiritual teachers

Another essential ingredient in the foundational Bahá'í beliefs relating to the logic behind the Creator's design for human enlightenment and progress—whether in this world or in the realms of the spirit where our lives continue after the body's death[14]—is the need for the divinely enlightened Educators who guide our spiritual progress. After all, students in the most refined and well-equipped classroom would learn little without someone who understands the subject and, furthermore, is adept at instructing the students to learn on their own, without becoming oppressive or domineering in their instruction. The purpose of the teacher in this metaphorical classroom is to show the students how to attain a degree of autonomy in their own journey toward enlightenment, although they will always have access to further assistance.

These divinely ordained teachers, Bahá'ís believe, are the Prophets of God—what the Bahá'í writings refer to as "Manifestations" inasmuch as They both articulate specific spiritual concepts, social ordinances, and a path to individual refinement and manifest perfectly the attributes and powers of God. In brief, the Manifestations are the perfect exemplars of Their own guidance, even while They also provide us the surest access to God Himself because They are a higher order of being and thus possess powers and comportment beyond anything we ordinary human beings are capable of developing or exercising.

It is in the context of this distinction that Bahá'u'lláh, in The Book of Certitude, describes in detail the "twin stations" of the Prophets—something we will discuss in more detail in chapter 3—to demonstrate that while Their otherworldly powers are largely concealed, the phenomenal attraction of Their comportment, personalities, and actions provide us with a paradigm or referent for our own personal spiritual aspirations. We thus may long to become like Them, knowing all the while that we should not lament our inability to emulate Their perfection: They are inherently perfect manifestations of Godliness as expressed through a human persona, while we are always works in progress, never achieving some final state of accomplishment but ever joyous in our endless journey. For while we will never become anything other than human souls, within that category of existence is the possibility of infinite refinement.

NEW WINESKINS FOR THE NEW WINE

Concomitant with the new knowledge infused into society by the Manifestations is a pattern of action that is intended as a means by which one can demonstrate an understanding of the spiritual principles that can be discerned in the utterances or scripture of the Prophets. This important action is necessarily social in nature—for until practiced in the crucible of interaction with others, virtue is mostly theoretical.

The acquisition and practice of virtue, in turn, induces in us an increased understanding of other ways in which spiritual virtues or principles can be expressed. Our sense of the nature of justice or kindness, for example, may begin with very basic interactions within our family or among other children, but as our social experience expands and becomes more complex, we must develop a more in-depth understanding of these spiritual attributes so that we can express them in increasingly more subtle and challenging applications.

As we have noted, then, an obvious but vitally important corollary of this educational process is the essentially social nature of enlightenment. Indeed, it is the essential premise of the science of sociology that we are inherently social beings. We cannot raise ourselves. We cannot live usefully as solitary beings—one reason, no doubt, that Bahá'u'lláh in His own teachings and laws for the advancement of human society has abolished asceticism or monasticism.

HISTORY AS A SPIRITUAL DYNAMIC

Another concept central to understanding the Bahá'í perspective—especially as regards the Bahá'í view of human history—is the belief that an essential function of the Manifestation is to advance human civilization. In this context, it is the Bahá'í belief that each successive Revelation in human history is carefully designed by the Manifestation or Prophet to befit both the requirements and capacities of the age in which He appears; it thus contains laws and guidance that will suffice to advance the peoples capable of having access to that Revelation. For when the regions of the world were diverse and isolated, it is reasonable to assume there may have been various Manifestations simultaneously at work in areas remote from one another.

Over the course of time, the world became increasingly contracted into a few expansive civilizations such that communication among all the peoples of the world became feasible. We can thus discern, in our understanding of human history, a coherent design in the sequence of Prophets, particularly in what is referred to as the Abrahamic line of Prophets, which has produced the world religions of Judaism, Christianity, Islam, the Bábí Faith, and the Bahá'í Faith.

It is essential to appreciate and comprehend this concept of "progressive Revelation" before attempting to examine the Súriy-i-Haykal through a Bahá'í lens. For included in this concept is the belief that human history is not a random sequence of events resulting from the laws of cause and effect, but rather is a logical continuum, a divinely guided process in which the Creator progressively advances human civilization by degrees as He continually sends Manifestations, each one of Whom provides the next step or stage (era or dispensation) in our shared understanding of human purpose and our subsequent collective implementation of that understanding in appropriate social laws, ordinances, norms, and governmental design.

A Bahá'í study of human history asserts the relentless material and spiritual advancement of human civilization through progressive stages of increased collaboration and cooperation. Most important of all, in relation to the Súriy-i-Haykal, is the Bahá'í belief that we are at this present time in history living in the midst of a critical and singular turning point in our collective progress on planet Earth, a transition from our collective childhood and adolescence to a stage of maturity.

This milestone, this point of transition and social transformation, is signified by the critical need—and present readiness—for global solutions to ever more pressing global dilemmas and challenges facing a planet that has been contracting into an interdependent global community: "Unification of the whole of mankind is the hall-mark of the stage which human society is now approaching. Unity of family, of tribe, of city-state, and nation have been successively attempted and fully established. World unity is the goal towards which a harassed humanity is striving. Nation-building has come to an end."[15]

The Temple and the Ontology of the Manifestations

As a final relevant axiom in this prefatory examination of the Bahá'í context in which we will study the vital importance of the Súriy-i-Haykal, we need to understand and appreciate the essential pertinence of the ontology or nature of the Manifestations. After all, there are many prominent spiritual teachers, philosophers, and enlightened souls who have advanced human understanding, whether regarding the sciences, the mystic powers latent within each of us, or the myriad other arenas of human capacities and endeavors.

But the Manifestations, Bahá'ís believe, are not merely extraordinarily wise or enlightened individuals. They are, rather, another order of being, as indicated by several essential distinctions between Their reality and that of the rest of us. First, whereas our reality begins during conception, the Manifestations are pre-existent in the spiritual realm prior to associating with a human persona in the physical realm.[16] Second, Their boundless knowledge is inherent; They do not require human instruction in order to advance in this life. Third, They are "omniscient at will."[17] Fourth, They inherently and perfectly manifest all the attributes and powers of God. Fifth, They know God, whereas our access to and knowledge of God, whether in this physical stage of our existence or in our subsequent eternal experience in the spiritual realm, will always be through the intermediary of the Manifestation: "We will have experience of God's spirit through His Prophets in the next world, but God is too great for us to know without this Intermediary. The Prophets know God, but how is more than our human minds can grasp."[18]

There is more that could be observed about the uniqueness of these Beings, but stated succinctly, the Manifestations are the most exact and complete expression of the Creator we will ever encounter. Thus, while Their Revelation is inspired by God—and, consequently, we correctly designate Their Revelation as "the Word of God," even as we designate Their personhood as "the Word made Flesh"[19]—They are the artificers of Their own utterances. For while some infer, especially from the Old Testament depictions of Abraham and Moses and from the story in the Qur'án of how God tells Muḥammad what to reveal by communicating to Him through the angel Gabriel, that the Manifestation is simply a transmitter of God's word adding nothing of His own, the Bahá'í writings assert clearly that the Manifestation is the author of His words, the designer of His laws and ordinances for humankind, and the architect of the social and political edifice that will disseminate and effectuate the stage of human advancement His advent is designed to bring about.[20]

Indeed, it is in the context of appreciating the Bahá'í concept of the Manifestation and its relationship to the advancement of human civilization that we start to understand why a study of the Súriy-i-Haykal is so crucial and why it is considered one of the more important works among the immense panoply of Bahá'u'lláh's revealed texts, an outpouring so appropriately described by Bahá'u'lláh Himself as a vast ocean: "Immerse yourselves in the ocean of My words, that ye may unravel its secrets, and discover all the pearls of wisdom that lie hid in its depths."[21]

In perhaps the most memorable or oft-recited passage from the Súriy-i-Haykal itself, Bahá'u'lláh alludes to the *Haykal* or temple (the human aspect of the Manifestation) with the following assertion, highlighting the crucial point that the appearance of the Manifestation in human form is the principal means by which we understand the Creator:

Say: Naught is seen in My temple but the Temple of God, and in My beauty but His Beauty, and in My being but His Being, and in My self but His Self, and in My movement but His Movement, and in My acquiescence but His Acquiescence, and in My pen but His Pen, the Mighty, the All-Praised. There hath not been in My soul but the Truth, and in Myself naught could be seen but God.[22]

Another passage from the Writings of Bahá'u'lláh confirms and elucidates this fundamental and overarching understanding of the station and powers of the Manifestation by stating that we should consider all the guidance and actions of the Manifestation as identical to the utterances and suggestions of God Himself:

> The essence of belief in Divine unity consisteth in regarding Him Who is the Manifestation of God and Him Who is the invisible, the inaccessible, the unknowable Essence as one and the same. By this is meant that whatever pertaineth to the former, all His acts and doings, whatever He ordaineth or forbiddeth, should be considered, in all their aspects, and under all circumstances, and without any reservation, as identical with the Will of God Himself.[23]

Meanings

THE BAHÁ'Í CONCEPT OF THE REVELATORY PROCESS

At this point, it may be well worthwhile to recount briefly what is intended by the concept of "Revelation" within the context of Bahá'í beliefs. The term "Revelation" as applied to the Bahá'í belief about the writings, utterances, and actions of the Prophets or Manifestations does not imply that what the Manifestation does and says is merely His response to precise words or commands the Creator conveys to the Prophet. Rather, the process portrayed in the Bahá'í texts implies that the Manifestation is inspired by God about what sort of guidance is needed to accommodate the exigencies of the age in which the Prophet appears to advance human spirituality and subsequently to create an "ever-advancing civilization."[24] But it is the genius or capacity of the Manifestation that enables Him to devise the precise language and literary form that, together with His exemplary personal comportment and actions, best convey this guidance.

One of my favorite passages illustrating the creativity of the Manifestation's vision and the artistry with which He constructs His dispensation is a description by Shoghi Effendi regarding the capacity of Bahá'u'lláh to fashion a blueprint or framework capable of bringing into being, and subsequently sustaining, a world commonwealth of nations. In what I regard as a wonderfully useful conceit—Bahá'u'lláh as master craftsman (specifically a metal worker in this case)—Shoghi Effendi emphasizes our inability at present to understand fully the ingenuity of Bahá'u'lláh's design for the future society and how it will come about:

Given a goal and He

> Not ours, puny mortals that we are, to attempt, at so critical a stage in the long and checkered history of mankind, to arrive at a precise and satisfactory understanding of the steps which must successively lead a bleeding humanity, wretchedly oblivious of its God, and careless of Bahá'u'lláh, from its calvary to its ultimate resurrection. Not ours, the living witnesses of the all-subduing potency of His Faith, to question, for a moment, and however dark the misery that enshrouds the world, the ability of Bahá'u'lláh to forge, with the hammer of His Will, and through the fire of tribulation, upon the anvil of this travailing age, and in the particular shape His mind has envisioned, these scattered and mutually destructive fragments into which a perverse world has fallen, into one single unit, solid and indivisible, able to execute His design for the children of men.[25]

The Manifestation is ever keenly aware of both the capacity and the limitations of those to whom He is speaking—most often the followers of the previous Manifestation Whom He succeeds and Whose teachings constitute the foundation upon which He forges a new Revelation. And yet, the Manifestation is also quite aware that He is preparing the peoples to Whom He appears for social and political conditions He is capable of foreseeing, even though they might not at the time comprehend them. It is in this sense, perhaps, that the traditional concept of "faith" is applicable—the notion that once you have established to your own satisfaction that the Manifestation is indeed Whom He claims to be, you follow His guidance even if some of it may at the time seem contrary to what you might think is the best course of action. Of course, even this "faith" is not "blind faith" because it is established on the logical foundation of one's prior investigation and study.

It is in this context that appreciating the continuity of religious history as delineated in the plenteous Bahá'í texts regarding progressive Revelation is essential in comprehending the underlying organic unity and the systematic coherence of the sequence of the world religions. Understanding this context is also essential if one is to grasp the major themes that Bahá'u'lláh has infused into the Súrih of the Temple.

we must understand Progressive Revelation to understand

THE HISTORY OF THE DELEGATION OF AUTHORITY

One other Bahá'í belief that features as a central theme of the Súriy-i-Haykal is the concept of the delegation of authority from God to humankind. Stated as a concomitant and essential part of the methodology by which God gradually advances society age to age through the advent of the Manifestations, this law is best described as gradualness, or the portioning out of knowledge: "Even as it hath been said: 'Not everything that a man knoweth can be disclosed, nor can everything that he can disclose be regarded as timely, nor can every timely utterance be considered as suited to the capacity of those who hear it.'"[26] Simply put, learning is constrained by degree, by the fact that, whether as individuals or as a society, we must acquire and implement new learning incrementally. New or more advanced or more complex social laws of organization and interaction are necessarily understood and put into practice incrementally according to the capacity and conditions latent within a given society during a specific period of time—an "era" or "dispensation" as regards the period of time during which a new Revelation is operant.

Any overview of the advancement of civilization bears out this principle, even at the most basic levels of living—obtaining food, building shelter, creating foundational forms of social order to facilitate survival. Likewise, as mentioned above, Shoghi Effendi notes how, having achieved increasingly complex forms of social order—family, tribe, city-state, and nation state—we are now, at this time in our collective history, in the dispensation begun in 1844 with the Báb's declaration of His station and mission, ready for the ultimate form of planetary social order, a global commonwealth constructed to maximize individual freedoms while securing stability and justice through a pact of collective security and a force comprised of individuals from all signatory states to enforce that security.

Of course, the Bahá'í description of how the plan of God is fulfilled on planet Earth goes beyond the political arena, from the evolution of human life according to scientific law to the evolution of human society as driven by necessity and as guided by the appearance and instructions of Manifestations Who describe and implement the relevant spiritual laws. But what might not be obvious in any study or recitation of the constituent components of this systematic process and the resulting gradually more complex social structures is that, through the evolving sophistication and increasingly encompassing application of these concepts instigated by the teachings of the successive Manifestations, authority, though today administered by a single body elected through universal suffrage,[27] is in actuality being systematically decentralized. We can observe this most obviously—as we will discover in the Súriy-i-Haykal—in the complete transformation of governance worldwide during the last two centuries. The vesting of power or authority to govern in the few—the king, the emperor, the oligarch, the dictator—was suddenly perceived to be anathema to the fundamental rights of the masses, the ordinary citizens, even as empires and monarchies gave way to the upheaval of those wishing to assume a role in their own governance, whether in the form of republics, democracies, or some other participatory version of self-rule.

Here we see how the Súriy-i-Haykal marks a critical development in the historical process of the delegation of authority. Human beings, having been created noble, have always had the *potential* to govern their own affairs collectively and with justice, but during the infancy of our social evolution, this potential had not yet emerged into actuality. Incapable of sustaining anything like a democratic culture beyond the scope of a city-state, humanity was thus ruled by the few: monarchs, oligarchs, and emperors. With the Súriy-i-Haykal, Bahá'u'lláh signals to these rulers that the authority delegated to them is not unconditional, that if they reject exercising their power in a manner befitting humanity's capacities and newly dawning requirements for a global commonwealth, that same power and authority will be taken from them.

Bahá'u'lláh speaks to this precise point quite directly in the Súriy-i-Haykal, most obviously in His compliment to Queen Victoria about the utilization of a parliamentary system whereby the people are empowered to elect representatives to whom they delegate the authority to articulate their concerns in the council chambers of government. This direct empowerment of the people, already emerging when He wrote the Súriy-i-Haykal and the epistles contained therein, has in the meantime accelerated exponentially. Indeed, it seems apparent that authority for self-governance is set forth in Bahá'u'lláh's design for a global commonwealth in which there is universal suffrage, with regard to both the secular and the sacred sectors of administration.

While all the features of this design are not spelled out in the letters to the rulers, in keeping with the methodology of the Manifestation for the gradual unfoldment of His laws and guidance, Bahá'u'lláh does

Historical of the concentration of Power from King/emperor to a more democratic way for humanity present the salient features of this world order in terms they can readily understand, supported by clear and logical initial steps that must be undertaken in time to avoid further warfare and suffering. Bahá'u'lláh thus enjoins them to abandon autocratic rule (largely inherited from the medieval notion of the divine right of kings) and minister to the needs of the populace who live under their sway, rather than striving to increase their power or amass great wealth, or deluding themselves that they can become immortal through any means other than recognizing the advent of a new Day, a new Era, and an abrupt and critical transformation in the structure of the body politic.

Meanwhile, the delegation of authority to humanity as a whole has advanced by its own momentum, as part of the Major Plan of God. The rulers could advance or delay this development according to how they responded to Bahá'u'lláh's advice, just as they could advance or delay the restructuring of their societies according to the imperatives of justice. However, these laws and exhortations are not merely suggestions about how human beings can best exhibit divine virtues; they are also descriptions of how extant forces determine social outcomes. If a government is unjust, in time it is doomed to fail, not merely as a matter of divine retribution, but because a just social order describes our reality accurately. We are all equal in the sight of God and are all deserving of certain inalienable rights. Consequently, governance devised according to this reality will prosper. Governance that denies or undermines this fact of our reality will falter, decline, and ultimately fail under the weight of this operant law.

This essential component of the Bahá'í teachings portrays human history on planet Earth as a work in progress whose divinely ordained journey is organic and ultimately predictable in its outcome. And even as the wise parents gradually assign or delegate autonomy and personal authority to their developing progeny—from embryo, to birth, to infancy, to childhood, to youth, to maturation and adulthood—so we find ourselves, as Bahá'u'lláh notes in the Súriy-i-Haykal, at a crucial stage of change and choice. We can, He informs the world leaders, easily attain global unity by accepting His station as the Manifestation for this Day or Dispensation; the peace that would result from acting according to this recognition is the Most Great Peace. Or, once these same rulers have rejected this easy path—as they have by the time Bahá'u'lláh writes His epistle to Queen Victoria[28]—they can strive to bring about a Lesser Peace by establishing a pact of collective security. However, since even this Lesser Peace was rejected by the rulers of Bahá'u'lláh's time, it too will necessarily require that humankind endure testing and turmoil, such as the horrendous world wars we have endured since the revelation of this work, as well as the various ongoing conflicts that even now threaten the stability of world order.

By usefully extending the parental analogy, we can consider how at every stage of our individual journey through life, we must be assisted from without. We begin as children, at the mercy of our parents, subject to their hopefully benign and enlightened methods for instructing us in manners, comportment, and some sense of spiritual attributes as borne out in our everyday activities. We then progress by degrees through more advanced forms of direct and indirect education, expanding our knowledge through the practice of virtue in ever-widening circles of social interaction. Finally, by the age of maturity, we are hopefully endowed with the capacity and desire to take charge of our own destiny and thereby to become responsible for our own choices and actions, though we are forever a work in progress and never without the periodic need for social assistance in all its myriad forms, whether from parents, friends, or others.

According to the Bahá'í Writings, the most important point in this individual process—the transition from adolescence to maturity—is precisely where humankind presently struggles in our collective progress on planet Earth. We are, as it were, experiencing the turmoil associated with the birth pangs of a new reality and redefined identity. And that rebirth or resurrection is portrayed by Bahá'u'lláh in great detail as the emergence in time of a commonwealth of nations. 'Abdu'l-Bahá observes how "Bahá'u'lláh declared the 'Most Great Peace' and international arbitration. He voiced these principles in numerous epistles which were circulated broadcast throughout the East."[29] 'Abdu'l-Bahá continues, "He wrote to all the kings and rulers encouraging, advising and admonishing them in regard to the establishment of peace; making it evident by conclusive proofs that the happiness and glory of humanity can only be assured through disarmament and arbitration."[30]

These letters calling for such a pact—five of the most important of which are included in the Súrih of the Temple—were written over one and a half centuries ago, but the principle of collective security outlined in those letters has been discussed and attempted time and again through noble but ultimately inadequate efforts—the League of Nations and the United Nations, for example. Even at this writing, alliances such as

NATO (the North Atlantic Treaty Organization) and the EU (European Union) are attempting to respond to and possibly deter the incursion of an aggressor nation into a neighboring sovereign nation—Russia's merciless and unjustifiable invasion of Ukraine, apparently with the sole motive of extending the range of its power. Were there a single global pact in place, we can imagine that the response to this incursion would have been swift and overpowering, especially inasmuch as the pact would have also effectively reduced the armaments available to individual nation-states and the collective force derived from this same pact would already have been in place to respond immediately to this violation of the sovereignty of a member state.

Early in His admonitions to the kings and rulers of His day, Bahá'u'lláh assured the world leaders that transition to a global community secured by a collective pact was accessible with relatively simple and totally available actions on their part. The first route was to recognize His station and heed all His counsels accordingly; thereby the world could attain a "Most Great Peace" in which a spiritualized global society would see fruits far beyond the mere cessation of war. The second route, offered in the letters to the rulers included in the Súriy-i-Haykal, was through their own dedication to unity among themselves. The rulers took neither route. Bahá'u'lláh is clear that they do not have the power to prevent either the Lesser or the Most Great Peace; both will still be achieved—but now only after turmoil, immense struggle, wars, a "tempest, unprecedented in its violence, unpredictable in its course, catastrophic in its immediate effects, unimaginably glorious in its ultimate consequences," but a tempest which, while not yet complete nor the totality or pitch of its furor yet experienced, has, according to the Bahá'í writings, already begun and "is at present sweeping the face of the earth. Its driving power is remorselessly gaining in range and momentum."[31]

THE STAGE OF MATURATION

Here we would do well to return to the principal ingredients of the Bahá'í perspective to discern our part, our responsibility, in this once-in-a-planetary-lifetime event, both as individuals and as a society. This is to say, while the Bahá'í writings assure us that the story of planet Earth is destined to experience a "happy ending," they also emphasize how our own efforts at present can play a strategic part in facilitating this propitious outcome and contributing, even at the most simple level of everyday living, to helping humankind endure the "tempest," establish a spiritual and social framework for the stage of maturity that will subsequently emerge by degrees, and even to some extent "mitigate the severity of impending catastrophe."[32]

From all that has thus far been said about Bahá'í views and beliefs regarding human history—its motive force, its progressive stages of enlightenment expressed in increasingly expansive and complex social structures—it can be inferred that the strategically important notion of the delegation of authority will not only resonate throughout the letters Bahá'u'lláh wrote to the rulers; it is indeed an essential ingredient in the Bahá'í view of reality from the planetary level to the unity and governance of the local community. The sad and unfortunate failure of the rulers to heed His message, which will be explored below, could not jeopardize the unfoldment of this delegation, which today is reflected in the work being done by those committed to Bahá'u'lláh's vision for human existence on this planet. In point of fact, one could summarize the history of planet Earth thus far with a simple declarative sentence: it begins with the God's wish to be known and ends with community-building as presently described and encouraged by the Universal House of Justice in its successive plans for establishing a framework for a sane, just, and secure life for every individual in every neighborhood and village throughout the world: "The unity of the human race, as envisaged by Bahá'u'lláh, implies the establishment of a world commonwealth in which all nations, races, creeds and classes are closely and permanently united, and in which the autonomy of its state members and the personal freedom and initiative of the individuals that compose them are definitely and completely safeguarded."[33]

WHY THE BAHÁ'Í PERSPECTIVE IS ESSENTIAL TO THIS STUDY

At this point, the reader should understand with relative clarity why the foregoing review of the fundamental axioms of Bahá'í belief and perspective is essential prior to any useful examination of the Súriy-i-Haykal. The work is situated in this context and is intended to be studied and comprehended as it relates to the entirety of what we have thus far established about the Bahá'í view of human history, the nature of reality as a whole, and, even more particularly, the strategic position the Súriy-i-Haykal itself occupies in the context of the Revelation which Bahá'ís believe to be the most recent dispensation from God, the transformative agent that is presently ushering in the long-awaited framework for a global community characterized by a system of collective justice to ensure world peace.

Nevertheless, I feel it important to appreciate how, without such an understanding, any study of Bahá'u'lláh's works, and the Súriy-i-Haykal in particular, as well as any study of the Bahá'í Faith as a whole, is likely to lead the scholar astray, or at least to misrepresent Bahá'í history and texts. The reason for such a cautionary assertion derives from two axioms regarding Bahá'u'lláh's Writings. The first of these concerns the very explicit Bahá'í philosophical/theological perspective, the knowledge of which is absolutely essential to anyone wishing to grasp the intended meaning of what Bahá'u'lláh is discussing in each of the myriad works that constitute the "ocean" of His Revelation. The second relates to the historical/cultural context that significantly informs the meaning of Bahá'u'lláh's texts.

THE PHILOSOPHICAL/THEOLOGICAL CONTEXT

From a Bahá'í theological perspective, Bahá'u'lláh as a Manifestation is not subject to the influences that might affect the thinking and themes of an ordinary human author. That is, while He was not impervious to the trials and tribulations He was made to endure, His utterances derived from His foresight—indeed, His omniscience—about the requisites for advancing human civilization far into the future. Therefore, the meaning and goals of His revealed works are tailored to objectives and exigencies about which the generality of those who hear Him or read His works may be totally oblivious. The oft-repeated metaphor Bahá'u'lláh uses to convey the meaning and sometimes temporarily concealed objectives of His works is that the body of humankind is a patient suffering from a potentially fatal malady, and He, alone, is the divinely empowered Physician capable of discerning the nature of the disease and prescribing the remedy.

If the reader approaches His work unaware of this context, one that most Bahá'í readers assume, then that individual will most likely be unable to appreciate or accept the authority of the otherworldly wisdom the Bahá'í reader attributes to this theological context—that Bahá'u'lláh is not an ordinary mortal but a Being specialized by God to possess the knowledge and capacity to present teachings sufficient both to deal with the present exigencies afflicting the body politic and outline the course of action that will enable society to undertake the next stage in its endless development. And here, of course, we are referring to increasingly more complex, rational, and just governance, characterized by increasingly refined expressions of efficiency, equity, and beneficence.

And yet, in another context, Bahá'u'lláh seems to imply that understanding the meaning of His utterances does *not* require knowledge regarding foundational Bahá'í beliefs, historical context, or the other prerequisites we have cited above. Instead, He seems to assure the reader that those who can best understand and appreciate the wisdom latent in His utterances are not those steeped in traditional forms of learning, which the information we have presented might seem to indicate as necessary. Rather, Bahá'u'lláh implies that those who will be best equipped to comprehend His words are those whose perspective is not beclouded by worldly distractions or personal aspirations. "None apprehendeth the meaning of these utterances," He states in the Book of Certitude, "except them whose hearts are assured, whose souls have found favour with God, and whose minds are detached from all else but Him. In such utterances, the literal meaning, as generally understood by the people, is not what hath been intended."[34] Similarly, in another passage, Bahá'u'lláh assures the reader, "The understanding of His words and the comprehension of the utterances of the Birds of Heaven are in no wise dependent upon human learning. They depend solely upon purity of heart, chastity of soul, and freedom of spirit."[35]

This is not a contradiction. Even as there is not merely one pathway to belief in God, nor only one prescribed method for acquiring spiritual virtues or attaining a state of nearness to God, so the pathways to acquiring certitude of belief in God or accepting His Manifestations—and thence becoming confirmed in the guidance They provide—can be equally varied according to the particular personality, capacities, and proclivities of the seeker. This accounts for Bahá'u'lláh's statement in the Súriy-i-Haykal about the various modes or styles He employs in His Writings so that all peoples may thereby discover a voice, a tenor, a literary form that works best for them, a methodology we will address more fully at the beginning of chapter 5.

The point is that while we can assume the Bahá'í reader is already capable of approaching the Súriy-i-Haykal with some degree of understanding about the philosophical/theological and historical/cultural context in which the work is revealed, the reader who is not a Bahá'í needs to know about the assumptions with which the Bahá'í reader approaches these works. And yet, what we can assume Bahá'u'lláh is stating about the comprehension of His utterances is that whether the reader is or is not a Bahá'í, understanding His often allusive and abstruse works—most of which have multiple layers of meaning—requires a spiritual attitude and an openness of heart and mind, as opposed to the acquisition of voluminous amounts of esoteric knowledge or august levels of academic prowess.

Another way of understanding these two modes of study or approaches is as complementary avenues to the same goal. But regardless of how much knowledge about the Bahá'í Faith and its teachings one may acquire, belief in and confirmation of the theological tenets of the Bahá'í Faith require an internal process that is inevitably personal and incapable of being easily defined. Let it suffice to conclude this distinction by noting that any cursory review of religious history—as recounted in the Bahá'í texts—demonstrates that the first followers of Manifestations are not often the clerics or divines of the previous religion, who, all too often, are vehement persecutors of the Manifestation and His early followers. Instead, most often the first to recognize the Manifestation are the lowly but purehearted souls who, undeterred by worldly affections or any aspirations for personal recognition, find comfort in the exhortations of the Manifestations, discern in His comportment and authentic love a confirmation of His claims, and have an instinctive sense of the essential meaning and intent of His teachings.

The Historical/Cultural Context

Of course, all literature is written in a context. And although there are some critical theories in the study of literature that attempt to assess the meaning of a work without regard to either the author's personal history or the cultural context in which the work emerged (the formalist approach of New Criticism, for example, the *explication de texte* or "close reading" of text[36]), such approaches, while often enlightening, are necessarily incomplete. And in the case of some literature—and this is particularly the case with the massive canon of Bahá'u'lláh's works—a knowledge of historical and social context is essential.

As we have already noted, Bahá'u'lláh is writing (or "revealing") His works in response to the specific needs of the evolution of human society at a critical period of transition—from a period of its adolescence to its adulthood, a maturation that will be characterized by the establishment of a global commonwealth as an expression of the fact that our planet has, by virtue of sudden and remarkable material advancement, become contracted into a single community. And according to Bahá'í belief, this unified, organic, interdependent, and collaborative enterprise, while in one sense the inevitable outcome and culmination of all previous social advancement, nevertheless requires a logically coherent structure to accommodate it.

Virtually every work revealed by Bahá'u'lláh relates to and derives its essential meaning from this context and this purpose—to usher in this new age, to provide the structure to administrate planetary governance, and to assign to each level of this structure (from the individual to some sort of world tribunal) the role it must play and the means by which that assignment can best be accomplished. Bahá'u'lláh thus speaks not merely as an astute observer of history, but as the Successor to Those previous Manifestations who have been the promulgators of history, however subtle, indirect, and unacknowledged Their role may have been. 'Abdu'l-Bahá states this axiom forthrightly as follows:

In like manner, the holy Manifestations of God are the focal Centres of the light of truth, the Wellsprings of the hidden mysteries, and the Source of the effusions of divine love. They cast Their effulgence upon the realm of hearts and minds and bestow grace everlasting upon the world of the spirits. They confer spiritual life and shine with the splendour of inner truths and meanings. The enlightenment of the realm of thought proceeds from those Centres of light and Exponents of mysteries. Were it not for the grace of the revelation and instruction of those sanctified Beings, the world of souls and the realm of thought would become darkness upon darkness. Were it not for the sound and true teachings of those Exponents of mysteries, the human world would become the arena of animal characteristics and qualities, all existence would become a vanishing illusion, and true life would be lost. That is why it is said in the Gospel: "In the beginning was the Word" [John 1:1]; that is, it was the source of all life.[37]

Insofar as the cultural context is concerned, it is vitally important to appreciate why the Báb and Bahá'u'lláh "chose" Persia as the place where this world-transforming resurrection of humankind would be instigated, something Shoghi Effendi elucidates: "the primary reason why the Báb and Bahá'u'lláh chose to appear in Persia, and to make it the first repository of their Revelation, was because, of all the peoples and nations of the civilized world, that race and nation had, as so often depicted by 'Abdu'l-Bahá, sunk to such ignominious depths, and manifested so great a perversity, as to find no parallel among its contemporaries."[38] He continues by noting that "no more convincing proof could be adduced demonstrating the regenerating spirit animating the Revelations proclaimed by the Báb and Bahá'u'lláh than their power to transform what can be truly regarded as one of the most backward, the most cowardly, and perverse of peoples into a race of heroes, fit to effect in turn a similar revolution in the life of mankind."[39] Whereas, had They appeared "among a race or nation which by its intrinsic worth and high attainments seemed to warrant the inestimable privilege of being made the receptacle of such a Revelation [it] would in the eyes of an unbelieving world greatly reduce the efficacy of that Message, and detract from the self-sufficiency of its omnipotent power."[40]

And such is the case with the appearance of each Manifestation. Yet there is another salient reason underlying the culture in which the Báb and Bahá'u'lláh appear that relates importantly to the concept of the succession of Revelations. For even as Christ appeared in the stronghold of Jewish authority and among the most enlightened and learned Jewish scholars of His day to confront them with the fulfillment of the long-awaited appearance of the Messianic prophecies, so the Báb and Bahá'u'lláh appeared in the stronghold of Shí'ih Islam, the one sect of Islam that accepts the authority of the Twelve Imams, and would thus be the most likely to recognize in the appearance of the Báb both the Qá'im and the return of the Twelfth or Hidden Imam.

It is in this context that so much of the works of both the Báb and Bahá'u'lláh are replete with elucidations of and allusions to various Súrih in the Qur'án, to authoritative ḥadíth, and to teachings of the Imams, even as virtually all of Christ's teachings contain allusions to passages from authoritative Jewish scripture. And while the teachings of the Báb and Bahá'u'lláh are intended to become circulated and studied worldwide, even as are the laws of Bahá'u'lláh over the course of time, it is important that the reader study Bahá'u'lláh's Súrih of the Temple with an awareness of both the philosophical/theological context and the historical/cultural context in which the work was revealed.

Bahá'u'lláh's Declaration of His Station and Mission

There is at least one more crucial feature of the context regarding Bahá'u'lláh's final version of the Súriy-i-Haykal that any reader would do well to take into consideration when attempting to understand and interpret the intended meaning of this work and why it assumes such an important place in the Revelation of Bahá'u'lláh. The Súriy-i-Haykal begins with the recounting of Bahá'u'lláh's first intimation of His mission, fifteen years prior. In so doing, He connects this work directly to the successive stages of His declaration, and effectively concludes them. In light of this relationship to His methodology, we would benefit from a review of those stages to provide the context for the study of the Súrih.

The Bahá'í texts affirm that although the Manifestation is fully aware of His station and mission prior to announcing His advent to others, He does not reveal or proclaim this information to others until the appropriate time. Therefore, while His immaculate character and otherworldly knowledge may be recognized by family, friends, or others attaining His presence, there comes a point in His life when He receives the intimation from God through the Holy Spirit that the time has arrived to unveil His station and commence His ministry.

For Abraham, this intimation occurs as He is about to sacrifice His son (Isaac, according to the Old Testament; and Ishmael, according to Muslim belief). For Moses, this intimation occurs when He encounters the burning bush on Mount Sinai. Christ receives this intimation while being anointed by John the Baptist. Muḥammad experiences this intimation when He is meditating in a cave on Mount Hira. The Báb experiences the first intimation of His mission in a dream vision about the martyred Imam Husayn. And Bahá'u'lláh receives this first intimation in a dream vision while imprisoned in the Síyáh-Chál in Tehran.

Thus, according to Bahá'í belief, these points of beginning do not indicate some transformation of the Prophet from one state to another—from being a very spiritual human being to becoming a Manifestation with all the powers and attributes associated with that station. 'Abdu'l-Bahá makes this point quite clear in *Some Answered Questions* by authoritatively interpreting what Bahá'u'lláh means in His letter to Naṣíri'd-Dín Sháh (a letter included in the Súriy-i-Haykal) when He states, "I was but a man like others, asleep upon My couch, when lo, the breezes of the All-Glorious were wafted over Me, and taught Me the knowledge of all that hath been. This thing is not from Me, but from One Who is Almighty and All-Knowing."[41] Where some might infer that Bahá'u'lláh is articulating the transformation of Himself from being an ordinary "man like others," 'Abdu'l-Bahá explains, "This is the station of divine revelation. It is not a sensible, but an intelligible reality. . . . It is a comparison and an analogy—a metaphor and not a literal truth. . . . Sleeping is the state of silence, and wakefulness is the state of utterance. Sleeping is the state of concealment, and wakefulness is that of manifestation."[42]

'Abdu'l-Bahá concludes this extremely important assertion about how the ontology of the Manifestation is distinct from that of ordinary mortals with an axiom that applies not solely to Bahá'u'lláh but to every Manifestation when They receive the first intimation of Their revelation: "Briefly, the Manifestations of God have ever been and will ever be luminous Realities, and no change or alteration ever takes place in Their essence. At most, before Their revelation They are still and silent, like one who is asleep, and after Their revelation They are eloquent and effulgent, like one who is awake."[43]

THE SECOND DECLARATION

This first declaration of Bahá'u'lláh's station and mission in October of 1852 is private and personal, an intimation that the time has come for Him to begin His ministry. However, complying with a request made by the Báb, Bahá'u'lláh delays any formal public declaration until what is referred to as the Riḍván announcement in April of 1863, almost eleven years later.

The reason for the Báb's request for this delay is obvious for anyone who has a passing knowledge of the events that transpired during the intervening years. The Báb, in "A Second Tablet Addressed to 'Him Who will be Made Manifest,'"[44] requests that Bahá'u'lláh, Whom the Báb knew was the One Who would fulfill that prophecy,[45] delay revealing His station and mission until such time as His followers (the Bábís) might have access to His own teachings that would prepare them for Bahá'u'lláh:

I, indeed, beg to address Him Whom God shall make manifest, by Thy leave in these words: "Shouldst Thou dismiss the entire company of the followers of the Bayán in the Day of the Latter

Resurrection by a mere sign of Thy finger even while still a suck-
ling babe, Thou wouldst indeed be praised in Thy indication. And
though no doubt is there about it, do Thou grant a respite of nineteen years as a token of Thy favour so that those who have embraced this Cause may be graciously rewarded by Thee."[46]

While the ministry and Revelation of the Báb, as prefatory to and
preparatory for the more encompassing Revelation of Bahá'u'lláh, was
foreordained to endure only nine years (from 1844 to 1853), the Báb
in His omniscience foreknew that the tribulations, persecutions, mass
executions and turmoil that had beset His followers would prevent
them from having ready access to His teachings about the advent of the
Promised Qayyúm,[47] "Him Whom God would Manifest," nor would
they be sufficiently organized and unified in the objectives of this Revelation to be prepared for the appearance of Bahá'u'lláh. In fact, during
Bahá'u'lláh's decade of extraordinary teaching and organization of the
Bábís in Baghdad (from 1853 to 1863), He not only began to reveal
some of His own important works—such as the Hidden Words, the Sev-
en Valleys, and, most important of all, the Kitáb-i-Íqán, an apologia for
the Báb and His Revelation[48] and the most important doctrinal work of
the Bahá'í Revelation—He also had the works of the Báb transcribed
and circulated among the community, both in Baghdad and in Persia.

The year nineteen thus signifies the nineteenth year of the Báb's
dispensation, the year 1863, in the spring of which Bahá'u'lláh spent
twelve days in the garden, henceforth designated as the Garden of
Riḍván (Paradise), proclaiming to all who attained His presence that
He was indeed the One promised by the Báb, the One Who would usher
in a New World Order to befit the earth having become contracted into
a single body politic.

THE THIRD DECLARATION OF BAHÁ'U'LLÁH

In his article "From Oppression to Empowerment," Nader Saiedi discusses three of these declarations of Bahá'u'lláh as alluding to the intimation in the Siyáh-Chál, the declaration during the twelve days of the
Riḍván gathering, and, finally, Bahá'u'lláh's declaration to the world at
large contained in His numerous letters to world leaders, both secular
and religious. And in a very important sense, the final writing and as-
sembling of the Súriy-i-Haykal marks the climax of this enouncement

to the world.⁴⁹ But shortly before the outpouring of these epistles, Bahá'u'lláh made another declaration of His station in the context of a momentous and strategically important event.

After Bahá'u'lláh's second exile, to Constantinople, on August 16, 1863, and His subsequent further exile to Adrianople four months later, His half-brother Mírzá Yaḥyá, whom He had raised after the death of their father and whose persistently vile actions attempted to undermine Bahá'u'lláh's authority, began to increase his grievous attacks on the One Who had consistently responded to his depravity and deceptive practices with forbearance and forgiveness. Mírzá Yaḥyá's intentions and tactics were no longer veiled or subtle. After inviting Bahá'u'lláh to his home, Mírzá Yaḥyá poisoned Bahá'u'lláh's teacup. The malady that this caused afflicted Bahá'u'lláh so grievously that He nearly died. His hand, which had so gracefully produced tablets in His own refined calligraphy, now shook with a tremor that endured through the rest of His life, as is evident in the samples of His writing from that time forward. On another occasion, Mírzá Yaḥyá tried to convince Ustád Muhammad-'Alíy-i-Salmání, the barber of Bahá'u'lláh, to slay Bahá'u'lláh as a service to Mírzá Yaḥyá and his claim to be the true leader of the Bábí Faith.⁵⁰

This troubling period that threatened to create the direst of consequences for the community of believers was designated by Bahá'u'lláh as "the *Ayyám-i-Shidád* (Days of Stress), during which 'the most grievous veil' was torn asunder, and the 'most great separation' was irrevocably effected."⁵¹ Bahá'u'lláh could no longer tolerate this succession of events, pernicious behaviors He had thus far endured so as not to cause a schism or disunity among the Bábís. Consequently, He instructed His amanuensis Mírzá Áqá Ján to deliver to Mírzá Yaḥyá a tablet called the Súriy-i-Amr (the Súrih of Command):

> The moment had now arrived for Him Who had so recently, both verbally and in numerous Tablets, revealed the implications of the claims He had advanced, to acquaint formally the one who was the nominee of the Báb with the character of His Mission. Mírzá Áqá Jan was accordingly commissioned to bear to Mírzá Yaḥyá the newly revealed Súriy-i-Amr, which unmistakably affirmed those claims, to read aloud to him its contents, and demand an unequivocal and conclusive reply.⁵²

This forthright and unambiguous declaration of His station as "Him Whom God will make manifest" foretold in the Writings of the Báb brought about several changes that mark this sequence of events as a milestone in the revelation of Bahá'u'lláh and in the history of the Bahá'í Faith.

After being granted "a one day respite, during which he could meditate his answer," Mírzá Yaḥyá responded to Bahá'u'lláh's exhortation to recognize His station with "a counter-declaration, specifying the hour and the minute in which he had been made the recipient of an independent Revelation, necessitating the unqualified submission to him of the peoples of the earth in both the East and the West."[53] Mírzá Yaḥyá now claimed to be the Prophet foretold by the Báb, an action that caused Bahá'u'lláh to instigate "the Most Great Separation." "So presumptuous an assertion," states Shoghi Effendi, "made by so perfidious an adversary to the envoy of the Bearer of so momentous a Revelation was the signal for the open and final rupture between Bahá'u'lláh and Mírzá Yaḥyá—a rupture that marks one of the darkest dates in Bahá'í history."[54]

For two months Bahá'u'lláh withdrew with His family and secluded Himself from everyone else, thereby forcing the Bábís to choose freely between Himself and Mírzá Yaḥyá. As part of this process, He had His brother Áqáy-i-Kalím divide equally all the material possessions, even the furniture, bedding, and the like. One half was sent to Mírzá Yaḥyá, and the other half He retained for Himself and His family.

This symbolic gesture marked the explicit division between the followers of Bahá'u'lláh, who now would be called "Bahá'ís," and those who chose to follow Mírzá Yaḥyá. These would now be known as "Bábís" or "Azalís" (after Mírzá Yaḥyá's title "Ṣubḥ-i-Azal"), while Bahá'u'lláh in His Writings would designate them as "people of the Bayán"—those who continued to consider themselves Bábís, even though the Báb Himself had cautioned His followers in His own writing that once "Him Whom God will Manifest" appeared, those who continued to follow "the Bayán" (the Revelation of the Báb) would be committing a grievous error: "How strange then that at the time of His appearance ye should pay homage by day and night unto that which the Point of the Bayán hath enjoined upon you and yet fail to worship Him Whom God shall make manifest."[55]

Soon after this separation, the traditional Bábí greeting of "Alláh-u-Akbar," a continuation of the Islamic greeting, was replaced among the

Bahá'ís with "Alláh-u-Abhá." And though this fracture, while unavoid-
able in light of Mírzá Yaḥyá's persistent claims (he even went so far
as to make his plaint to the government authorities), helped precipitate
the final and most grievous exile of Bahá'u'lláh to the prison colony
of 'Akká, it also permanently removed Mírzá Yaḥyá from further influence among the followers of Bahá'u'lláh because he was exiled in
perpetuity to the island of Cyprus, ironically designated by the Turks as
"the Island of Satan."[56]

THE FOURTH DECLARATION

What can be considered as the fourth declaration of Bahá'u'lláh's station and mission to the world at large consists of His proclamation in
the multitude of epistles He sent to kings, rulers, religious leaders, and
other governmental bodies during the Adrianople period and continuing after His exile to 'Akká. Of course, the first of these was sent in
Constantinople to Sultan 'Abdu'l-Azíz prior to Bahá'u'lláh's further
exile to Adrianople. And while no copy of this document remains, two
statements hint at the power and tone of its contents.

   According to Balyuzi's account, The Lawh-i-Abdu'l-Aziz-Va-Vuka-
la to the Sultan "was revealed on the very day that the brother-in-law
of the Grand Vizier came to inform Bahá'u'lláh of the edict [regarding
further exile] which had been issued against Him."[57] Balyuzi further recounts that Bahá'u'lláh refused to meet the envoy and "delegated 'Abdu'l-Bahá and Aqay-i-Kalim [Mírzá Musa] to receive it, and promised
to reply within three days. Next morning the Tablet was delivered by
Shamsi Big directly to 'Ali Pasha [the Grand Vizier to 'Abdu'l-Azíz],
with a message from its Author that 'it was sent down from God.'"[58]

   The reaction of the grand vizier upon reading its contents provides
us with a clear sense of what Bahá'u'lláh had written: "'I know not
what that letter contained,' Shamsi Big subsequently informed Aqay-i-
Kalim, 'for no sooner had the Grand Vizir perused it than he turned the
color of a corpse, and remarked: 'It is as if the King of Kings were issuing his behest to his humblest vassal king and regulating his conduct.'
So grievous was his condition that I backed out of his presence.'"[59]

   Regarding this same tablet, Shoghi Effendi cites a remark by
Bahá'u'lláh that provides even further insight into its content and tone:
"'Whatever action,' Bahá'u'lláh, commenting on the effect that Tablet
had produced, is reported to have stated, 'the ministers of the Sulṭán

took against Us, after having become acquainted with its contents, cannot be regarded as unjustifiable. The acts they committed before its perusal, however, can have no justification.'"[60] But this was merely the beginning of the epistles that began to flow so copiously from the pen of Bahá'u'lláh over the course of the next four years in Adrianople, continuing into His final exile to 'Akká, and reaching a climax with Bahá'u'lláh's final configuration of the Súriy-i-Haykal, a tablet that in its original form had been revealed in Adrianople.

Shoghi Effendi, in his incomparable prose, captures the amazing scope of this relentless and astounding outpouring in the following summation of this period in which Bahá'u'lláh declared His station and its import to the world at large. It also responds to anyone who might question why, if Bahá'u'lláh was the Promised One of all ages—and if He possessed the solution and guidance that could bring about global unity and a just and lasting peace—He did not announce this to the world. The answer, of course, is that this is precisely what He did do, and He did so as forcefully, eloquently, clearly, and effectively as could have been done at the time:

> Tablets unnumbered were streaming from the pen of Bahá'u'lláh, in which the implications of His newly-asserted claims were fully expounded. The Súriy-i-Amr, the Lawh-i-Nuqtih, the Lawh-i-Ahmad, the Súriy-i-Asháb, the Lawh-i-Sayyáh, the Súriy-i-Damm, the Súriy-i-Hajj, the Lawhu'r-Rúh, the Lawhu'r-Ridván, the Lawhu't-Tuqá were among the Tablets which His pen had already set down when He transferred His residence to the house of 'Izzat Áqá. Almost immediately after the "Most Great Separation" had been effected, the weightiest Tablets associated with His sojourn in Adrianople were revealed. The Súriy-i-Múlúk, the most momentous Tablet revealed by Bahá'u'lláh (Súrih of Kings) in which He, for the first time, directs His words collectively to the entire company of the monarchs of East and West, and in which the Sultán of Turkey, and his ministers, the kings of Christendom, the French and Persian Ambassadors accredited to the Sublime Porte, the Muslim ecclesiastical leaders in Constantinople, its wise men and inhabitants, the people of Persia and the philosophers of the world are separately addressed; the Kitáb-i-Badí', His apologia, written to refute the accusations levelled against Him by Mírzá Mihdíy-i-Rashtí, corresponding to the Kitáb-i-Íqán, revealed in

defense of the Bábí Revelation; the Munáját̲h̲áy-i-Ṣiyám (Prayers for Fasting), written in anticipation of the Book of His Laws; the first Tablet to Napoleon III, in which the Emperor of the French is addressed and the sincerity of his professions put to the test; the Lawḥ-i-Sulṭán, His detailed epistle to Náṣiri'd-Dín S̲h̲áh, in which the aims, purposes and principles of His Faith are expounded and the validity of His Mission demonstrated; the Súriy-i-Ra'ís, begun in the village of Kás̲h̲ánih on His way to Gallipoli, and completed shortly after at Gyáwur-Kyuy—these may be regarded not only as the most outstanding among the innumerable Tablets revealed in Adrianople, but as occupying a foremost position among all the writings of the Author of the Bahá'í Revelation.[61]

Shoghi Effendi continues at length in recounting the plenitude of these epistles and tablets in which Bahá'u'lláh proclaims a turning point in human history, what this declaration portends by way of transforming human society, as well as Bahá'u'lláh's elucidation of the obligations that the critical circumstances of this historical turning point immediately imposed upon the governments of the world.

Of course, the focus of this study is on demonstrating how Bahá'u'lláh's final rendering of the Súriy-i-Haykal can be viewed as both a fitting climax to this proclamation to world leaders and a poetic overview of exactly how God's purpose in creating and then assisting the progress of an "ever-advancing civilization" must be understood by leaders at every level of society, leaders who are called on to enthusiastically endorse and participate in carrying out the plentiful guidance Bahá'u'lláh offers in this ongoing process of the reformation of human governance and the principles that must underlie a just and secure global social order.

Consequently, in the subsequent chapter, we will discuss further how the Súriy-i-Haykal helps encapsulate and convey this conclusive guidance by examining further the context in which it is revealed. But prior to that, we will first examine what exegetical methodologies might be most appropriate to our examination of this work. We will also assess why some contemporary critical theories might prove inadequate for this task or, when misapplied or applied poorly, could actually give rise to major misapprehensions about the Súriy-i-Haykal, as well as other works of the Báb and Bahá'u'lláh.

Chapter 2

$2\backslash 3\backslash 23$

Exegesis and the Súriy-i-Haykal

To understand the approach to exegesis taken in this study, it will be helpful to consider two related but distinct approaches to exegesis that create epistemological issues with respect to the study of the Revealed Word. The first occurs when the scholar operates within a framework of ontological materialism and the second when they assume that they have privileged access to the meaning of the text, either because of their membership in a clerical order or because of their expertise in a particular academic field.

THE EPISTEMOLOGICAL LIMITATIONS OF A MATERIALIST PERSPECTIVE

Much contemporary scholarship about literature and history begins with the a priori assumption that the authors or actors are products of events beyond their control and often beyond their understanding, whether these be inherited genetic predispositions, a panoply of life events, or social and cultural influences and perspectives. But another and extremely relevant presumption, especially in postmodern critical approaches examining history, is that while figures do not operate within a vacuum, they are a part of all they have met, as the persona of Ulysses affirms in Tennyson's marvelous dramatic monologue.[62] Accordingly, one cannot or should not consider the possibility of metaphysical or spiritual forces as extant, or at least as operant in the physical world.

If one does not accept or allow for the possibility of a metaphysical reality and, additionally, the feasibility of an interplay or interpenetration between the metaphysical and physical realms (for example, God to man via the Manifestation, or even soul to body), then the scholar or student is forced to devise material explanations for the events that occur in the lives of the Manifestations and, mostly importantly, to explain Their sudden display of astounding knowledge and eloquence, especially since, One and All, the Manifestations are not formally trained or educated by others but demonstrate from the beginning of their declaration inherent knowledge and, additionally, an ability to cite verbatim the words of texts to which They have had no physical access, something Bahá'u'lláh explains in the Lawḥ-i-Ḥikmat (The Tablet of Wisdom):

> Thou knowest full well that We perused not the books which men possess and We acquired not the learning current amongst them, and yet whenever We desire to quote the sayings of the learned and of the wise, presently there will appear before the face of thy Lord in the form of a tablet all that which hath appeared in the world and is revealed in the Holy Books and Scriptures. Thus do We set down in writing that which the eye perceiveth. Verily His knowledge encompasseth the earth and the heavens.[63]

How is a scholar to approach the study of Writings whose Author explicitly claims that there is a metaphysical reality underpinning material creation, that this greater reality interpenetrates and influences the limited world to which we have sensory access, and—perhaps most remarkably—that the Author Himself has a uniquely privileged access to and understanding of this metaphysical reality? While there are many ways to study a text, each of which can unlock certain insights, it is clear that assuming a materialist ontology from the outset creates certain limitations, whatever other strengths such a framework may possess. Most critically, the reader who adopts a materialist perspective in examining the texts of Bahá'u'lláh must conclude that any claim of the Author to divine inspiration necessarily results from the Author's delusion or else from some feigned or baseless claim to authority, made in order to promote personal prestige and power. Conversely, it is solely by adopting the perspective of the beliefs contained in the Bahá'í writings themselves that their underlying themes can appropriately be understood on their own terms, whether or not the reader or scholar chooses to accept the metaphysical assumptions behind the text as true.

WHY A BAHÁ'Í PERSPECTIVE DISALLOWS SOME CRITICAL THEORIES

Perhaps one salient example can help demonstrate the limitations of a materialist analysis of revealed religion. Abbas Amanat's *Resurrection and Renewal: The Making of the Bábí Movement in Iran, 1844–1850* is a historical study of the origin and development of the Bábí Faith. A superbly researched and informative study, the work attempts to explain how the unlearned and self-educated Siyyid 'Alí-Muhammad (the Báb) could suddenly and inexplicably become capable of producing a work as erudite, comprehensive, and eloquent as the Qayyúmu'l-Asmá'—the Báb's commentary on the Súrih of Joseph from the Qur'án.

Amanat does not consider the possible veracity of the Báb's claim that He is a Manifestation and thus endowed with inherent capacity and divine knowledge, making Him capable of expressing that guidance in the most eloquent of literary forms, even as Muḥammad before Him, Who was similarly "unlearned" in any formal sense, became suddenly capable of issuing forth the divine utterance that became the standard of eloquence for the Arabic language from that time forward. In other words, the scholar of religious history and scripture is faced with a simple choice: either these individuals were extraordinary, another order of being, and divinely inspired as They claimed, or there is some materialist explanation for Their sudden ability to cite scripture from the past and produce commentaries and studies that far excel in depth and style the ability of any among the most learned of Their "Day" or Dispensation.

Of course, the most grievous and egregious explanation, at least from a Bahá'í perspective, would be that They were dissimulators whose words were actually devised by learned compatriots who acted as ghostwriters for these charismatic founders of religions. Amanat outright rejects this claim, countering the assertions of certain "opponents of the Báb" that it was the learned student Mullá Husayn—the first to recognize the Báb and the one to whom the Báb revealed the opening passages of the Qayyúmu'l-Asmá' on the evening of May 23, 1844— who "instigated and even induced Siyyid 'Alí-Muhammad to claim" He was the promised return of the Twelfth Imam.[64] Amanat also counters the assertion that Mullá Husayn himself "was the author of the writings attributed to the Báb."[65] However, in an apparent attempt to reconcile an academically acceptable explanation for the Báb's sudden erudition and eloquence despite his lack of formal training with the claims of the

Báb that He was divinely appointed by God as a Manifestation and the Primal Point from which the long-awaited Resurrection would unfold, Amanat attempts to offer a somewhat ambiguous middle ground: "One can suggest, then, that if Mullá Husayn at that particular moment had not met him [the Báb] in Shiraz, the course of Siyyid 'Alí-Muhammad's spiritual development might have taken a very different direction."[66]

Amanat seems understandably constrained by his position as a scholar of history to attribute all events—whether individual or collective—to material causes. Thus, throughout his informative survey of the historical, religious, and cultural context in which the Báb appeared, it seems apparent that he was not willing to countenance or even articulate the Bahá'í theory of explicit divine interventions in history as the motive force propelling civilization forward.

How might scholars, working within the expectations of their academic discipline, grapple with this issue? To begin with, it would certainly be possible to describe the same events from a Bahá'í perspective without implying the acceptance of such assertions, but rather simply portraying the account in terms of Bahá'í belief. For example, one could cite the account by Mullá Husayn of how the Báb asserted to him that He was the Promised One foretold by Siyyid Kázim-i-Rashtí, the teacher of Mullá Husayn, and how the Báb offered certain specific proofs of that assertion, the most convincing of which to Mullá Husayn was the Báb's spontaneous unfolding during the course of one evening the first chapter of His commentary on the Súrih of Joseph from the Qur'án: "I sat spellbound by His utterance, oblivious of time and of those who awaited me," Mullá Husayn recalls. "Suddenly the call of the Mu'adhdhín, summoning the faithful to their morning prayer, awakened me from the state of ecstasy into which I seemed to have fallen. All the delights, all the ineffable glories, which the Almighty has recounted in His Book as the priceless possessions of the people of Paradise—these I seemed to be experiencing that night."[67]

The problem Amanat faces is important and understandable. If he were to rely solely on material derived from authoritative Bahá'í sources to portray the course of this history, the objectivity of his account might be called into question. The same problem holds true for anyone else who might wish to approach the life and works of the Báb and Bahá'u'lláh from a postmodern critical lens or any other theoretical stance relying solely on materialist explanations.

Another result of this dilemma, as demonstrated in Amanat's account, is evident in a statement where he observes that the Báb "was beginning to believe that he must have been chosen for a divine mission," the nature of which "remained unclear to him for some time."[68] While Amanat in no way implies that the Báb was insincere in this belief or aspiring to power, he clearly implies that the Báb's belief was a logical result of the His interest in the "the esoteric tradition elaborated by Aḥsá'í [Shaykh Aḥmad Aḥsá'í, founder of the Shaykhí movement] and Rashtí [Siyyid Káẓim-i-Rashtí, his successor and teacher of Mullá Husayn]," further suggesting that "his interest in secrets of occult sciences increasingly drew his attention to eschatological themes."[69]

While such an interpretation appears valid within the framework of materialist critical theory, it is unlikely to satisfy a well-informed reader who is not committed to that framework, i.e., not necessarily one who believes in the Báb's claim to privileged metaphysical insight, but even one who is "agnostic" as to the metaphysical question. The attempt to explain the Báb's life and ministry in materialist terms appears on its face inadequate and insufficient when it does not at least call into account the explanation so plainly set forth by the Báb, by Mullá Husayn, and by evidence derived from the remarkable outpouring of works revealed by the Báb when He was a solitary prisoner in the mountain fortress of Máh-Kú without access to the works of others or assistance from anyone else. Indeed, it was during the Báb's nine-month imprisonment in this site that He revealed unaided the Persian Bayán, the major doctrinal work of the Bábí dispensation, a work of some 8,000 verses which Shoghi Effendi describes as the "monumental repository of the laws and precepts of the new Dispensation and the treasury enshrining most of the Báb's references and tributes to, as well as His warning regarding, 'Him Whom God will make manifest.'"[70]

Again, it is not imperative that Amanat express his agreement with the Báb's own explanation for the sudden ability of the unlearned merchant to bring forth such an amazing canon of works. But one would think that in an attempt at presenting an objective analysis of this history, he would be obliged at the very least to articulate what the participants in that history assert occurred, as well as what it is clear they believed to be the logical explanation for these events.

This is not to deny that scholarship in this vein can produce valuable insights but only to suggest that it cannot help us with the core question of what the "Revealed Word" means—what message it may have for

humanity and how we might make use of it. Consequently, inasmuch as
it is this core question that the present study seeks to address, this work
must necessarily adopt a Bahá'í perspective in approaching its subject
matter.

SOME CLARIFICATIONS ABOUT BAHÁ'Í SCHOLARSHIP

Two relevant compilations of passages from authoritative statements
about learning and scholarship have been prepared by the Research
Department of the Universal House of Justice. The first of these, titled
simply *Scholarship*, was published in 1995[71] and consists of three sections: "The Station of Scholarship," "The Function of Scholarship," and
"General Principles and Guidelines" (regarding scholarship).

The passages in the first compilation are largely devoted to encouraging the study of the texts and lauding the scholarly pursuits of those
who wish to pursue various academically sound approaches to examining the history of the Bahá'í Faith, the theological and philosophical principles and theories of the Faith, as well as comparative studies
demonstrating how Bahá'í concepts are borne out in the scripture and
history of prior revealed religions. But in the third section on "General
Principles and Guidelines" are several pertinent cautionary statements
about certain practices and assumptions of contemporary scholarship
that in some cases might cause Bahá'í scholars to assume an entirely
materialistic approach, which can often lead to an inaccurate understanding or interpretation of the Bahá'í texts and Bahá'í history.

Thus, on the one hand, a letter included on behalf of the Universal
House of Justice in 1979 assures Bahá'í scholars that in no way is academic study to be constrained; rather, it is to be encouraged: "The fact
that the Faith, as the Guardian states, 'enjoins upon its followers the
primary duty of an unfettered search after truth', should reassure any
aspiring Bahá'í historian that there can be no question of any requirement to distort history in the so-called 'interests' of the Faith. On the
contrary, the combination of profound faith and freedom of thought is
one of the great strengths of the Bahá'í religion."[72]

At the same time, this first compilation includes several statements
cautioning against "taking for granted the a priori assumptions of modern non-Bahá'í scholars and of allowing their thinking and their understanding of the Faith to be limited by criteria which they themselves, as
Bahá'ís, would know to be in error."[73] Even more to the point, another

statement by the House of Justice warns that by attempting to comply with the tenor of some contemporary trends in religious studies, the Bahá'í scholar can become entrenched in a misrepresentation of verities about reality so clearly articulated in the Bahá'í teachings:

> The principal concern of the House of Justice is over a method-ological bias and discordant tone which seem to inform the work of certain of the authors. The impression given is that, in attempting to achieve what they understand to be academic objectivity, they have inadvertently cast the Faith into a mould which is essentially foreign to its nature, taking no account of the spiritual forces which Bahá'ís see as its foundation. Presumably the justification offered for this approach would be that most scholars of comparative re-ligion are essentially concerned with discernable phenomena, ob-servable events and practical affairs and are used to treating their subject from a western, if not a Christian, viewpoint. This approach, although understandable, is quite impossible for a Bahá'í, for it ig-nores the fact that our world-view includes the spiritual dimension as an indispensable component for consistency and coherence, and it does not beseem a Bahá'í to write . . . about his Faith as if he looked upon it from the norm of humanism or materialism.[74]

This same letter to a National Spiritual Assembly, written on October 4, 1994, concludes with guidance to Bahá'í scholars who have become swayed by these materialistic academic approaches to comparative re-ligion about the obvious dangers of complying with such constraints:

> In other words, we are presented in such articles with the spectacle of Bahá'ís trying to write as if they were non-Bahá'ís. This leads to these authors' drawing conclusions and making implications which are in conflict with Bahá'í teachings and with the reality of the Faith. A good Bahá'í author, when writing for such a publication, should be fully capable of adopting a calmly neutral and exposi-tory tone, without falling into the trap of distorting the picture by adopting what is, in essence, a materialistic and localized stance.[75]

However, as the issue of some Bahá'í scholars assuming materialistic and relativistic approaches to religious studies continued apace in the mid-1990s, the Universal House of Justice found it necessary to issue a second compilation dealing more pointedly with the problem of trying to approach religious study while denying, or else ignoring, the possibility of the existence of a metaphysical reality. Related to this concern was the subsequent need to reject or else avoid considering a reciprocal relationship between the metaphysical realm and the physical realm—that is, the notion that revealed religion plays a significant and continuous role in the evolution and progress of human society.

In a March 14, 1996 letter included in this second compilation, titled *Issues Related to the Study of the Bahá'í Faith: Extracts from Letters Written on Behalf of the Universal House of Justice*, there is, once again, explicit assurance that study of the Bahá'í Faith and its teachings is not only allowed, but fervently encouraged: "As you know, Bahá'u'lláh says that the pursuit of knowledge has been enjoined upon everyone, and knowledge itself is described by Him as 'wings to man's life' and 'a ladder for his ascent.' Those whose high attainments in this respect make it possible for them to contribute in important ways to the advancement of civilization are deserving of society's recognition and gratitude."[76]

In this same compilation is a letter, issued on February 8, 1998, that once again affirms emphatically that in no way can an accurate study of the Bahá'í Faith or its teachings be approached if the author out-of-hand denies, rejects, or excludes from scholarly study the feasibility of Bahá'í foundational beliefs in the existence of a metaphysical realm, in the revelatory process, or in the interpenetration between physical and metaphysical reality, and, therefore, between science and religion:

> The purpose of scholarship in such fields [comparative religion and history] should obviously be the ascertainment of truth, and Bahá'í scholars should, of course, observe the highest standards of honesty, integrity and truthfulness. Moreover, the House of Justice accepts that many scholarly methods have been developed which are soundly based and of enduring validity. It nevertheless questions some presumptions of certain current academic methods because it sees these producing a distorted picture of reality.[77]

That distortion, the letter goes on to observe, especially as it is promulgated in the training of scholars in such fields as religious studies and history, "seems to have restricted their vision and blinded them to the culturally determined basis of elements of the approach they have learned."[78] The letter continues by noting that such a limited and limiting approach can cause the scholar "to exclude from consideration factors which, from a Bahá'í point of view, are of fundamental importance. Truth in such fields cannot be found if the evidence of Revelation is systematically excluded and if discourse is limited by a basically deterministic view of the world."[79]

EXEGESIS, HERMENEUTICS, AND THE ASSUMPTION OF AUTHORITY

There are various approaches associated with the deep study of a text—such as exegesis, hermeneutics, and various forms of literary criticism: historical critical theory, formalist theory or "new criticism," modernism, feminist literary criticism, postmodernism (new historicism), and cultural studies, to cite some of the most familiar approaches to literary analysis in scholarly studies.[80] Common to all of these is the assumption that beneath the surface or literal meaning of a work are other layers of meaning, whether or not intended by the author. Within the materialist framework discussed above, approaches that focus on unintentional or socially conditioned meanings will often be favored. But in regard to the deep analysis of religious texts, or scriptural study, exegesis is the most appropriate term to apply and, historically, the traditional approach in unearthing the symbolic or figurative meaning that, most scholars assume, is intentionally implanted by the writer or prophet and subsequently deciphered authoritatively by clerics and divines who are deemed—or who deem themselves—qualified to discern the spiritual or metaphysical intent of the author. This assumed capacity most often derives from an authority conferred on them by some systematic approach to scholarly training, such as has previously emerged among those world religions in which recognized clerics or divines establish what is then forthwith considered to be the correct or authoritative interpretation or application of scriptural texts.

In the context of exegetical study, then, the reader or scholar most often assumes the true meaning, the intended meaning, is purposefully veiled by the author so that only those endowed with this special capacity can discern the spiritual or divine purpose and application of the text. For example, when Christ on the cross seems to lament that God has abandoned Him—"Why hast thou forsaken me?"—the student of scripture will recognize in this apparent despair the echo of precisely the same words and even the foreshadowing of the entire episode of the crucifixion in Psalm 22, penned prophetically hundreds of years before.

The informed reader will thus discern in Christ's words no lament or despair but yet another attempt on the part of the Messiah to caution His persecutors of their grievous error in failing to recognize the anointed One sent by God precisely as prophesied, the very One Whose advent they have awaited for so long.

On a less scholarly level for those not familiar with the Old Testament, the creative reader will discover throughout the language employed by Christ in His brief ministry a consistent use of accessible symbols, such as His frequent use of imagery related to bread and nourishment. Clearly in these tropes or figurative images, physical food symbolizes or metaphorizes spiritual nourishment, a source of life that endures beyond this life. In this same context, for example, Christ refers to Himself as "The Bread of Life."[81]

Of course, these are fairly simple and obvious examples that hardly require any academic expertise. But it is fair to say that with regard to scripture, whether of the Old Testament, the New Testament, the Qur'án, or the writings of the Bábí Faith or Bahá'í Faith, the intent of the authors—whether the Prophets Themselves or other devoted and spiritually inspired followers—is not to confine true understanding to those with scholarly acumen or those whose have dedicated their lives to such study. Rather, according to statements by Christ, by Muḥammad, and by the Báb and Bahá'u'lláh, one of the great ironies of exegesis is that those who are most often oblivious to the symbolic or deeper meaning of the words are the very scholars and divines whose own learning has become a veil between them and the spiritual intent of scripture, even as Christ notes in Matthew 13:15: "For this people's heart is waxed gross, and their ears are dull of hearing, and their eyes they have closed; lest at any time they should see with their eyes, and hear with their ears, and should understand with their heart, and should be converted, and I should heal them."

Understanding with the heart—as opposed to objective scholarly analysis through some formulaic methodology—is a process Bahá'u'lláh also commends when He notes in the Kitáb-i-Íqán, "No man shall attain the shores of the ocean of true understanding except he be detached from all that is in heaven and on earth."[82] Later in the same work He affirms this axiom with a passage already cited in the previous chapter: "The understanding of His words and the comprehension of the utterances of the Birds of Heaven are in no wise dependent upon human learning. They depend solely upon purity of heart, chastity of soul, and freedom of spirit."[83]

Thus, whether we consider Biblical exegesis, Qur'ánic *tafsir* (interpretation), or the study of and commentary on Bahá'í texts, there is an
underlying assumption that the purpose of this concealment or veiling
of meaning—whether in parables, allegories, symbols, allusions, or
other literary devices—is not to relegate comprehension of scriptural
texts to exegetes or some esoteric class of academics. When Christ's
disciples query Him as to why He responds to the taunting questions put
to Him by the learned divines of that day—principally, the Pharisees
and Sadducees—with puzzling and, for the learned, somewhat inscrutable or abstruse parables, He responds, "Because it is given unto you
to know the mysteries of the kingdom of heaven, but to them it is not
given. For whosoever hath, to him shall be given, and he shall have
more abundance: but whosoever hath not, from him shall be taken away
even that he hath." He concludes, "Therefore speak I to them in parables: because they seeing see not; and hearing they hear not, neither do
they understand." He then cites this same verity as prophesied in Isaiah
6:9: "And in them is fulfilled the prophecy of Esaias, which saith, 'By
hearing ye shall hear, and shall not understand; and seeing ye shall see,
and shall not perceive.'"[84]

In the same vein, Bahá'u'lláh cautioned the learned of His Day that
"the highest and last end of all learning [is] the recognition of Him Who
is the Object of all knowledge; and yet behold how ye have allowed your
learning to shut you out, as by a veil, from Him Who is the Dayspring
of this Light, through Whom every hidden thing hath been revealed."[85]

And yet by no means does Bahá'u'lláh disdain learning, so long as
it does not cause one to become haughty, disdainful, or oblivious to the
fact that all learning has as its ultimate objective the enlightenment,
advancement, and spiritual transformation of humankind: "Great is the
blessedness of that divine that hath not allowed knowledge to become a
veil between him and the One Who is the Object of all knowledge, and
who, when the Self-Subsisting appeared, hath turned with a beaming
face towards Him. He, in truth, is numbered with the learned."[86]

THE DISTINCTION BETWEEN AUTHORITATIVE INTERPRETATION AND PERSONAL STUDY

It should be clear from the above discussion of both the materialistic
perspective and the nature of Bahá'í exegesis that while a willingness

to consider a Bahá'í text through the lens of Bahá'í beliefs is extremely valuable, there is no implication that a student or author who takes such an approach will thereby unlock the "correct"—or even "a correct"— reading of Bahá'u'lláh's works. Instead, it is the contention of this study that the reader who fails to consider these beliefs when attempting to understand the meaning of the work is likely to apprehend far less of what Bahá'u'lláh intends and will be especially hard put to discern the myriad allusions, metaphors, and other figurative devices, the great majority of which derive their meaning from the contextualization we discussed in the previous chapter.

Therefore, in order to assist the reader in appreciating the limitations on any personal claims to authoritative understandings or elucidation of the works of Bahá'u'lláh—by this or any other author—let us make a few observations about the concept of authoritative textual interpretation as defined in the Bahá'í Faith, a point which is, itself, part of the framework of Bahá'í beliefs that is essential to any study of Bahá'í texts.

In the study of what is considered to be the authentic scripture of those religions accepted in the Bahá'í teachings as belonging to the Abrahamic line of Revelations from God—most prominently Judaism, Christianity, Islam, the Bábí Faith, and the Bahá'í Faith[87]—interpretation of the sacred or "revealed" scripture is not only allowed, but encouraged, whether by those appointed for such a lofty purpose or by the ordinary believer. And yet, in each of these religions except the two most recent—the Bábí and Bahá'í Faiths—there emerged bodies of scholars explicitly recognized and sanctioned by those who had assumed authoritative control of the religion, clerics or divines who were looked upon to render binding interpretations of scripture, from which, in many cases, religious and secular law derived.

It should be noted as an aside that what Bahá'u'lláh has prevented through the abolition of the clerical class in His Dispensation should not be allowed to re-emerge through the back door of secular scholarship. The same issue of an implied claim to authoritative interpretation can arise under a different guise when secular scholars of religion adopt a stance of assumed authority because of their academic expertise. In a letter dated March 14, 1996, cited above from the compilation *Issues Related to the Study of the Bahá'í Faith*, the Universal House of Justice praises the various branches of scholarship that can help inform understanding of the Bahá'í Faith, whether for other scholars or for the generality of Bahá'ís and non-Bahá'ís alike. But it then cautions that Bahá'u'lláh has forbidden the formation of a class of scholars charged with creating, and thence imposing, some authoritative interpretation of the Bahá'í texts or Bahá'í history: "Collateral with His summons to the pursuit of knowledge, Bahá'u'lláh has abolished entirely that feature of all past religions by which a special caste of persons such as the Christian priesthood or the Islamic 'ulama came to exercise authority over the religious understanding and practice of their fellow believers."[88]

It is unnecessary and needless here to rehearse the history of how these bodies of learned divines emerged and precisely how they shaped—and too often misshaped—the history of each religion. But it might serve us well before we set out on our own venture in studying Bahá'u'lláh's abstruse and milestone work, the Súriy-i-Haykal, to mention at least two examples of how profoundly the religions were affected by aberrant interpretations from those in authority, examples that underly the guidance in the Bahá'í teachings that no such body of the learned be devised, either now or in the future; that authoritative exegesis be confined to Bahá'u'lláh, 'Abdu'l-Bahá, and the Guardian (Shoghi Effendi); and that authoritative elucidation of the sacred texts be confined to the Universal House of Justice. The rationale for this assertion is that according to Bahá'í belief, the Manifestation has inherent infallibility but also is endowed with the authority and power to confer infallibility (including in interpretation) on others—in this case, on 'Abdu'l-Bahá, Who subsequently bestowed the same on the Guardian. These powers are spelled out in detail in the authoritative testament of Bahá'u'lláh (the Kitáb-i-Ahdí or "The Book of My Covenant") and in the authoritative Will and Testament of 'Abdu'l-Bahá.

RELIGIOUS EXEGESIS GONE AWRY

Nothing can help us better appreciate Bahá'u'lláh's prohibition regarding the creation of an authoritative class of the learned or scholarly divines than what He alludes to as having occurred in the past. And while we could set forth a vast list of instances where such a class of learned divines or scholars has inappropriately assumed authority in matters of interpretation and elucidation of scripture, or where it has been endowed with such authority without intentionally arrogating it to itself, it is useful to cite specific cases where interpretation of scriptural texts has caused the distortion of the teachings of the Founder of a religion, or else has resulted in the creation of baseless laws and constraints on the believers. To highlight the problems caused by this issue—distinct from the materialist denial of divine intervention or the interpenetration of metaphysical and physical realities, and yet often resulting in the reduction of spiritual truths into the purely physical phenomena used to symbolize them in scripture—let it suffice for our limited purposes here to cite two examples of literalist exegesis of text that resulted in the perversion, if not the eventual destruction, of the intended course for each religion.

The Deification of Christ

Nothing became more troublesome, controversial, or divisive in the history of the Christian religion than the attempt by the church fathers to define the ontology of Christ. The study of Christology is complicated and to outline it in full would serve little purpose for the point we are making. Suffice it to say that almost from the point of Christ's death, the question arose as to whether Christ was divine but distinct from God or was God become incarnate.

Reading certain passages out of context would seem to confirm the conclusion by some that Christ was indeed God in the flesh. In John 14:9, Christ responds to Phillip's request to show the disciples this "Father" (to Whom Christ says He is soon going) by asserting, "Have I been so long time with you, and yet hast thou not known me, Philip? he that hath seen me hath seen the Father; and how sayest thou *then*, Shew us the Father?"

How similar this passage is to the most familiar passage we have cited above from the Súriy-i-Haykal where Bahá'u'lláh states, "Naught is seen in My temple but the Temple of God, and in My beauty but His Beauty, and in My being but His Being, and in My self but His Self."[89] And were we to interpret this literally, we might conclude, as did the Christian exegetes and subsequently the Church itself, that Bahá'u'lláh is the incarnation of God, rather than the correct meaning—as noted in chapter 1—that the Manifestation is the perfect incarnation of the virtues, attributes, and powers of God, but not the essence of God (that is, God Himself).

Yet the early Church fathers interpreted this passage literally, even though in the continuation of this same discussion, Christ seems to make clear that He is ontologically distinct from the Father. For example, He states, "I am the true vine, and my Father is the husbandman," and He repeatedly notes that He does and says only as He is directed by the Father: "I can of mine own self do nothing: as I hear, I judge: and my judgment is just; because I seek not mine own will, but the will of the Father which hath sent me."[90]

Yet because so many of Christ's statements about His reality, station, and purpose are imagistic, enigmatic, or symbolic, and inasmuch as He performed what the believers perceived to be palpable miracles, the controversy regarding His station and essential reality accelerated such that by the time of the Council of Nicaea—convened by the Emperor Constantine in 325 in an attempt to arrive at some consensus regarding the ontology of Christ—the issue had become a pitched battle among the most prominent Christian bishops and clerics.

The result of this council was the devising of the beginning of what became known as the Nicene Creed, the central assertion of which is that Jesus Christ is of one and the same essence as the Father. This doctrine, at Constantine's insistence, became further clarified to denote that Christ and God are one and the same, a change the emperor instituted to quell the political implications of the division between the followers of Arius, who asserted that Christ, though divine, was distinct from God, and the followers of Athanasius, who upheld what became the literal trinitarian doctrine—that God the Father, God the Son, and God the Holy Spirit are one and the same reality.

MUHAMMAD AS SEAL OF THE PROPHETS

The literal trinitarian doctrine was explicitly and repeatedly rejected by Muḥammad three hundred years later in the Qur'án. Muḥammad asserts that the eternal and everlasting God is far beyond deigning to bring forth a literal, physical son; that the concept or title of "Son" relates to Christ's station as a Messenger (*Rasul*); and that Christ in no wise disdained such a lofty station as being a Messenger:

O People of the Book! commit no excesses in your religion: nor say of Allah aught but truth. Christ Jesus the son of Mary was (no more than) a Messenger of Allah, and His Word, which He bestowed on Mary, and a Spirit proceeding from Him: so believe in Allah and His Messengers. Say not "Trinity": desist: it will be better for you: for Allah is One Allah: glory be to Him: (for Exalted is He) above having a son. To Him belong all things in the heavens and on earth. And enough is Allah as a Disposer of affairs.

Christ disdaineth not to serve and worship Allah, nor do the angels, those nearest (to Allah): those who disdain His worship and are arrogant, He will gather them all together unto himself to (answer).[91]

From a Bahá'í perspective, Muḥammad authoritatively clarifies this ongoing misunderstanding of Christ's station or ontology—a most grievous exegetical mistake that, among other unfortunate consequences, induced intractable chauvinism in Western Christianity, because no other Abrahamic religion claimed to be founded by God becoming incarnate. And yet, Islam became no less chauvinistic through a similar exegetical misinterpretation of scripture, at least from a Bahá'í view.

In the Qur'án 33:40, Muḥammad famously states that He is the "Seal of the Prophets": "Muhammad is not the father of any of your men, but (he is) the Messenger of Allah, and the Seal of the Prophets: and Allah has full knowledge of all things."[92] Thus, while Muḥammad affirms and explicates in detail throughout the Qur'án the belief that the religions of God are continuous, that each Revelation is part of a single, divinely ordained and coherent organic process whereby the religion of God unfolds in successive and progressive stages, this one passage was, and has continued to be, interpreted by the majority of Muslims to imply that there would be no further Revelations from God, that Muḥammad is the final Messenger, and that Islam is, therefore, the complete and final expression of the religion of God.

While we could examine in detail how this inference came to be accepted as authoritative and why alternative understandings were deterred and rejected, it is sufficient here to note Bahá'u'lláh's explanation of the true meaning of this statement inasmuch as we are employing the Bahá'í lens to examine these issues—a lens the reader is, of course, free to accept or reject.

Succinctly stated, Bahá'u'lláh explains that all the Messengers of God are effectively the "Seal," even as They are also the "Beginning." Thus, in the Book of Revelation, we find four different passages in which Christ asserts, "I am Alpha and Omega, the beginning and the ending."[93] The sense of this, Bahá'u'lláh explains in the Kitáb-i-Íqán, is that each Messenger or Manifestation is the end point for all previous Revelations—the objective foreshadowed and prophesied by previous

Revelations—and the point of beginning in preparation for all future Revelations that will follow without ceasing:

> [H]ow many are those who, through failure to understand its meaning, have allowed the term "Seal of the Prophets" to obscure their understanding, and deprive them of the grace of all His manifold bounties! Hath not Muḥammad, Himself, declared: "I am all the Prophets"? Hath He not said as We have already mentioned: "I am Adam, Noah, Moses, and Jesus"? Why should Muḥammad, that immortal Beauty, Who hath said: "I am the first Adam" be incapable of saying also: "I am the last Adam"? For even as He regarded Himself to be the "First of the Prophets"—that is Adam—in like manner, the "Seal of the Prophets" is also applicable unto that Divine Beauty. It is admittedly obvious that being the "First of the Prophets," He likewise is their "Seal."[94]

While the clerical interpretations mentioned here are not materialist in the same sense as the work of a scholar who rules out the possibility of metaphysical influence in the world, they do show how a literalist approach ends up veiling the spiritual import of the Word. If Christ is literally the Son of God, or Muḥammad is literally the seal or final Manifestation, then these are not assignments of spiritual realities or conditions.

BAHÁ'U'LLÁH'S CAUTION ABOUT SO-CALLED AUTHORITATIVE EXEGESIS

Of course, Bahá'u'lláh's statement about the failure to understand meaning comes in the context of the Kitáb-i-Íqán, His own discourse about how to interpret scripture that is dedicated in part to explaining how the failure of the followers of the prior Revelations to recognize the advent of the succeeding Revelations has resulted in almost entirely misleading interpretations of scripture by religious leaders—clerics and divines—who fail to appreciate the symbolic or figurative meaning underlying the literal text of their own scripture. In short, they became dogmatic in their literalism and thus became unable to read and interpret creatively the prophecies of scripture as these become manifest in the historical and spiritual events to which they allude.

After recounting some salient examples of the irony that the succession of Manifestations was typically rejected by the most prominent followers of the previous Revelation, Bahá'u'lláh concludes this point by observing that the principal reason for this failure was blatant misunderstanding, or else a desire on the part of religious authorities to retain positions of leadership:

> Leaders of religion, in every age, have hindered their people from attaining the shores of eternal salvation, inasmuch as they held the reins of authority in their mighty grasp. Some for the lust of leadership, others through want of knowledge and understanding, have been the cause of the deprivation of the people. By their sanction and authority, every Prophet of God hath drunk from the chalice of sacrifice, and winged His flight unto the heights of glory. What unspeakable cruelties they that have occupied the seats of authority and learning have inflicted upon the true Monarchs of the world, those Gems of divine virtue! Content with a transitory dominion, they have deprived themselves of an everlasting sovereignty. Thus, their eyes beheld not the light of the countenance of the Well-Beloved, nor did their ears hearken unto the sweet melodies of the Bird of Desire. For this reason, in all sacred books mention hath been made of the divines of every age.[95]

With these caveats and this specific guidance in mind, therefore, let us attempt in the exegesis of the Súriy-i-Haykal that follows to employ the creativity and purity of motive, the openness of heart and mind, encouraged by Bahá'u'lláh. All the while, let us bear in mind that no part of the following exegetical exercise, however soundly derived or imaginatively and logically deduced, has any authority, nor is it shared in any spirit but that of the mutual joy of plunging into the vast ocean of Bahá'u'lláh's texts to meditate on the purpose and various levels of meaning of one of the most important and abstruse works revealed by Him. In short, the ultimate goal is simply to encourage other readers and students of the Bahá'í Faith to delight in this same sort of endeavor.

THREE TYPES OF BAHÁ'Í EXEGESIS

While there are no official forms or categories of interpretations of Bahá'í texts, nor any set guidance on how to approach interpretation, we can discern, for the purposes of the concerns we are addressing in this work, three of the most common sorts of interpretation that have emerged in Bahá'í studies.

The first level of interpretation of text occurs when a scholar or a team of scholars translates a text by the Báb, Bahá'u'lláh, or 'Abdu'l-Bahá from the Persian or Arabic into English or into another language. While the intention of such important work is not to impose a certain meaning on a sentence or an entire work, often the original Persian or Arabic is so allusive, figurative, or connotative that it cannot be rendered literally word for word. The translator is thus forced to discover "the intended meaning" of the writer in order to replicate the work as accurately as possible, thereby choosing words that may not be the exact translation of the original words but that do serve to capture the central idea of the work.

Obviously, such an endeavor requires an intimate familiarity with both the original language and the culture in which it is situated, especially the culture that existed at the time of the writing. For example, the Writings of the Báb and Bahá'u'lláh are replete with allusions to the Qur'án, to well-known ḥadíth, and to cultural practices, even though the works are intended to have universal applicability. Consequently, it is most often the case, especially when the Bahá'í World Centre is undertaking the creation of an authoritative translation of a work, that a team of translators will be employed to begin the process of accomplishing this multifaceted task.

In such cases, this endeavor will draw on the services of those who are well versed in the Persian and Arabic languages as well as the cultural history and social context in which the work was written. Fortunately for those working with the Bahá'í texts, exact and complete commentaries about the circumstances surrounding the writing of these works are available in the Bahá'í archives. Such availability of resources does not lessen the amount of study and research required for each work, but it does mean that at the first level of research, gaining access to the relevant materials is not problematic.

Also required for the translation of the Bahá'í authoritative texts is for all those involved to be well versed in Bahá'í teachings and history. Likewise, it is important for some part of such a team to be equally well versed in the subtleties of grammar and idioms of the language into which the text is being translated. And while there have been, and increasingly exist, scholars who are well versed in both languages involved (the language of the original text and the language into which the text is being translated), it is still necessary for several levels of further review to occur to ensure that the translation has captured as nearly as possible what the author intended to say. The ultimate review thus takes place at the level of the Universal House of Justice itself, the final arbiter of how successful the effort has been.

And yet there is always the possibility of a need for further improvement or refinement of translated works, even as has occurred relatively recently with the 2014 re-translation of 'Abdu'l-Bahá's *Some Answered Questions*, which refines and renders more accurate the 1930 translation. In other words, a translation, even if authoritative, will never perfectly replicate the original text.

In this regard, it is well worth noting that while Persian and Arabic are the languages utilized by Bahá'u'lláh for a Revelation intended to guide humanity through this dispensation, it is the authoritative English translation of these texts by Shoghi Effendi to which the members of the Universal House of Justice turn when they are determining the intent or elucidating the text of Bahá'u'lláh's works.

One reason for the primacy of the English language can be found in a statement by 'Abdu'l-Bahá in the authoritative Bahá'í texts. He asserts, "This American nation is equipped and empowered to accomplish that which will adorn the pages of history, to become the envy of the world and be blest in both the East and the West for the triumph of its people . . . . The American continent gives signs and evidences of very great advancement. Its future is even more promising, for its influence and illumination are far-reaching. It will lead all nations spiritually."[96] Therefore, Shoghi Effendi, in preparation for serving 'Abdu'l-Bahá and translating Persian and Arabic into English, studied the language rigorously, first at the American University of Beirut in Lebanon and subsequently at Balliol College at Oxford.

Another attribute of English that makes it particularly capable of capturing the intended meaning of Bahá'í scripture is that it has the richest vocabulary among the languages of the world, is receptive to "loan-words,"[97] and has, during the contemporary era, effectively become the international language of communication for travel and trade.[98] In addition, English is the official language of a number of major global institutions, and it has become the accepted language of the scientific community, being the most-learned language in the world.

In sum, when the Universal House of Justice, or any scholar or ordinary reader, wishes to understand the intended meaning of the original

Arabic or Persian in the Writings of 'Abdu'l-Bahá or Bahá'u'lláh, they can find exactitude and precision in the Guardian's English translation of those passages that might be ambiguous or allusive in the original text. Likewise, because 'Abdu'l-Bahá conferred upon Shoghi Effendi the authority to provide infallible guidance, including interpretation of the sacred texts, his translations into English assume indisputable authority.

Therefore, while Shoghi Effendi translated only portions of the Súriy-i-Haykal, the authorized translation of the remainder of the work utilized several teams of translators who were able to observe how the Guardian had translated the same words or similar passages in the numerous works he did render authoritatively into his stellar and highly acclaimed English prose.

HISTORICAL REVIEW AND INTERPRETATION

As we noted in the introduction, one of the first places to look to discover some authoritative insight into the meaning of a work revealed by the Báb, Bahá'u'lláh, or 'Abdu'l-Bahá is in Shoghi Effendi's *God Passes By*. This text, a gift by the Guardian to the Bahá'ís of the West in centennial commemoration of the founding of the Bahá'í Faith—the Declaration of the Báb in 1844—serves as a foundational chronological review of and commentary on the Bahá'í Faith until the time of its writing in 1944.

In this book, Shoghi Effendi does not always go into great detail about most of the works he mentions, nor does he refer to all of the works penned by these three Figures. But his explication of the major themes of the most important texts can provide the reader with a reliable, authoritative, and insightful starting point in the attempt to study and understand these works in depth. Another service *God Passes By* renders is to assess the relative importance of the various works—in the introduction, we noted his comments about the Súriy-i-Haykal.

A second example of interpretation as a secondary or subsidiary outcome of a historical review of the Bahá'í Faith is the extremely useful and rigorous four-volume study by Adib Taherzadeh, *The Revelation of Bahá'u'lláh*, which surveys the body of works by Bahá'u'lláh. Functioning as both a history of the four major divisions of the life of Bahá'u'lláh and a recounting of the major works revealed in each of these periods, this remarkable undertaking also contains useful comments, plentiful citations about the works from authoritative sources, and Taherzadeh's personal—albeit non-authoritative—summaries of the content, themes, and meanings of these same works.[99]

Here, too, it is not the purpose of Taherzadeh to provide interpretations or exegesis per se, and yet his information about the context in which each work was revealed, as well as his personal assessment of what is contained in each work, offers the student of the Bahá'í Faith and the works of Bahá'u'lláh a most valuable head start. The obvious rationale for a student to utilize Taherzadeh's research and personal understanding of the meaning and import of the works is that a knowledge of the context—when the work was revealed, to whom it was written, and the main themes of the discourse—is extremely valuable, if not essential, when one sets out to study intensively the various levels of symbolic or figurative meaning that might lie veiled beneath the surface.

EXPLICIT INTERPRETATIONS OR EXEGESIS

What we attempt in this examination of the Súriy-i-Haykal falls primarily in a third category of Bahá'í exegesis, the one that is most explicitly exegetical, consisting of attempts at the elucidation of the various levels of meaning of a particular work. For once the reader understands the general context of the work, then a deeper and more creative or imaginative exploration of the text becomes possible.

As we have already noted, individual exploration and creative speculation is both allowed and encouraged, regardless of whether the reader is a believer in the Bahá'í Faith and its teachings. There is always more being communicated in these works than might appear on a first reading. Indeed, some revealed works, especially those by Bahá'u'lláh, warrant numerous examinations, each of which will provide an entirely different experience for the reader; often a panoply of meanings becomes apparent at every successive level of interpretation, each of which may well result in further insights into the "intended meaning" of the work. It is in this context that at the conclusion of the Kitáb-i-Íqán, Bahá'u'lláh cites Sádiq, the sixth of the Shí'ih Imams, to acknowledge that "We speak one word, and by it we intend one and seventy meanings; each one of these meanings we can explain."[100], [101]

Keeping in mind all the plentiful prefatory background, requirements, and caveats we have reviewed regarding the study of Bahá'í texts, let us now begin what is admittedly an incomplete and personal attempt to discern some of the varied purposes Bahá'u'lláh had in mind with His final rendering of the Súriy-i-Haykal.

Chapter 3

Context and Key Symbols

A central objective of our study of the Súriy-i-Haykal is to understand how Bahá'u'lláh through this work illuminates the wisdom with which the Creator, through the intermediary of the Manifestation, progressively portions out authority to human governance and thence to the generality of humankind. This process unfolds in a manner proportional to humankind's evolving needs, and its increasing capacity to understand spiritual concepts and implement them in an ever more complex and expansive social framework for human interaction, a framework in which our physical/social experience can become an increasingly refined expression of the spiritual realm.

This concept, as already noted in the review of the Bahá'í lens through which we are examining this work, is most generally expressed as progressive Revelation, the Bahá'í concept of the progress of human history by means of the periodic divine intervention of the Manifestations. And clearly, as noted in the introduction, the Súrih of the Temple examines this process through various levels of symbolic application of this abiding conceit—the Temple as a place of worship, the Temple as the human body, the Temple as the body of the Manifestation, and finally, the Temple as physical reality as a whole—that is, a symbolic expression of the Body of God.

We noted at the outset that Bahá'u'lláh has the work artistically rendered in the calligraphic form of another symbol—the pentacle or five-pointed star, a device commonly utilized in Islamic culture and art to represent the human body. As we have also previously noted, Bahá'u'lláh's principal use of this device is to proclaim that God has once again made Himself accessible through the advent of a Manifestation for this era, this Day of Days[102] foretold by the Báb and designated by Bahá'u'lláh in the Kitáb-i-Íqán as "the Latter Resurrection."[103]

As stated in the introduction, the Súriy-i-Haykal was first revealed "during His [Bahá'u'lláh's] banishment to Adrianople and later recast after His arrival in 'Akká,"[104] but the expanded version of the work included five letters selected from those He had penned to the various secular and religious rulers: Pope Pius IX, Napoleon III, Czar Alexander II, Queen Victoria, and Naṣíri'd-Dín Sháh. He then added a concluding paragraph so that the Súriy-i-Haykal effectively encompasses the five letters: "It was this composite work which, shortly after its completion, Bahá'u'lláh instructed be written in the form of a pentacle, symbolizing the human temple. To it He added, as a conclusion, what Shoghi Effendi has described as 'words which reveal the importance He attached to those Messages, and indicate their direct association with the prophecies of the Old Testament.'"[105]

Likewise, one major clue to the importance Bahá'u'lláh assigned to this work is indicated by the fact (also cited in the introduction) that it was among the works which, during the last years of His ministry, Bahá'u'lláh Himself had published and disseminated, something noted by 'Abdu'l-Bahá in regard to the specific prophecies included in some of the epistles, as we will note later.

We have also discussed this work as effectively representing the culmination of Bahá'u'lláh's fourth and most forthright declaration of His advent, station, and ministry. No longer concealing His identity or His purpose, He boldly announces in this work His function as the Temple of God among us, asserting that His principal purpose is nothing less than articulating the necessary steps for world leaders to take in beginning to bring forth a global polity, through the attainment of an initial "Lesser Peace"—a peace which will in turn pave the way, by the end of His dispensation, for the establishment of the Golden Age of "the World Order of Bahá'u'lláh," the ultimate paradigm for human governance at the planetary level:

The emergence of a world community, the consciousness of world citizenship, the founding of a world civilization and culture—all of which must synchronize with the initial stages in the unfoldment of the Golden Age of the Bahá'í Era—should, by their very nature, be regarded, as far as this planetary life is concerned, as the furthermost limits in the organization of human society, though man, as an

individual, will, nay must indeed as a result of such a consummation, continue indefinitely to progress and develop.[106]

Throughout the five epistles He includes, Bahá'u'lláh admonishes
the leaders He addresses to recognize His station, to follow His guidance in order to unite the peoples of the world under the banner of a single global polity and social order, to bring about just policies among the
populace who abide under their aegis, and to be just in their treatment
of the Bahá'ís, as well as the peoples of all other religions. He further
cautions certain of these leaders that if they fail to heed His advice, they
will reap retributive consequences. For some, He indicates that their
fate has already been sealed as the direct result of their prior treacherous
actions and their unjust and immoral policies.

In his own comments about the importance of the Súriy-i-Haykal,[107]
Shoghi Effendi alludes to the fact that the work fulfills the prophecy by
Zechariah (6:12–13) regarding the rebuilding of the temple, which is
actually an eschatological reference to the advent of Bahá'u'lláh, as opposed to an allusion to an actual third temple building to be constructed
after the destruction of the second temple in 70 CE by the Romans. It
is also worth noting that in his article "An Introduction to the Súratu'l-
Haykal (Discourse of The Temple)," Mohamad Ghasem Bayat states
that even the second temple as alluded to by Zechariah "actually refers
to the Person of Jesus and not the perishable building of the Temple of
Solomon."[108]

When describing the import of Bahá'u'lláh's first intimations of His
Revelation in the Siyáh-Chál, Shoghi Effendi refers to this same prophecy, together with other prophecies from the Old Testament that likewise allude to the advent of Bahá'u'lláh and the building of the Temple
of the Lord:

> To Him Isaiah, the greatest of the Jewish prophets, had alluded as
> the "Glory of the Lord," the "Everlasting Father," the "Prince of
> Peace," the "Wonderful," the "Counsellor," the "Rod come forth
> out of the stem of Jesse" and the "Branch grown out of His roots,"
> Who "shall be established upon the throne of David," Who "will
> come with strong hand," Who "shall judge among the nations,"
> Who "shall smite the earth with the rod of His mouth, and with
> the breath of His lips slay the wicked," and Who "shall assemble
> the outcasts of Israel, and gather together the dispersed of Judah

from the four corners of the earth." Of Him David had sung in his Psalms, acclaiming Him as the "Lord of Hosts" and the "King of Glory." To Him Haggai had referred as the "Desire of all nations," and Zachariah as the "Branch" Who "shall grow up out of His place," and "shall build the Temple of the Lord." Ezekiel had extolled Him as the "Lord" Who "shall be king over all the earth," while to His day Joel and Zephaniah had both referred as the "day of Jehovah," the latter describing it as "a day of wrath, a day of trouble and distress, a day of wasteness and desolation, a day of darkness and gloominess, a day of clouds and thick darkness, a day of the trumpet and alarm against the fenced cities, and against the high towers." His Day Ezekiel and Daniel had, moreover, both acclaimed as the "day of the Lord," and Malachi described as "the great and dreadful day of the Lord" when "the Sun of Righteousness" will "arise, with healing in His wings," whilst Daniel had pronounced His advent as signalizing the end of the "abomination that maketh desolate."[109]

Additionally, the Súriy-i-Haykal effectively represents the climax, and communicates the overarching purpose, of Bahá'u'lláh's proclamation to these world leaders regarding the strategic actions they can take to change the course of human history and, by doing so, achieve a historical status that no other expression of power or prestige could garner for them.

As discussed in some detail in *The Ocean of His Words*,[110] by no means are these "form letters." Each epistle is precisely tailored to the character and personality of the recipients, as well as to the social and political policies they have implemented. This tailoring, including in passages in which Bahá'u'lláh reveals His omniscience, strongly suggests that these leaders had reason to pay careful attention to these letters as being from someone of spiritual insight, as opposed to being merely one from among the many aberrant messages the monarchs and leaders doubtlessly received frequently.

For example, the careful reader will note that in some of these letters, Bahá'u'lláh includes allusions to specific words these leaders have said or actions they have undertaken in private, Bahá'u'lláh's knowledge of which, one would imagine, should have caused them to be shocked, bewildered, astounded, especially since the Writer was not even a citizen of their countries or someone moving in the same political circles who might be capable of an educated guess as to the private thoughts, words, and deeds of the monarchs. No, these eloquent epistles were conveyed to them from a then-unknown Persian imprisoned by the mighty Ottoman government.

The reactions to, and impact and outcomes of Bahá'u'lláh's epistles—each message carefully tailored to the personality, leadership, and intentions of these renowned figures—is one of the central themes of Shoghi Effendi's *The Promised Day is Come*, which reveals how Bahá'u'lláh's foreshadowing of the future was fulfilled for each of the recipients, something we will also examine in more detail later.

We would also do well to take note of a statement by 'Abdu'l-Bahá in a talk made in New York on November 15, 1912 indicating that the Súriy-i-Haykal had been published and circulated in India thirty years before (ca. early 1880s), thereby causing the peoples aware of this work to await with great anticipation the fulfillment of Bahá'u'lláh's dire prophecies for some of these recipients, all of which had come true, or else were in the process of taking place:

> The book containing these Epistles to the kings was published in India about thirty years ago and is known as the Súratu'l-Haykal ("Discourse of the Temple"). Whatever is recorded in these Epistles has happened. Some of the prophecies contained in them came to pass after two years; others were fulfilled after five, ten and twenty years. The most important prophecies relative to events transpiring in the Balkans are being fulfilled at the present time though written long ago. For instance, in the Epistle which Bahá'u'lláh addressed to the Sulṭán of Turkey, the war and the occurrences of the present day were foretold by Him. These events were also prophesied in the Tablet He addressed to the city of Constantinople, even to the details of happenings now being witnessed in that city.[111]

Of course, any assessment of the context in which this important work was revealed, the epistles included, and its final calligraphic form crafted, would be incomplete without mentioning the memorable events surrounding the delivery of the final and most extensive letter included among the five letters in the Súriy-i-Haykal: the Lawḥ-i-Sulṭán, the letter to Naṣíri'd-Dín Sháh, the most lengthy and complex synthesis of behests, warnings, chastisement, and guidance among these epistles.

Prior to being copied into calligraphic form as part of the pentacle in the Súriy-i-Haykal, the letter, having been revealed earlier in

Adrianople, would be delivered to the Sháh after Bahá'u'lláh had been exiled to 'Akká by one whom Bahá'u'lláh had especially chosen for this mission: Áqá Buzurg, a seventeen-year-old whom Bahá'u'lláh titled "Badí'" ("Wonderful"). Even though Bahá'u'lláh had cautioned that whoever conveyed the tablet to the Sháh would most certainly be killed, many vied for this honor, yet Bahá'u'lláh chose the young Badí'.

As Bahá'u'lláh had prophesied, after Badí' traveled to Persia on foot and presented the Lawḥ-i-Sulṭán to the Sháh, he was tortured and killed in a most grotesque manner:

> It was reserved for Násiri'd-Dín Sháh, however, to wreak, at the instigation of the divines, his vengeance on One Whom he could no longer personally chastise by arresting His messenger, a lad of about seventeen, by freighting him with chains, by torturing him on the rack, and finally slaying him.[112]

Even today Bahá'ís marvel at the pictures of the brave young man, both before his mission and in chains just moments before he was martyred.

Badí', aged fifteen. The photo was taken approximately two years before he undertook his mission on behalf of Bahá'u'lláh[113]

Badí', aged seventeen, chained before his execution[114]

For his bravery, Bahá'u'lláh bestowed upon him the title of *Fakh-ru'sh-Shuhadá'* ("Pride of Martyrs"). And later in this study as we examine the letter he delivered, we will come to appreciate how Bahá'u'lláh foreknew the anger this epistle would provoke in this presumptuous and pretentious king who held an obsessive, unquenchable hatred for the Bábís, the Bahá'ís, and most especially for Bahá'u'lláh Himself.

SOME STRATEGIC SYMBOLS

But with all this prefatory information, it is now possible and appropriate to begin trying to discern how this symbolic work portrays the descent of authority from the realm of the spirit, through the utterances and actions of the Manifestations, to human governance, and ultimately to the level of the community and the neighborhood.

First, let us examine the major symbol overarching all the subordinate literary devices. As stated above, the title "Súriy-i-Haykal" (Súrih of the Temple) announces the major symbol unifying the work—the human temple as symbolized so potently in the final calligraphic configuration of the work in the form of a pentacle, a five-pointed star: the top point of the pentacle represents the head; the two side points, the arms; and the bottom two points, the legs.

While, so far as we know, the original of this completed work cannot be found, we do have a useful example of a similar calligraphic design in the so-called "Star Tablet" of the Báb, which, like Bahá'u'lláh's final rendering of the Súriy-i-Haykal, is constructed entirely of the calligraphy that is the work itself:

Written in the Báb's own hand, this exquisite work demonstrates the remarkable calligraphy of this supposed "unlearned" merchant, who, early in His youth, had already demonstrated knowledge beyond the ken of His own teachers.[115]

I include the star tablet here to illustrate how the final rendering commissioned by Bahá'u'lláh might have looked, but I also theorize how the five tablets to the representative kings and rulers might have been included in the final version of the Súriy-i-Haykal. That is, it would seem logical, given this design, that Bahá'u'lláh would have had the five epistles positioned in each of the five points of the *haykal*, with the Súriy-i-Haykal itself possibly occupying the center.

THE USE OF THE HAYKAL IN THE RINGSTONE SYMBOL

A parallel symbolic representation of the Manifestation as the Intermediary between God and humankind occurs in 'Abdu'l-Bahá's calligraphic design of what is called "the ringstone symbol," which also utilizes the pentacle to represent the human temple, the *haykal*.

Bahá'í scholar Abu'l-Qasim Faizi has provided a detailed explanation of this symbolic design, and we would do well to review some of his conclusions.[116] Faizi demonstrates how this arrangement can be understood as a succinct visual statement of the Bahá'í concepts of both how creation itself is arranged and how the Creator oversees and directs the course of human history by delegating authority to the Manifestations, Who, in turn, delegate authority to whatever form of human governance best befits the needs and challenges of a particular era or dispensation in human history.

Faizi begins by noting how the lines (which are actually a combination of the letters "b" and "h") comprise three horizontal levels. The first or topmost level represents the world or realm of God as Creator. The second or middle level represents the world of the Prophets or Manifestations, from Whom the Cause, or Command of God, emanates. The third or lowest horizontal line represents the world of man, the realm of physical reality or the created world.

As discussed in the first chapter, in the Bahá'í conception the Creator guides human social, spiritual, and material progress is by sending the Prophets—the Vicegerents or Manifestations—Who, though pre-existent in the realm of the spirit, "accept descent from their realms on high and suffer the abasement of living in human temples, walking amongst men and speaking their languages."[117] The two five-pointed stars in this symbolic arrangement are placed on either side of the middle line and represent the attributes of God made perceptible or manifest when the Prophets of God assume a bodily or physical form and a persona. In particular, the two stars represent the twin Manifestations—the Báb and Bahá'u'lláh—come in this Day to guide humankind to make the transition from its previous stages of infancy, childhood, and adolescence to maturity and adulthood. In short, this is a singular event in the course of human history, for, having attained adulthood, humankind, the Bahá'í writings assert, will never regress to former stages. Like any other organism, the evolving human body politic achieves maturation only once.

Finally, the descending line represents the Holy Spirit as It emanates from the realm of the Creator, inspires and animates the Manifestations, and through Them brings about creation itself. And, over the course of time, the Manifestations guide and direct the course of human affairs, including the development of an increasingly more complex political structure to befit more encompassing and complex social structures—tribes, villages, cities, city-states, nation-states, and finally, a global commonwealth.

Faizi further explains the symbolism of the two letters that are employed in this symbolic arrangement. The letter "b" (beh) in the original Arabic script is written as ب and "h" (ha) is written as ه. The "b" symbolizes the name "Bahá," and "h" symbolizes the name of "the Báb." The symbolic numerical value of these two letters according to the *abjad* system is also important to this arrangement. In fact, it is still common today to find poets, "doctors of religion," and other writers who will convey ideas through the symbology of the numerical value of letters.

For example, this methodology was often employed by the Báb in bestowing titles that contained the same numerical value as the recipients' original names. Faizi cites several of these: "For example, he called 'Mahku,' 'Basit' (open). Mahku and Basit have the same numerical value of 72. He called Chihrig 'Shadid' (Grievous). Both of these have a numerical value of 318. Likewise, the great author of *The Dawn-Breakers* was named Muhammad, but surnamed 'Nabil'; both names have a numerical value of 92."[118]

But let us return to the symbolic numerical value of letters, as this *abjad* system is utilized in the calligraphic design in the ringstone symbol. As stated, the letters "b" and "h" stand for the names of Bahá'u'lláh and the Báb, respectively. The numerical value of the word "Báb" is 5: "b" = 2, "a" = 1, and "b" = 2, thereby totaling 5. The numerical value of Bahá is 9: "b" = 2, "a" = 1, "h" = 5, and "a" = 1, thereby totaling 9. And nine is traditionally considered the ultimate or perfect number because to increase value beyond nine, one must start repeating previous numbers. Consequently, nine is traditionally deemed in Islamic cultures to be endowed with mystical qualities and powers and connotes the idea of completeness or sufficiency.

Finally, as noted, the inclusion of the two five-pointed stars in the ringstone symbol represents the "twin Manifestations"—the Báb and Bahá'u'lláh—while the vertical line passing through the three horizontal lines represents the Holy Spirit emanating from God, descending to the intermediary level of the Manifestations (the realm of command) and from there to the created realm, where it is manifested in physical reality that humankind might become enlightened and transformed.

THE SYMBOLIC MEANINGS OF THE WORD "HAYKAL"

The pentacle as employed by Bahá'u'lláh in the literal shape of the work and as symbolically utilized within the tablet would thus seem to represent divine guidance translated into human expression and delegated to human governance—through both the words of the Manifestations (Their written or revealed utterances) and through Their exemplary character and actions when They appear among us in the guise of ordinary human beings.

Of course, as already noted, the *haykal* as a symbol by itself does not necessarily represent the Manifestations—Who, as stated before, are another and higher level of being—but rather the human temple, the human appearance, or the material aspect of the Manifestation. It is in this sense that we may reasonably conclude that in the Súriy-i-Haykal the Will of God is conveyed to human governance indirectly through the advent and subsequent guidance provided by the Manifestations to kings and rulers and other forms of human governance, and simultaneously to the human body politic as a whole. Thus, in its most inclusive usage, the "temple" symbolizes the implementation of God's plan for humankind, whether in just forms of governance, civil laws, social norms, a spiritual regimen for the individual, or, over the course of time, an "ever-advancing civilization."[119]

But again, the notion of the human body—whether of an ordinary human or of the Manifestation— as a temple is itself symbolic, the temple being literally a place of worship and thus figuratively the abode of God or a place where the worshiper can gain access to the Holy Spirit. Symbolically, then, the human body is the figurative abode of our essential reality, the means by which our soul—our consciousness and all our other human faculties—commune and interact with material reality and, as alluded to through the classroom analogy in chapter 1, learn spiritual and abstract lessons through physical exercises.

Yet another important but less obvious figurative significance of the *haykal* in the tablet is the symbolic value of the letters in the word "*haykal*." Explicated concisely in a footnote to the text, the symbolic value of each letter is described as follows: "The word *Haykal* (Temple) is composed in Arabic of the four letters *Há', Yá', Káf* and *Lám* (HYKL). Its first letter is taken to symbolize the word *Huvíyyah* (Essence of Divinity); its second letter the word *Qadír* (Almighty), of which *Yá'* is the third letter; its third letter the word *Karím* (All-Bountiful); and its fourth letter the word *Faḍl* (Grace), of which *Lam* is the third letter."[120]

A more poetic and spiritual explanation of the letters is provided by Bahá'u'lláh in the body of the tablet when the Maid of Heaven addresses each letter individually, bestows upon it a spiritual signification, and foreordains for it the purpose it will serve in fulfilling the Will of God. In paragraphs 36–47, as each letter is addressed, the third letter representing "the All-Bountiful" is given the greatest attention with a succession of six demonstrations of how the Manifestation will bestow bounty upon humankind.

VARIOUS ANCIENT AND CONTEMPORARY MEANINGS OF THE PENTACLE

While it is needless here to examine in exhaustive detail the storied history of the symbolic usage of the pentacle or pentagram, before we proceed to examine further how Bahá'u'lláh has employed this device it will be helpful for the reader to become aware of at least two other categories of usage that have occurred in the context of cultural, theological, and normative discourse.

Because of the exploration of Satanism, Occultism, and the modern pagan religion of Wicca in popular culture—particularly in contemporary cinema—most people are familiar with the pentagram as symbolizing such beliefs. In conjunction with these beliefs, the pentagram is often portrayed as a means of conjuring spirits from the underworld.

The origins of this connotation of the pentacle or pentagram is complex. The pentagram features in such prominent literature as Christopher Marlowe's play *The Tragical History of the Life and Death of Doctor Faustus*, composed in the Elizabethan era of the late 16th century, but there are far earlier uses of the pentacle: in ancient Mesopotamian religion, around 3500 BCE, to represent the goddess Inanna; in Greek Pythagoreanism in the 6th century BCE and in Neoplatonism in the 3rd century CE as a symbol of human health; in the Taoist Chinese tradition to symbolize the five elements (earth, metal, water, wood, and fire); and finally and most importantly in Heinrich Cornelius Agrippa's *Three Books of Occult Philosophy*, 1533 CE, where the human body is inscribed in, and symbolized by, a pentagram:

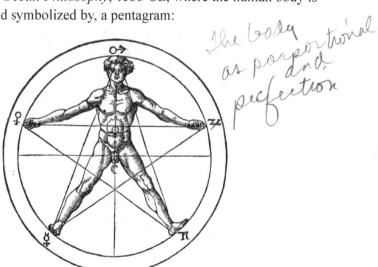

Symbols of the sun and moon are in center, while the five signs in the perimeter represent the five known planets or the cosmos[121]

An obvious counterpoint to Agrippa's association of the pentagram with the human body in the context of occult philosophy is found in Leonardo da Vinci's more famous and artistically accomplished "Vitruvian Man" (1490). Here, while the intent is not to specifically highlight the pentacle, that shape is nevertheless suggested by the extension of the limbs within geometric forms. The effect is to highlight the human body as a symbol of proportionality and perfection—an understanding that brings us closer to the second category of usage of the pentacle that we wish to highlight.

THE PENTANGULAR KNIGHT

For students of English literature, one of the most notable uses of the "pentangle" (yet another term for the five-pointed star) in representing humankind occurs in the anonymous Middle English poem *Sir Gawain and the Green Knight*. Composed during the height of the popularity of the evolving Arthurian legend, this narrative depicts in alliterative verse the testing of one who epitomizes the five categories of chivalric virtue. He is, as it were, the perfect knight.[122]

Without going too deeply into the marvelous symbolic structure of the work, we can consider a few of its most important allusions in order to derive a valuable comparison between how this author employs the symbolic pentangle and how Bahá'u'lláh utilizes the same device in the Súriy-i-Haykal. First and most obviously, the pentangle is the symbol displayed on the outside of Gawain's shield, which on the inside features an image of the Virgin Mary. As a device for protecting the knight in battle, the shield thus symbolizes both outward or physical protection, and inward or spiritual protection.

The outward symbolism of the pentangle therefore represents those attributes that should govern the conduct of a knight—the chivalric code—as the author spells out in detail. Each point represents one of the five categories of the knight's perfection: 1) perfection in his five senses; 2) perfection in his five fingers (his physical strength and prowess); 3) perfection in his faith, found in the five wounds of Christ; 4) the five joys of Mary (whose image, as we have noted, is on the inside of the shield); and 5) the five courtly virtues of friendship, fraternity, purity, politeness, and pity.

Interestingly, the work also can be seen as demonstrating how the knight gains a sort of further wisdom and, in my opinion, a further perfection, at least as far as the human condition is concerned. Gawain undergoes three tests in which he is tempted by the wife of his host as he prepares for his encounter with the infamous Green Knight, who most surely will slay him. For the first two nights, Gawain resists admirably without in any way insulting the beautiful lady of the castle. But on the third night, while still resisting her physical charms, he does accept from her the gift of a scarf, a talisman which, she assures him, will protect him in his forthcoming battle.

Without rehearsing the rest of the story, when he encounters the Green Knight at the climax, he discovers that the host himself is that fearsome creature and that the three temptations were the real tests, not the confrontation with the Green Knight. Therefore, Gawain receives three strokes from the Green Knight's blade, the first two of which are withheld from cutting his flesh, but the third of which inflicts a slight "nick."

When Gawain returns from his venture to the court of King Arthur, he is greatly celebrated for undertaking this quest and, even more importantly, having succeeded. And yet Gawain feels himself a failure. Instead of relying on his shield and all it symbolizes—his pentangular virtues, as well as his faith in the Virgin Mary to protect him—he relied on a supposedly magic green totem as a sort of backup protection.

The rest of the knights joke about his all-too-serious sense of failure and decide to wear scarfs on their sleeves as a sign of their desire to attain such honor and bravery as Gawain has achieved. Gawain also wears the scarf, but for him it is a reminder of his failure, his reliance on something other than the very values—both chivalric and religious—to which he has dedicated his life and allegiance.

In sum, Gawain confronts his own humanity. He is, as it were, as perfect as a man might be, but being human, he will always fall short of complete perfection, a station reserved for Christ or Mary. In this sense, then, the pentangle represents that expression of perfection that is available to a human being. Even as 'Abdu'l-Bahá notes, no matter how virtuous a man can become, there is always room for improvement; we never attain some final condition beyond which no further advancement is feasible—not with respect to a single virtue, let alone with regard to the panoply of all possible virtues: "Thus, however learned a man may be, it is always possible to imagine one even more learned."[123]

Thus, we see from *Sir Gawain and the Green Knight* that the pentacle has a long history of usage that, far from signifying some attempt to gain power through occult practices, speaks to the religiously-informed pursuit of spiritual perfection.

The Historical Context

Before we begin assessing other symbols and the multiple layers of meaning to which they allude, we would benefit from first reviewing the historical context in which the work was initially revealed. We can then comprehend more easily how and why Bahá'u'lláh had it reconstructed into its final form as we have described it.

An Allegorical Dialogue in the Siyáh-Chál

As one begins to read this challenging work, it is valuable to be aware of two crucial points. First, this tablet is written as an account of the first intimation of Bahá'u'lláh's Revelation while imprisoned in the Siyáh-Chál, even though more than fifteen years had passed since that milestone event when the tablet was penned. Second, the work is portrayed by Bahá'u'lláh as a dialogue between His rational soul and the Holy Spirit abiding in Him, portrayed analogically by the Maid of Heaven.

We are thus introduced to the principal narrative voice in the work, which is most familiarly described in the *Lawḥ-i-Sulṭán*, the tablet to Naṣíri'd-Dín Sháh, composed around this same time in Adrianople: "O King! I was but a man like others, asleep upon My couch, when lo, the breezes of the All-Glorious were wafted over Me, and taught Me the knowledge of all that hath been. This thing is not from Me, but from One Who is Almighty and All-Knowing. And He bade Me lift up My voice between earth and heaven, and for this there befell Me what hath caused the tears of every man of understanding to flow."[124]

Bahá'u'lláh illuminates His experience in the Siyáh-Chál by depicting an allegorical dialogue between the Maid of Heaven and Himself. This is the "Luminous Maid," "clad in white," as described by Bahá'u'lláh in the *Lawḥ-i-Ru'ya* ("Tablet of the Vision"), revealed in 1872.[125] In the Súriy-i-Haykal, Bahá'u'lláh portrays the Maid and her first interaction with Him as follows:

While engulfed in tribulations I heard a most wondrous, a most sweet voice, calling above My head. Turning My face, I beheld a Maiden—the embodiment of the remembrance of the name of My Lord—suspended in the air before Me. So rejoiced was she in her very soul that her countenance shone with the ornament of the good pleasure of God, and her cheeks glowed with the brightness of the All-Merciful. Betwixt earth and heaven she was raising a call which captivated the hearts and minds of men. She was imparting to both My inward and outer being tidings which rejoiced My soul, and the souls of God's honoured servants.[126]

Bahá'u'lláh then describes the first major proclamation by the Maid in this dream vision, the beginning of the dialogue between the Maid—as the voice of the Holy Spirit—and the Temple, which is the personage of Bahá'u'lláh:

Pointing with her finger unto My head, she addressed all who are in heaven and all who are on earth, saying: By God! This is the Best-Beloved of the worlds, and yet ye comprehend not. This is the Beauty of God amongst you, and the power of His sovereignty within you, could ye but understand. This is the Mystery of God and His Treasure, the Cause of God and His glory unto all who are in the kingdoms of Revelation and of creation, if ye be of them that perceive. This is He Whose Presence is the ardent desire of the denizens of the Realm of eternity, and of them that dwell within the Tabernacle of glory, and yet from His Beauty do ye turn aside.[127]

Of course, this is not the complete statement of the Maid, as she announces to "all who are in heaven and all who are on earth" the advent of Bahá'u'lláh and what His appearance signifies regarding this long-awaited turning point in human history.[128] But in terms of understanding the narrative architecture of the work, it is important that we take note of some important points about the literary structure.

First of all, because this is a dream vision, we are not supposed to imagine that a literal maiden appeared in the Siyáh-Chál, nor that Bahá'u'lláh was actually asleep upon a couch. His feet were bound in stocks and His neck bowed by the weight of the infamous chains—the Qará-Guhar and the Salásil—even as Bahá'u'lláh notes in *Epistle to the Son of the Wolf*:

Thou canst well imagine what befell Us. Shouldst thou at some time happen to visit the dungeon of His Majesty the Sh́áh, ask the director and chief jailer to show thee those two chains, one of which is known as Qará-Guhar, and the other as Salásil. I swear by the Daystar of Justice that for four months this Wronged One was tormented and chained by one or the other of them. "My grief exceedeth all the woes to which Jacob gave vent, and all the afflictions of Job are but a part of My sorrows!"[129]

To state the sense of this dialogue in more mundane terms, this is but one of the countless examples where Bahá'u'lláh utilizes various creative literary modes and devices to make complex spiritual concepts and processes more comprehensible to ordinary readers. Thus, in literal terms, the dialogue maintained throughout the Súriy-i-Haykal is dominated by the voice-persona of the Maid of Heaven. Yet, as Adib Taherzadeh helpfully notes in his discussion of this work, "It is fascinating to know that the One Who speaks with the voice of God in this Tablet is identical with the One spoken to."[130] It is in this context that the dialogical part of the Súriy-i-Haykal might call to mind for the reader 'Abdu'l-Bahá's description of the process that takes place when an ordinary individual enters a state of reflection or meditation: "It is an axiomatic fact that while you meditate you are speaking with your own spirit. In that state of mind you put certain questions to your spirit and the spirit answers: the light breaks forth and the reality is revealed."[131]

But even though the dialogue is portrayed in this figurative framework, we can presume that the internal meditative process between the Holy Spirit operating through Bahá'u'lláh and His own consciousness is quite real. That is, in the Kitáb-i-Íqán, Bahá'u'lláh lays out in full the distinction between the dual stations occupied by each Manifestation—the station of essential unity and the station of distinction, a concept we will soon address. Furthermore, the information that emerges from this internal reflection (or conversation) is serious and illuminating, laying out as it does during the first intimation of Bahá'u'lláh's Revelation (even if written down by Bahá'u'lláh years later, and thus in retrospect) the tribulations He must endure, the powers He must wield if He is to succeed, and the capacities or attributes He must employ if He is to survive adversity and, thereby, courageously and unstintingly carry out His world-transforming mission.

The outline I have assembled for this study in the appendix should assist the reader in appreciating exactly how the voice-persona of the Maid (the Holy Spirit manifesting Itself through the mind and soul of Bahá'u'lláh) predominates the majority of the work. Indeed, the closing paragraph that follows the last of the five letters—the letter to Naṣíri'd-Dín Sháh—is also in the voice of the Maid, or symbolically, the voice of the Holy Spirit associating with Bahá'u'lláh.

As we have already noted, "Temple" has various levels of symbolic significance. But inasmuch as the Temple at the second level of symbolism (after the Temple as a physical place of worship) represents the physical aspect of the manifest condition of Bahá'u'lláh, one might well think of this entire work in terms of a period of reflection and meditation by Bahá'u'lláh, cautioning Himself about how He must gird His loins and steel His courage and constancy to endure all that He was then undergoing in the Síyáh-Chál, and all the suffering—both physical and psychological—that He would subsequently be forced to endure.

Of course, at the time of the revelation of this tablet in Adrianople, Bahá'u'lláh had already experienced grievous tribulations and attacks. Most notable, perhaps, were the Ayyám-i-Shidad, "the Days of Stress" discussed earlier in the context of what I have called Bahá'u'lláh's third Declaration—the period when Mírzá Yaḥyá openly rebelled against Bahá'u'lláh. Indeed, Shoghi Effendi describes the actions of Mírzá Yaḥyá, which precipitated the "Most Great Separation," as more grievous and devastating than all the previous tribulations that had plagued the twenty-five-year-old Faith. "Neither the tragic martyrdom of the Báb nor the ignominious attempt on the life of the sovereign, nor its bloody aftermath, nor Bahá'u'lláh's humiliating banishment from His native land, nor even His two-year withdrawal to Kurdistan, devastating though they were in their consequences," Shoghi Effendi eloquently asserts, "could compare in gravity with this first major internal convulsion which seized a newly rearisen community, and which threatened to cause an irreparable breach in the ranks of its members."[132] Shoghi Effendi then compares the betrayal of Mírzá Yaḥyá to the betrayals wrought in previous dispensations—on Muḥammad by His uncle Abu-Jahl, on Christ by Judas Iscariot, on Joseph by his brothers, on Noah by one of His sons, and on Cain by Abel. The rupture resulting from this betrayal, as also noted earlier, gives context to Bahá'u'lláh's use of the phrase "people of the Bayán," including in the Suríy-i-Haykal, as shall be discussed later.

As grievous as were the *Ayyám-i-Shidad*, they constituted only one of the many tribulations Bahá'u'lláh endured in the execution of His divine mission. In this sense, the Súriy-i-Haykal represents Bahá'u'lláh's recollection of His internal reflection, years earlier in the Siyáh-Chál, on all He foreknew He would have to endure, and on the need to steel Himself to undergo all the further animosity and tribulations He was aware would be His lot—much as Christ did in His symbolic confrontation with Satan in the wilderness in preparation for His own sacrificial ministry.[133]

As previously noted, at the most basic level of meaning, the word *haykal* means "temple," one of whose enduring symbolic referents is the human body. And as already discussed in the first chapter regarding foundational Bahá'í beliefs about the soul, the human temple or body is believed to be the means or mechanism through which the spiritual essence (the soul) associates with physical reality during the mortal stage of our eternal existence. And as I have also explained in chapter 1, and at great length in *The Face of God Among Us*, the Manifestations, while ontologically distinct from us, in order to accomplish Their objective must become manifest through a human temple and consequently endure the common lot of humanity: pain, afflictions, "other heartache, and the thousand natural shocks / That flesh is heir to."[134]

Doubtless Bahá'u'lláh, like every Manifestation before Him, is well aware of the perilous journey He has ahead of Him—all the pain, suffering, and rejection He will encounter—even before receiving the first intimations of His Revelation, possibly even in the realm of the spirit before willingly agreeing to become God's Vicegerent to advance the education and enlightenment of humankind. Consequently, we may well presume that the recounting of the dialogue between the Holy Spirit within Bahá'u'lláh and His rational soul is for our benefit more than it is an indication that this was a crucial point of enlightenment in the life of the Prophet.

At the same time, even if the sharing of this experience through the revelation of the tablet serves primarily to teach us how we, too, must be prepared to undergo hardship if we are to perform our own special role in assisting the Cause of God—to become heroic in our service even as did exemplary figures like Badí'—we must also be willing to appreciate that such a reflection, such an internal dialogue, accurately represents the mental and spiritual process that took place as Bahá'u'lláh readied Himself to begin the treacherous and challenging journey His ministry would entail.

The temple thus represents not merely the flesh and bone dimension of the Prophet's reality, but the entirety of the mortal experience that will be His lot. Perhaps it also presents us with an understanding of the distinction between the foreknowledge that challenges will occur and the actual experience of enduring the dramatic series of events that will characterize the ministry of Bahá'u'lláh. And even though this is not the beginning of His suffering—five years prior to this experience in the Siyáh-Chál, He had been made to endure imprisonment and even the excruciatingly painful bastinado during the upheaval in Mázindarán as He attempted to join His coreligionists at the siege of Fort Shaykh Ṭabarsí—what better time than this, in the pitch-black stygian darkness and putrid atmosphere of the Siyáh-Chál, weighted down by chains and with every expectation that He might be the next to be taken out and executed, to prepare Himself for all else that must follow as He, like the Manifestations before Him, sacrifices every human comfort and every concern for personal safety and welfare to serve and assist the very same people who, during His lifetime, largely reject the salutary remedy He, as the Divine Physician, has come to provide.

THE TWIN STATIONS OF THE PROPHETS OF GOD

The temple is not merely representative of the mortal reality of the Manifestation, nor solely a symbol of the implementation in human or material form of the spiritual principles of the heavenly realm, though certainly it is an important symbolic demonstration of the ultimate goal of all heavenly guidance—the promulgation of an "ever-advancing civilization" as a result of our following the instructions provided by each successive Manifestation.[135] As Bahá'u'lláh states so memorably in the Súriy-i-Haykal itself, His "temple" also represents nearness to the presence of God, at least such nearness as human beings are capable of attaining:

> Say: Naught is seen in My temple but the Temple of God, and in My beauty but His Beauty, and in My being but His Being, and in My self but His Self, and in My movement but His Movement, and in My acquiescence but His Acquiescence, and in My pen but His Pen, the Mighty, the All-Praised. There hath not been in My soul but the Truth, and in Myself naught could be seen but God.[136]

This statement is reminiscent of the words of the Báb—the Forerunner and Herald of Bahá'u'lláh—Who in like manner proclaimed, "I am the Primal Point from which have been generated all created things. I am the Countenance of God Whose splendour can never be obscured, the Light of God Whose radiance can never fade."[137] And it is in this context that Bahá'u'lláh alludes to the station of "essential unity" shared by all the Manifestations; They are all part of one ongoing organic process of enlightenment, whereas in Their station of distinction, They can provide only that guidance that humankind is capable of understanding and implementing for a particular era or dispensation. In the station of essential unity, then, all the Manifestations function as one soul appearing in various personae, a concept Bahá'u'lláh discusses at great length in the Kitáb-i-Íqán.

He begins discussing this distinction with the observation that "These Manifestations of God have each a twofold station. One is the station of pure abstraction and essential unity. In this respect, if thou callest them all by one name, and dost ascribe to them the same attribute, thou hast not erred from the truth. Even as He hath revealed: 'No distinction do We make between any of His Messengers!' For they one and all summon the people of the earth to acknowledge the Unity of God, and herald unto them the Kaw<u>th</u>ar of an infinite grace and bounty."[138]

In the continuation of this same discussion (revealed in 1862), Bahá'u'lláh explicitly alludes to the metaphor of the temple as He provides further insight into the station of essential unity of the Prophets: "It is clear and evident to thee that all the Prophets are the Temples of the Cause of God, Who have appeared clothed in divers attire."[139] He continues, "If thou wilt observe with discriminating eyes, thou wilt behold them all abiding in the same tabernacle, soaring in the same heaven, seated upon the same throne, uttering the same speech, and proclaiming the same Faith. Such is the unity of those Essences of being, those Luminaries of infinite and immeasurable splendour."[140]

CONSTRUCTING THE TEMPLE

From the already cited concluding paragraph added by Bahá'u'lláh to encapsulate the five epistles in His final rendering of the work, we see that the central symbolic and structural device found in the Súriy-i-Haykal, within the aforementioned dialogue between the voice of the Maid as the Holy Spirit and the Temple as the human incarnation of that spirit in the personage of Bahá'u'lláh, is the symbolic or figurative account of the construction of the Temple.

THE LITERAL EDIFICE

As mentioned earlier in this chapter, on the most basic level, the building of the temple alludes to the long-awaited building of the third Temple in Jerusalem in fulfillment of both Judaic and Christian prophecy. Of special interest is that passage cited previously from Zechariah 6:12–13: "Even he shall build the temple of the LORD; and he shall bear the glory." The term "glory" here is obviously stunning inasmuch as the title "Bahá'u'lláh," assumed by Mírzá Husayn-'Alí, also embodies the same term and concept—*Bahá* means "glory" or "splendor."

This connection made between the Temple in the Súriy-i-Haykal and a literal edifice may also bring to the mind of a Bahá'í reader the construction and emergence of the buildings of the Bahá'í World Center on Mount Carmel, a site associated with biblical prophecy and situated less than a hundred miles from the Temple Mount in Jerusalem. In a very real sense, these buildings were built by Bahá'u'lláh: not only did they emerge under the supervision and through the toil of His designated successors in the leadership of the Bahá'í community and in fulfilment of His design, but He Himself designated the spot of their construction. This connection may assume greater significance when considered in light of the theme of the delegation of authority in the Súriy-i-Haykal, and the text's role in illuminating the first steps of the pathway towards a global commonwealth. Shoghi Effendi gives us a glimpse of the glory of this ultimate form of global governance:

> This final and crowning stage in the evolution of the plan wrought by God Himself for humanity will, in turn, prove to be the signal for the birth of a world civilization, incomparable in its range, its character and potency, in the history of mankind—a civilization which posterity will, with one voice, acclaim as the fairest fruit of the Golden Age of the Dispensation of Bahá'u'lláh, and whose rich harvest will be garnered during future dispensations destined to succeed one another in the course of the five thousand century Bahá'í Cycle.[141]

Shoghi Effendi elsewhere highlights that the World Order of Bahá'u'lláh, now embryonic but destined to unfold in time until it manifests the world civilization which he describes, finds its "nucleus and pattern" in the Bahá'í Administrative Order—the system, ordained by Bahá'u'lláh, through which the Bahá'í community governs itself.[142] He asserts: "The Bahá'í Commonwealth of the future, of which this vast Administrative Order is the sole framework, is, both in theory and practice, not only unique in the entire history of political institutions, but can find no parallel in the annals of any of the world's recognized religious systems."[143] And this Administrative Order, which must thus play such an indispensable role in the progress towards the global civilization that represents the ultimate design for the delegation of authority by God to humanity—the theme of the Súriy-i-Haykal—has its world headquarters in the very heart of Mount Carmel, in those noble edifices that so many today see as the truest successors to the biblical Temple.

THE SYMBOLIC EDIFICE

As we have noted, an essential part of the Súriy-i-Haykal is the symbolic construction of the temple that is the human appearance of Bahá'u'lláh. As we have also noted, it is presented to us by Bahá'u'lláh for our benefit as we attempt to understand the thematic heart of this work. It thus focuses on those powers and capacities that Bahá'u'lláh must utilize; however, we should not ignore the possibility that the description of the construction of the temple and the attributes that best characterize its constitution, comportment, and actions may also establish a paradigm that we ordinary humans should attempt to emulate. From this perspective, the work is not solely a recounting of the internal reflections of the Manifestation as He steels Himself for all He must endure; it also becomes guidance for all those who would dedicate themselves to the service of humankind by attending to the spiritual construction of their own temple.

Chapter 4

The Construction and Preparation of the Temple

Having reviewed the central symbols of the Súrih, we can now explore the dramatic unfoldment of the dialogue between the Holy Spirit, personified by the Maid of Heaven, and the mind of Bahá'u'lláh. Understanding how this dialogue forms the narrative framework for the entire work is important because the narrative never breaches what in theater is called "the fourth wall." Put simply, Bahá'u'lláh, as the Creator of the tablet, never speaks to the audience directly, except perhaps in the beatitudes at the outset, which would seem to serve as a prologue or introit to the narrative proper.

Throughout, it is the voice of the Maid of Heaven that is dominant, sometimes speaking to Bahá'u'lláh as a physical being (the "Temple"), introducing Him to the worlds of heaven and earth, and at other times instructing Bahá'u'lláh as to what He must proclaim to the peoples of the world. The latter parts of the narrative constitute the majority of the tablet prior to the inclusion of the five letters, but these occur only after the Temple has been constructed and its duties prescribed.

The passages in which the Maid ordains what Bahá'u'lláh should reveal usually begin with the imperative "Say:" and contain a variety of subjects, some cautionary, but the majority in the form of announcing to the world the momentous occasion of the advent of the Promised Manifestation and the transformative, long-awaited age that the religions and peoples of the world have anxiously anticipated.

One of the defining clues or keys enabling the reader to distinguish between those passages Bahá'u'lláh is to proclaim to the world and the instructions and comfort the Maid provides to "the Temple"

(Bahá'u'lláh in His "station of distinction"[144]) are the twenty or so epithets or appellations the Maid employs as nominatives of direct address
when she speaks to or about Bahá'u'lláh.

We could simply list them according to the order in which they
occur to demonstrate their variety. For example, as we have already
cited, after Bahá'u'lláh proclaims the beatitudes (paragraphs 1–5), He
describes His condition while imprisoned in the Siyáh-Chál when the
Maid of Heaven first appears to Him. But She utilizes a series of ma-
jestic epithets in the seventh paragraph to introduce Bahá'u'lláh as "the
Best-Beloved of the worlds," "the Beauty of God amongst you," "the
power of His sovereignty within you," "the Mystery of God and His
Treasure," "the Cause of God and His glory," and "He Whose Presence
is the ardent desire of the denizens of the Realm of eternity, and of them
that dwell within the Tabernacle of glory."[145]

However, rather than examining these epithets in the order in which
they appear, it will likely be of greater service to the reader for us to as-
semble them in groups according to the attributes they contain or imply.
For example, most obviously related to the title and theme of the tablet
are those epithets that allude to Bahá'u'lláh in relation to His station as
the "Temple" of God. In this context, Bahá'u'lláh is addressed as "this
Temple," the "Living Temple," the "Temple of Holiness," the "Temple
of My Cause," the "Temple of Divine Revelation," and the "Temple
of Divine mysteries." Some of these are used more than once, but the
intent for each is clear. The word "Temple" represents the human dimension, station or function of the Manifestation through which the
peoples of the world can gain access to the spiritual realm, can obtain divine knowledge, and can unseal the long-guarded mysteries of
religious prophecies, promises, and scriptural enigmas. In this sense,
the Temple is the vehicle through which we gain access to God; this
includes being the entity through which God exercises authority over
humanity. In this respect, the delegation of authority to the Temple itself
is a necessary first step to the further delegation of authority from the
realm of command to the realm of human polity, which we see reflected
in the five representative epistles speaking to those whose function it is
to receive this trust.

A second category we might employ in grouping these epithets
has to do with specific functions or powers of the Manifestation. In
Bahá'u'lláh's capacity as Revealer of the Word, the Maid addresses
Him as "O Pen of the Most High" and "Pen of Eternity." In His function

as the means by which we gain access to God—and to the spiritual realm in general, as well as the means by which we are assisted by God—she addresses Him as "The Path of God" and the "Manifestation of Our own Self," and the "Hand of God."

Two of the most commonly employed and well-known appellations employed by the Maid are "This Youth" and "Ancient Beauty." Some may find it perplexing that Bahá'u'lláh continues to employ "this Youth" in tablets where He is referring to Himself. After all, He was still revealing works until the last years of His life when He was more than seventy years of age. The unofficial explanation for this epithet lies in words uttered by the Guardian to a number of pilgrims where he is said to have explained that the term alludes to the fact that He was only twenty-seven years old when He signaled His recognition of the Báb, and thirty-five years of age when He received the first intimations of His Revelation, the very same event in the Síyáh-Chál that constitutes the setting for the Súriy-i-Haykal.

The appellation "Ancient Beauty" alludes to the fact that Bahá'u'lláh is descended from the early Prophets in the Abrahamic line, even from Abraham Himself. In this sense, He represents the Beauty of God as revealed successively from ancient times down through the ages. Shoghi Effendi mentions this epithet, among a number of others, in discussing the titles possessed by Bahá'u'lláh:

> He was formally designated Bahá'u'lláh, an appellation specifically recorded in the Persian Bayán, signifying at once the glory, the light and the splendor of God, and was styled the "Lord of Lords," the "Most Great Name," the "Ancient Beauty," the "Pen of the Most High," the "Hidden Name," the "Preserved Treasure," "He Whom God will make manifest," the "Most Great Light," the "All-Highest Horizon," the "Most Great Ocean," the "Supreme Heaven," the "Pre-Existent Root," the "Self-Subsistent," the "Day-Star of the Universe," the "Great Announcement," the "Speaker on Sinai," the "Sifter of Men," the "Wronged One of the World," the "Desire of the Nations," the "Lord of the Covenant," the "Tree beyond which there is no passing."[146]

We find in yet another group of titles bequeathed Bahá'u'lláh by the Maid of Heaven the most lofty, celebratory, and laudatory terms of praise, all of which are additional to those mentioned by Shoghi

Effendi in the previous citation. There is no need to explore the meaning of these beauteous terms—they are self-explanatory. But they are well worth reciting and equally worthy of our personal reflection as they portray in poetic and symbolic phrases the attitude of respect with which we should regard Bahá'u'lláh. These include "the Best-Beloved of the worlds," "He Who hath ever been the Desire of every perceiving heart," "the Object of the adoration of all that are in heaven and on earth," "the Cynosure of the former and the latter generations," and "this resplendent Beauty."

THE FUNCTIONS AND CAPACITIES ASSIGNED
TO THE VARIOUS PARTS OF THE TEMPLE

Among the most dramatic parts of the Súriy-i-Haykal occurring during the course of the Maid of Heaven's dialogue with Bahá'u'lláh are her instructions to the various parts of the human temple that is the Manifestation's earthly persona. Here She specifies the capacities He must acquire or demonstrate in order to be successful in attaining the objectives set out before Him, and in responding to the challenges that, though befalling all of God's Vicegerents, will be especially onerous at this, the most momentous turning point that has yet occurred or that will ever occur again in course of human history on planet Earth.

Here we would do well to remember that while this dialogue is what we presume to be an inner reflection between Bahá'u'lláh and His own spirit—or the Holy Spirit operating through Him and inspiring Him—the voice of the Holy Spirit within Him is describing to His conscious mind how He has been prepared (and is constantly being reinforced) to endure all the trials to which He has already alluded as He converses with the Maid, as well as the further tribulations and challenges He will face from the time of the Súriy-i-Haykal's Revelation in Adrianople (ca. 1868) until His death some twenty-four years later.

Beginning with paragraph 19 and continuing to paragraph 67, six different faculties of the Temple are addressed by the Maid of Heaven, and in each case, she addresses the faculty; explains its purpose, goal, or duty; and also portrays the powers and attributes with which it has been endowed that it might carry out its objective. The creativity in this symbolic dialogue is so remarkable as to defy any easy or simple analysis, but for the reader, it is beneficial to list each faculty and mention a couple of the features cited in the Maid's address to them.

One might think that the Maid would address those parts represented by the *haykal* itself—the five-pointed star—namely, the head, the arms, and the legs, but even as Bahá'u'lláh's art is organic and rarely constrained by formalistic modes, so the Maid addresses those facilities most relevant to spiritual preparation and powers. In this same vein, Her instructions to the six faculties are scattered throughout the work, much as the laws are scattered throughout the equally organic structure of the Kitáb-i-Aqdas.

O EYES OF THIS TEMPLE!

The Maid addresses the Eyes of the Temple in paragraph 19, beginning with the exhortation that they should not become distracted by anything in the heavens or on the earth: "We have created you to behold Our own Beauty: See it now before you!" One aspect of the complexity of the dramatic dialogue here is that, as we have already noted, the voice is that of the Maiden addressing the eyes of the physical persona with which Bahá'u'lláh associates during His earthly life. Thus, the pronoun "you" is not capitalized.

Likewise, when She states, "Erelong shall We bring into being through you keen and penetrating eyes that will contemplate the manifold signs of their Creator and turn away from all that is perceived by the people of the world," She is stating that the peoples of the world will learn to discern the true nature of reality through Bahá'u'lláh's own eyes and understanding as His critical perceptions about reality are unfolded in the ocean of Bahá'u'lláh's revealed works. On another level, Bahá'u'lláh is using this indirect symbolic discourse to inform us what we, as humans, need to do by way of emulating the Manifestation to the extent possible in "constructing" our own "temples." In this sense, all the advice of the Maiden in preparing Bahá'u'lláh to confront the tribulations He will endure is equally applicable to us, at least to the extent we are able to follow it.

When the Maid concludes Her instruction to the "Eyes of the Temple" about the charge She has laid upon them, She notes that it is through the eyes or observations of Bahá'u'lláh that people will be judged as to whether or not they employ their own vision to attend to mundane or even sensual matters or focus, instead, on matters of the spirit: "Through you [the eyes of the Temple] shall We [the Holy Spirit] bestow the power of vision upon whomsoever We desire, and lay hold upon those who have deprived themselves of this gracious bounty. These [those who turn away from the vision Bahá'u'lláh unfolds before them], verily, have drunk from the cup of delusion, though they perceive it not."[147]

This analysis may at first seem overly complicated, but once the reader comes to appreciate the narrative structure Bahá'u'lláh has masterfully devised, the intended meaning of the work as a whole, as well as these particular creative features He has included, become increasingly accessible. Likewise, once the reader comprehends the sense of the narrative voices at work—realizing all the while, of course, that all the voices ultimately derive from Bahá'u'lláh's own literary design and not from literal characters—the underlying logic of the fictional construct unfolds before us, but only if we are willing to invest our energies at the outset so that we can discern the design of this masterpiece of Revelation.

O EARS OF THIS TEMPLE!

The Maiden's address to the Ears follows much the same theme as her guidance to the Eyes. She cautions the Ears to turn away from "idle clamour and hearken unto the melodies of your Lord."[148] Allegorically, this would seem to portray the process by which the Manifestation "hears" or receives divine guidance "from the Throne of glory," and thence shares it with humankind so that those whose own ears are receptive may discern in the revealed words of Bahá'u'lláh naught but the voice of God, "the sweet accents of Divine Revelation that proceed from these most blessed and hallowed precincts."[149]

Needless to say, the voice of Revelation ("the sweet accents") to which the Ears attend is essentially spiritual or metaphysical. It is also obvious, as with the address to the Eyes of the Temple, that the admonitions and advice to the faculties of the Temple are equally relevant to the faculties of those receptive souls who are exposed to the Revelation of Bahá'u'lláh.

O TONGUE OF THIS TEMPLE!

The Maid as the Holy Spirit then addresses the "Tongue of the Temple," rehearsing what information has been bestowed upon the utterance of Bahá'u'lláh. She first proclaims that the Tongue has been

taught "whatsoever had remained concealed in the Bayán" (the principal work of Báb) and has been given "the power of utterance" that the
Tongue "might bring into being through thee eloquent tongues—the
voices of the followers—that will praise and extol Me amongst the
Concourse of eternity and amidst the peoples of the world." Through
these "tongues"—the voices of the true believers—"all created things
shall arise to glorify the Lord of names and to bear witness that there
is none other God save Me, the All-Powerful, the Most Glorious, the
Best-Beloved."[150]

She cautions, however, that none will be capable of accomplishing
this mandate unless first inspired by Bahá'u'lláh: none will "make
mention of Me" unless first "inspired by this Tongue." She further
forewarns the Tongue that only a few will understand what the Tongue
proclaims: "Few, however, are they who understand! No tongue is there
that speaketh not the praises of its Lord and maketh not mention of His
Name. Amongst the people, however, are those who understand and
utter praises, and those who utter praises, yet understand not."[151]

While this observation would seem to indicate that ultimately everyone realizes their subservience to God—whether in this life or the life
to come—and some will recognize the Manifestation and the authority
of His utterance, few will have the capacity to discern the various levels
of meaning that lie concealed beneath the surface or literal meaning
of the Revealed Word. As even the casual student of Bahá'í history
is well aware, this observation is borne out in the fact that despite the
stalwart efforts of those followers who did recognize the Báb and then
Bahá'u'lláh—even to the point of sacrificing their lives—the vast majority of those exposed to the teachings of Bahá'u'lláh paid little heed
to His Revelation at the time. And indeed, this same process or pattern
is evident as we reflect on the history of all the revealed religions, even
as Christ acknowledges in His conclusion to the parable of the wedding
feast when He observes, "many are called, but few are chosen."[152]

O FEET OF THIS TEMPLE!

Between the address to the "Tongue of the Temple" and the Maid's
guidance to the "Feet of the Temple," much takes place: the dialogue between the persona of Bahá'u'lláh and the Holy Spirit coursing through
Him, the additional explication of symbols contained in the four letters (*hykl*) of "Haykal" or "Temple," and other important information

regarding what Bahá'u'lláh—or the Tongue—must say to the peoples of the world, matters we shall discuss when we examine the logical framework of the work.

It suffices to note here that we should not assume that everything between paragraph 21, where the Tongue is addressed, and paragraph 61, where the Feet of the Temple are addressed, is an extension of the address to the Tongue of the Temple. The structure of the text, as in many works of Bahá'u'lláh, is complex, and what might seem to be digressions are sometimes parts of the overall flow of themes.

For example, we discover in some works that when Bahá'u'lláh does digress, He informs the reader He has done so. We note this in the *Gems of Divine Mysteries* where He states, "It is Our wish at this juncture to digress from Our theme to recount that which befell the Point of the Qur'án, and to extol His remembrance, that perchance thou may-est gain into all things an insight born of Him Who is the Almighty, the Incomparable."[153] Likewise, in the midst of His "argument" in the Kitáb-i-Íqán, He digresses about the different sorts of knowledge; however, in what I infer to be a humorous and loving vein, He returns to His discourse by stating, "We have digressed from the purpose of Our argument, although whatsoever is mentioned serveth only to confirm Our purpose. By God! however great Our desire to be brief, yet We feel We cannot restrain Our pen. Notwithstanding all that We have mentioned, how innumerable are the pearls which have remained unpierced in the shell of Our heart!"[154]

In any case, the theme of the address to the Feet of the Temple is straightforward and brief. The Holy Spirit admonishes the feet—which have been "wrought . . . of iron"—to "[s]tand firm with such constancy as to cause the feet of every severed soul to be strengthened in the path of God."[155] Again we note here that the virtues assigned to the various parts of the Temple are also meant to serve as guidance to be exemplified by those who follow Him. The Maid of Heaven thus cautions the Feet of the Temple, even as She cautions the persona of Bahá'u'lláh, that they will endure tests and hardship but must demonstrate constancy so that the believers themselves will emulate this staunchness and will thereby remain firm and steadfast. She warns, "Beware lest the storms of enmity and hatred, or the blasts of the workers of iniquity, cause you to stumble. Be immovable in the Faith of God, and waver not."[156] She assures the Feet of the Temple that soon believers will arise to follow their example of constancy: "Erelong shall We bring into being through you other feet, firm and steadfast, which shall walk unwaveringly in Our path, even should they be assailed by hosts as formidable as the combined forces of the former and latter generations."[157]

Of course, it is obvious to the reader that this analogy is directed by the Holy Spirit to Bahá'u'lláh Himself, Who must demonstrate firmness, a virtue that Bahá'u'lláh in the Kitáb-i-Íqán had designated toward the end of the work as one of the major proofs of the Manifestation:

> Another proof and evidence of the truth of this Revelation, which amongst all other proofs shineth as the sun, is the constancy of the eternal Beauty in proclaiming the Faith of God. Though young and tender of age, and though the Cause He revealed was contrary to the desire of all the peoples of earth, both high and low, rich and poor, exalted and abased, king and subject, yet He arose and steadfastly proclaimed it. All have known and heard this. He was afraid of no one; He was regardless of consequences. Could such a thing be made manifest except through the power of a divine Revelation, and the potency of God's invincible Will?[158]

O Breast of this Temple!

In the paragraph prior to addressing the "Breast of this Temple," the Maid of Heaven has already asserted to the Temple that "We, verily, have cleansed Thy breast from the whisperings of the people and sanctified it from earthly allusions, that the light of My beauty may appear therein and be reflected in the mirrors of all the worlds."[159] Obviously, the allusion to the "mirrors" is a reference to the faithful believers who—like the Manifestation, Who is also often compared to a perfect Mirror reflecting flawlessly and completely all the attributes of God—reflect the attributes of the Holy Spirit that others may discern in them the bounties or spiritual effects of the new Revelation. In fact, the Maid refers to these stalwart believers as "mirrors" eight different times in the tablet.

In the next paragraph (¶ 64) addressing the Breast of the Temple, the Maid once again employs the mirror analogy, beginning with the assertion, "O Breast of this Temple! We, verily, have caused all things to mirror forth thy reality, and made thee as a mirror of Our own Self." After explaining that it is the purpose of the Breast to reflect "the splendours of the light of thy Lord" to free others from attachment to base instincts—to "allusions and limitations"—she concludes by describing how, through the Breast of the Temple, the "mirrors" will emerge, "men with sanctified and illumined breasts, who will testify to naught save My beauty and show forth naught but the resplendent light of My countenance."[160]

Here, too, Bahá'u'lláh is reiterating a proof of the Manifestation He has cited in the Kitáb-i-Íqán. After establishing the revealed verses of the Manifestation as the foremost proof of Their station,[161] Bahá'u'lláh describes a second proof: "Amongst the proofs demonstrating the truth of this Revelation is this, that in every age and Dispensation, whenever the invisible Essence was revealed in the person of His Manifestation, certain souls, obscure and detached from all worldly entanglements, would seek illumination from the Sun of Prophethood and Moon of divine guidance, and would attain unto the divine Presence."[162]

O INMOST HEART OF THIS TEMPLE!

The "Inmost Heart," we might reasonably suppose, is synonymous with the Breast of the Temple. Certainly, we may presume that it abides therein. But the connotation of the original word *fu'ád* is complex and weighty, alluding not merely to the physical heart. In its broadest sense, the word refers to one's sensitivity, receptivity, dedication, and spirituality. Beyond these connotations, the term connotes the powers of consciousness, reason, reflection, abstract thought, and other capacities that distinguish our ontology as humans from that of animal life, however sensitive, emotive, and noble the station of the animal might be.

Therefore, as a preface to Her address to this most essential power or faculty, the Maid of Heaven refers to the knowledge to which the Inmost Heart of the Manifestation is privy, and the wisdom with which the Manifestation must adhere to the principle by which God portions out knowledge according to the capacity of the recipient and the timeliness of that knowledge within the historical context. Often cited independently from the Súriy-i-Haykal, this paragraph is quite correctly attributed to Bahá'u'lláh—the Maid is, after all, Bahá'u'lláh's own spirit:[163]

Within the treasury of Our Wisdom there lieth unrevealed a knowledge, one word of which, if We chose to divulge it to mankind, would cause every human being to recognize the Manifestation of God and to acknowledge His omniscience, would enable every one to discover the secrets of all the sciences, and to attain so high a station as to find himself wholly independent of all past and future learning. Other knowledges We do as well possess, not a single letter of which We can disclose, nor do We find humanity able to hear even the barest reference to their meaning. Thus have We informed you of the knowledge of God, the All-Knowing, the All-Wise. Were We to find worthy vessels, We would impart unto them the treasures of hidden meanings and apprise them of a knowledge, one letter of which would encompass all created things.[164]

This passage is astounding in many ways. The assertion is so complete, so impactful, that it feels very much like an aside or a tablet unto itself, and clearly the insight it provides is well worthy of being studied independently. Yet it is still part of the Maid's guidance to the Breast and, more importantly, a preface to what she is about to impart to the "Inmost Heart" of Bahá'u'lláh in His station of distinction, as the Temple of God among us.

Speaking about the knowledge that *can* be imparted (as opposed to that knowledge She has just mentioned that would require beings adequate to receive it), the Maid declares to the Inmost Heart of this Temple its station as "the dawning-place of Our knowledge and the dayspring of Our wisdom unto all who are in heaven and on earth."[165] Continuing with this theme, the Maid makes an announcement that is amazingly accurate, indeed prophetic, when we recall that this tablet is being revealed during latter half of the 19th century, when major reformation of virtually all the sciences was taking place. Perhaps most fundamental was the rapid and radical advancement being achieved in the field of physics, which would, with the emergence of "New Physics" during the following decades of the 20th century, result in the reformation of our current thought about physical reality, whether at the cosmic or quantum levels:

From thee [the Inmost Heart of the Temple] have We caused all sciences to appear, and unto thee shall We cause them to return. And from thee shall We bring them forth a second time. Such, indeed, is Our promise, and potent are We to effect Our purpose. Erelong shall We bring into being through thee exponents of new and wondrous sciences, of potent and effective crafts, and shall make manifest through them that which the heart of none of Our servants hath yet conceived.[166]

At this point, it would be useful to rehearse the chronology of all the astonishing scientific discoveries and revolutionary inventions that were taking place during these decades of the Revelation of Bahá'u'lláh. But here again we are constrained by the limitless depth and breadth of the revealed tablets of Bahá'u'lláh. Most especially, whether as readers, students, or scholars, we are overwhelmed by our inability to explicate in full a single tablet, let alone encompass a significant portion of Bahá'u'lláh's works and thought.

And frankly, that is a principal joy in this labor of love—that the reader-writer-student-scholar, fully aware of these limitations, can delight in playing some small part in beginning to explore even a few of the pearls of wisdom contained in the ocean of Bahá'u'lláh's revealed works. Therefore, it would seem we should in no wise lament that we must leave it to others in the future to explore how this succinct statement about advancement in the sciences is borne out in reality or to discern precisely that to which it might be alluding.

For example, when the Maid asserts, "And from thee shall We bring them forth a second time," She may be alluding to the new sciences and understandings that emerged after the fullness of the industrial revolution and the ostensible completeness of understanding that men of science thought they had achieved around the end of the 19th century, prior to the work of Curie, Einstein, and the like. But this assumption would only be speculation from our present perspective as we now struggle to assess our immediate future from within a veritable maelstrom of change in every aspect of our collective life as a global community.

Some Conclusions about These Symbolic Allusions

As we study this remarkable allegory, we cannot help marveling once more at the various layers of symbols and images. For example, the Maid of Heaven, as the figurative personification of the Holy Spirit operating through Bahá'u'lláh, addresses the Breast of the Temple (the heart and passion of Bahá'u'lláh), comparing it to a mirror. And that Mirror, by reflecting the light of the Holy Spirit (the outpourings of the Revelation through the pen of Bahá'u'lláh), will bring forth others who, also like mirrors, will shed light that will illumine the rest of humankind. And the illumination they will receive from that same Holy Spirit is manifest through the Mirror of Divine perfection that is the appearance of Bahá'u'lláh.

And yet, as we pause to reflect on the literary complexity of what Bahá'u'lláh has wrought in this work, we might wonder why such indirection must be employed to explain things that, we suppose, might be said more simply and directly. But if we imagine these same intricate and subtle concepts being attempted in a more direct manner, we quickly realize that the effect would be diminished in so many ways.

For example, Bahá'u'lláh—like the Manifestations before Him—is not shy or hesitant to proclaim His station, His power, His mission, or the tribulations He must endure to transform humankind and bring forth a global polity. Or stated in another way, it might sound self-serving or even a bit strange were Bahá'u'lláh to enumerate matter-of-factly all these same verities about His own person without employing this analogy to explain how Bahá'u'lláh must prepare Himself to endure, to persist, and thereby to transform the world.

This is not to say that Bahá'u'lláh, or any of the Manifestations, are not forthright in describing Their own power or perfection. Christ is so often portrayed and thought of as meek and mild, bringing healing and comfort to all whom He meets. And yet, as we noted in a previous chapter, He proclaims forcefully and openly to His disciples, "I am the way and the truth and the life. No one comes to the Father except through me. If you really know me, you will know my Father as well. From now on, you do know him and have seen him."[167] As we have also noted previously, Muḥammad likewise affirms forthrightly, "Muhammad is not the father of any of your men, but [He is] the Messenger of Allah, and the Seal of the Prophets: and Allah has full knowledge of all things."[168]

The point is that by creating what T. S. Eliot referred to as an "objective correlative"[169]—in this case, an allegorical narrative that alludes to this reality, rather than an impassioned, sententious homiletic pronouncement—Bahá'u'lláh has enabled us to examine and discover for ourselves the pain and tribulation He has endured as He presents His plaint to the Maid (the Holy Spirit dwelling within Him). By portraying this complex matter using a poetic or indirect method, Bahá'u'lláh has effectively allowed us to have a glimpse into His own psyche, something that would be much less effective and poignant were He to present something like the following: "as I was imprisoned in the stench-filled, pitch black dungeon, my feet in stocks and my neck bowed by the galling weight of the infamous Qará-Guhar and the Salásil chains, I started thinking to Myself about my suffering and felt my own spirit comfort me with such thoughts as these."

I think the point is clear. As constructed, the tablet presents this matter in the form of an intriguing story, a pitched dialogue between two characters—one representing the human station of the Prophet who feels pain (who suffers, who endures betrayal by His own family and some of His closest followers), and the other, the Holy Spirit operating through Him (Who assists Him, reassures Him). And yet, once again, this mystical encounter is not with a Figure other than Him, but rather His own soul become fictionally portrayed for us in a manner we can understand.

Chapter 5

What "The Maid" Inspires Bahá'u'lláh to "Say"

Now that we have reviewed some of the major symbols and figurative imagery employed by Bahá'u'lláh in His ingenuous rendering of a totally internal metaphysical experience into a quasi-fictional situation wherein twin aspects of His own reality are expressed as characters, we are ready to examine some of the more direct or unveiled information Bahá'u'lláh is exhorted to impart.

REVEALING THE WORD OF GOD

The first subject the Maid commands Bahá'u'lláh to pronounce concerns the fact that He is revealing the Word of God. And in paragraph 50, the Maid explains how He should respond to those who reject His assertion that His words are a Revelation from God: "Say: The Holy Spirit Itself hath been generated through the agency of a single letter revealed by this Most Great Spirit,[170] if ye be of them that comprehend. And that innate and untaught nature in its essence is called into being by the verses of God, the Help in Peril, the All-Glorious, the Best-Beloved."[171]

In the following paragraph, Bahá'u'lláh is admonished to disclose the complex nature of His verses; this is the well-known passage in which He alludes to the various styles or modes He will employ in the multitude of His revealed works:

Say: We have revealed Our verses in nine different modes. Each one of them bespeaketh the sovereignty of God, the Help in Peril, the Self-Subsisting. A single one of them sufficeth for a proof unto all who are in the heavens and on the earth; yet the people, for the most part, persist in their heedlessness. Should it be Our wish, We would reveal them in countless other modes.[172]

I have discussed this passage at length in *The Ocean of His Words*, where I note that Bahá'í scholar Jináb-i-Fádil Mazandarání is cited by Adib Taherzadeh as having determined these nine styles, modes, or categories primarily according to subject.[173] As I note in that examination of this passage, it is my own sense that Bahá'u'lláh's statement alludes instead to literary genres. Therefore, in chapter 4 of *The Ocean of His Words*, I discuss nine possible examples of what those genres or modes might be: the mystical treatise, the lyric mode, the doctrinal or philosophical essay, gnomic verse, the epistolary mode, the allegorical mode, supplications and meditations, the homiletic or oratorial mode, and the legal or covenantal mode. My point in that discussion is not to assert that all the works of Bahá'u'lláh are necessarily assigned by Him to some distinct category or that He felt Himself constrained by the formalism of some established literary forms. As Bahá'u'lláh says in this same passage, "Should it be Our wish, We would reveal them in countless other modes."

My sense of this statement is that Bahá'u'lláh is providing access to His Revelation and the teachings it contains to readers from a variety of backgrounds, religious inclinations, and spiritual orientations. As I further note in that same discussion, even as the nine portals to the Mashriqu'l-Adhkár represent the idea that there is sufficiency of access for people of all faiths and spiritual orientations, so also in His utilization of a variety of literary styles has Bahá'u'lláh has provided scriptural pathways for all people to attain the presence of God, regardless of their level of education or literary proclivity.

I know that personally I have, during my more than six decades as a Bahá'í, often heard other Bahá'ís express a preference for a particular work that gave them their first sense of intimacy with and access to the presence of God through Bahá'u'lláh's revealed word. For the mystically oriented, it might have been The Seven Valleys or The Tablet of the Holy Mariner. For the poetically inclined, the Persian Hidden Words; for the scholar, a theological essay or argument, such as the Kitáb-i-Íqán, which contains a highly structured analysis of how to interpret scripture, logical proofs regarding the Báb as Qá'im, and a detailed examination of the ontology of the Manifestations. In this sense, the use of "nine" here is most likely not intended to be taken literally, but represents completeness or sufficiency.

In a letter written on behalf of Shoghi Effendi, we find an explanation of the symbolic possibilities of this allusion. He begins by noting that the significance of "nine" as having symbolic value "lies in three facts." The first of these, he notes, is that "it symbolizes the nine great world religions of which we have any definite historical knowledge, including the Bábí and Bahá'í Revelations." The second symbolic value he notes relates most appropriately, I feel, to our explication of its meaning in relation to the nine literary modes inasmuch as "it represents the number of perfection, being the highest single number." Finally, Shoghi Effendi notes that according to the *abjad* system, "it is the numerical value of the word 'Bahá.'"[174]

THEMES THE MAID EXHORTS THE TEMPLE TO DISCLOSE

Another point worth noting here is that each of the revealed passages in the Súriy-i-Haykal that follow the imperative "Say" occurs in a such a context that we can, if we are attentive, discover certain ongoing themes among them. And if we are to appreciate the purposeful structure that Bahá'u'lláh has devised in His exposition on the preparing of the Temple (Bahá'u'lláh Himself) for all He must undertake and endure, we will benefit at this point from rehearsing some examples of how and where these themes appear.

THE THEME OF GRACE

This discussion about the various forms or modes with which Bahá'u'lláh will speak to us through His revealed work comes in the context of the Maid's explanation of the fact that the fourth letter of the word "temple" symbolizes *Fadl* or "Grace,"[175] and that possibly the most obvious and consequential demonstration of the grace of God to men is the Manifestation Himself, through Whom and from Whom all other bounties derive.

Of course, the major source of the grace emanating from God through this Temple—the Manifestation—are the revealed utterances, but the Maid once again cautions Bahá'u'lláh that not everyone will be ready to perceive or receive this expression of God's beneficence:

O Temple of the Cause! Grieve not if Thou findest none ready to receive Thy gifts. Thou wast created for My sake; occupy Thyself therefore with My praise amidst My servants. This is that which hath been ordained for Thee in the Preserved Tablet. Having found upon the earth many a soiled hand, We sanctified the hem of Thy garment from the profanity of their touch and placed it beyond the reach of the ungodly. Be patient in the Cause of Thy Lord, for erelong shall He raise up sanctified hearts and illumined eyes who shall flee from every quarter unto Thine all-encompassing and boundless grace.[176]

The Maid then exhorts the Temple to explain to those who reject His words, or who are not yet receptive, that He has revealed the Word of God in nine different modes, that they should fear God Who has created "all that are in heaven and on earth," and that whoever turns towards "this blessed Countenance shall manifest the potentialities of that inborn nature, and whosoever remaineth veiled therefrom shall be deprived of this invisible and all-encompassing grace."[177] She continues by telling tell Him to announce that all have been dealt with equitably, that the grace is available to all alike. However, because everyone has free will, it is up to every individual's choice whether or not to accept and follow the revealed Word. Indeed, this is a test—the Judgment Day that occurs whenever a Manifestation appears.

But this is not the end of the discussion of grace. The Maid continues to reveal what she desires Bahá'u'lláh to say, especially to the unbelievers, regarding the fact that such grace as has been described—especially the Revealed Word itself—is accessible only to those who believe, and that their belief is contingent on their ability to discern in the Temple a power and wisdom beyond that which they themselves possess. In short, they must humble themselves before the utterance of God and before the Word made flesh in the form of an earthly Temple, or human form.

Constancy in Proclaiming the Faith of God

As we have already noted repeatedly above, following the Maid's explanation about the attribute of grace signaled and symbolized by the fourth letter of HYKL, the Maid addresses the Feet of the Temple, describing how they have been constructed so as to tread the arduous pathway that lies before the Temple and to remain steadfast in carrying out the mission so that others will follow.

Of course, there is little need to reiterate what we have previously noted in the analysis of the instructions the Maid gives to each of the several parts of the Temple so that the Revelation of God to the people might be conveyed unfettered and immaculate once the Temple has been properly prepared and cleansed of any base desires or distracting concerns. But later in the work, after the Temple has been constructed, the Maid provides more lengthy homiletic matter with which the Temple can teach and admonish the peoples of the world that they might be receptive to the Word of God.

THE MIRRORS

We have already mentioned the numerous times the Maid employs the metaphor of "mirror,"[178] both as an allusion to the faithful believers who will heed the words of the Temple and reflect His example by following His pathway, and also in reference to the Temple itself: "O Living Temple! We, verily, have made Thee a mirror unto the kingdom of names, that Thou mayest be, amidst all mankind, a sign of My sovereignty, a herald unto My presence, a summoner unto My beauty, and a guide unto My straight and perspicuous Path."[179]

She then exhorts the Temple to bring forth from among the peoples of the world those who, like Him, will reflect the attributes of God: "Bring then into being, by Our leave, resplendent mirrors and exalted letters that shall testify to Thy sovereignty and dominion, bear witness to Thy might and glory, and be the manifestations of Thy Names amidst mankind."[180] She continues by noting, "We have caused Thee again to be the Origin and the Creator of all mirrors, even as We brought them forth from Thee aforetime." She concludes by assuring Him that when His task is done—presumably when His duty on this earthly plain is accomplished—He will return to His former dwelling place in the spiritual realm: "We shall cause Thee to return unto Mine own Self, even as We called Thee forth in the beginning."[181]

The Maid continues with this metaphor for the next three paragraphs, just prior to an extensive series of homilies wherein she admonishes the Temple to inform the people about the Revelation that has transpired and how they should respond. First, she cautions the Temple to warn the mirrors to be wary of becoming prideful in what they have discovered and thereby become hesitant to humble themselves before God: "Warn, then, these mirrors, once they have been made manifest, lest they swell with pride before their Creator and Fashioner when He appeareth amongst them, or let the trappings of leadership debar them from bowing in submission before God, the Almighty, the All-Beauteous."[182]

She continues in this vein by exhorting the Temple to tell the mirrors that their insight and power derives from the will of God emanating from the Temple, not from their own learning, accomplishments, or capacity: "Say: O concourse of mirrors! Ye are but a creation of My will and have come to exist by virtue of My command. Beware lest ye deny the verses of My Lord, and be of them who have wrought injustice and are numbered with the lost."[183] She then tells the Temple to warn the mirrors about being moribund and constrained by clinging "unto that which ye possess" or taking "pride in your fame and renown." Rather, the Temple should caution them that what will sustain them "is to wholly detach yourselves from all that is in the heavens and on the earth."[184]

The Maid concludes the "mirror" analogy by exhorting the Temple to inform the peoples that since He has it in His power "to transform, in a single moment, all things into mirrors of My Names," then "how much more [is this] in the power of My Lord, Who hath called Me into being through His all-compelling and inscrutable command."[185] She then exhorts Bahá'u'lláh to further assert that should He choose to do so, He could "revolutionize the entire creation in the twinkling of an eye," and that if such power is possible to Him as a Manifestation of God, then "how much more" is it possible for "that sovereign Purpose enshrined in the Will of God, My Lord and the Lord of all the worlds."[186]

THE FINAL AND MOST LENGTHY HOMILETIC MATTER

While to the knowledgeable reader, the voice conveying this guidance to the people is actually that of Bahá'u'lláh, we would do well to take note of the effectiveness of the narrative-persona device that Bahá'u'lláh employs in this and other works. While the persona of the Maid in the Súriy-i-Haykal may represent or symbolize an actual metaphysical force (the Holy Spirit emanating from the Creator), the voice She is portrayed as using represents Bahá'u'lláh's own inmost spirit and thoughts. Thus, this strictly literary device constructed by Bahá'u'lláh helps the reader appreciate how the Manifestation, though capable of doing whatsoever He wishes, considers Himself but a Vehicle or Mirror of the true source of power, God the Creator. As Bahá'u'lláh famously expresses this same idea in His letter to the Sháh, He considers Himself in this context "but a leaf which the winds of the will of thy Lord, the Almighty, the All-Praised, have stirred."[187]

In works such as the Kitáb-i-Aqdas or the *Epistle to the Son of the Wolf,* Bahá'u'lláh does not veil His station, authority, or voice with a persona device. However, in some other works, He does. In the Hidden Words, for example, the narrative persona is clearly the voice of God Himself providing humankind with a synthesis of "the inner essence" of "that which hath descended from the realm of glory . . . revealed unto the Prophets of old."[188] Likewise, in the Tablet of the Holy Mariner, there is an objective third-person narrator describing all that happens to the Mariner (Bahá'u'lláh) as He navigates the perilous seas (the trials and tribulations Bahá'u'lláh endures).

Bahá'u'lláh acknowledges His use of different narrative voices or modes in the *Epistle to the Son of the Wolf* when He describes these variable literary forms as one example of His desire to create unity amongst the peoples of the world by providing different avenues of access to His words:

> So long, however, as the thick clouds of oppression, which obscure the daystar of justice, remain undispelled, it would be difficult for the glory of this station to be unveiled to men's eyes. These thick clouds are the exponents of idle fancies and vain imaginings, who are none other but the divines of Persia. At one time We spoke in the language of the lawgiver; at another in that of the truth-seeker and the mystic, and yet Our supreme purpose and highest wish hath always been to disclose the glory and sublimity of this station. God, verily, is a sufficient witness![189]

In one sense, this statement seems to echo the observation Bahá'u'lláh makes in the Súriy-i-Haykal regarding the nine modes of His Revelation, as discussed above. But more importantly, it demonstrates Bahá'u'lláh's keen awareness that His major objective for this dispensation is to unite the peoples of the world; He thus creatively employs a variety of literary forms and narrative devices so that none can assert that they can discover no pathway to the truth Bahá'u'lláh reveals.

The use of the persona device in the Súriy-i-Haykal in particular provides a pathway for the reader to experience with Him all He recalls enduring in the Siyáh-Chál, and to appreciate how He was well aware of all the turmoil and tribulation He would willingly undergo from that point forward. Thus, Bahá'u'lláh begins by recalling that while He was "engulfed in tribulations" He "heard a most wondrous, a most sweet voice, calling above My head."[190] And while what follows is His recollection of this dream vision, by casting the dialogue with the Maid, as well as Her lengthy advice to Him in the form of a literal conversation, Bahá'u'lláh provides us with an intimate firsthand sense of what He experiences when, in the stygian gloom of the Síyáh-Chál, He first begins to receive the intimations that the time has come to initiate His own Revelation.

As we have noted, while Bahá'u'lláh foreknew His station and His mission, the experience of receiving "a Revelation direct from God"[191] must have a momentous impact on the Manifestation. For even if He well appreciated what He would have to endure—especially since He was in the midst of experiencing some of the direst physical consequences of being a leading Bábí—knowledge about the experience is hardly the same as the impact of the experience itself. At least, this is what we can infer from Bahá'u'lláh's narrative about the experience that He rehearses in the Súriy-i-Haykal, especially as alluded to in the letter to Naṣíri'd-Dín Sháh, an experience that Shoghi Effendi portrays in dramatic detail in citing a passage from Bahá'u'lláh about this remarkable event:

> In another passage He describes, briefly and graphically, the impact of the onrushing force of the Divine Summons upon His entire being—an experience vividly recalling the vision of God that caused Moses to fall in a swoon, and the voice of Gabriel which plunged Muḥammad into such consternation that, hurrying to the shelter of His home, He bade His wife, Khadíjih, envelop Him in His mantle. "During the days I lay in the prison of Tihran," are His own memorable words, "though the galling weight of the chains and the stench-filled air allowed Me but little sleep, still in those infrequent moments of slumber I felt as if something flowed from the crown of My head over My breast, even as a mighty torrent that precipitateth itself upon the earth from the summit of a lofty mountain. Every limb of My body would, as a result, be set afire. At such moments My tongue recited what no man could bear to hear."[192]

The remainder of what precedes the five letters consists of the Maid conveying to the Temple (Bahá'u'lláh) what He should tell several

categories of recipients about His message, even as He has already been
told what to say to the faithful believers, the near ones, and the mirrors.

Ye Manifestations of My Names

Bahá'u'lláh is to inform those who aspire to be followers that should
they "offer up all ye possess" in the path of God, even their very lives,
and pray to God ceaselessly, and yet oppose the Manifestation when He
appears, their works will be meritless in the eyes of God. Conversely,
should they "neglect all righteous works and yet choose to believe in
Him in these days, God perchance will put away your sins."[193]

As an illustration of this verity, Bahá'u'lláh is told to remind these
potential followers about the many who purport to be religious, "who
expend all their wealth in the path of God,"[194] but who end up being
rebellious and froward. For example, there are those who fast but then
reject the One who created the ordinance to fast. Likewise, there are
those who endure physical hardship but who then claim to be spiritually
superior. Similarly, there are those who live austere lives, but for the
purpose of acquiring renown, not as a service to God or to humankind. Consequently, "no mention shall remain of them." Whereas—and
this observation is particularly potent and relevant to those who today
dedicate their lives to promulgating the teachings of the Bahá'í Faith
and supporting its plans—there are those whose actions are altruistic
and whose deeds are pure, whose names will "fade from every mortal
mind," but with whom God will "be well pleased," and they will be
"numbered among the treasures of His name, the Most Hidden."[195]

Finally, He exhorts those who would be followers, who would bear
His name, to follow His commandments—to "abstain, then, from all
that hath been forbidden unto you in the Book"—but not to deprive
themselves of what "God hath provided for your sustenance" nor to endure "excessive hardships"—for example, not to become ascetics—but
simply to "follow the way" and "be not of the negligent."[196]

O Concourse of Divines and Learned Amongst Men

The next-to-last group the Temple is exhorted to address are, importantly, the religious leaders and those who are deemed to be the learned,
the clerics, the divines. The Temple is to caution them that merely following the Qur'ánic laws on abstention from wine and other similar

transgressions is to be expected from them and thus should not be considered a sign of their ascendancy. After all, such actions are merely a sign of compliance incumbent upon every believer. Neither should they allow their knowledge of the past Revelation to become a cause for their repute. Rather, the true indication of their spiritual supremacy is their ability to recognize and then turn toward the new Manifestation when He appears and follow whatsoever He ordains.

They should likewise call to mind that they are even as springs from which streams emanate, or trees whose roots, if they become corrupted, will cause the tree's "branches, and its offshoots, and its leaves, and its fruits" to become corrupted. But if they detach themselves from the vanities of this world and "[a]rise above the horizon of utterance to extol and praise your Lord, the All-Merciful,"[197] they will have fulfilled the purpose with which God has adorned them.

The Temple is then to explain to these followers of past laws and traditions that nothing is sacred or holy in and of itself, that only the endowment of a place or object with the power of the Holy Spirit ascribes to it power or spiritual prominence. For example, the Black Stone of the Kabih or the Mosque of Aqṣá have no inherent value as physical objects; their worth derives solely from their relationship to Muḥammad as a Manifestation of God.

The "People of the Bayán"

The last group the Temple is to address, prior to sounding the trumpet, are the followers of the Báb, or "the people of the Bayán," as Bahá'u'lláh designates those who, though having recognized and professed to be followers of the Báb, have thus far failed to recognize Bahá'u'lláh as the fulfillment of the Báb's exhortation that His followers recognize and follow "Him Whom God will manifest."

Writing on this theme, Shoghi Effendi cites a passage from a tablet of Bahá'u'lláh in which He expresses the same sort of concern about the Bahá'ís regarding what will happen to the Manifestation Who will succeed Him: "My fears are for Him Who will be sent down unto you after Me—Him Who will be invested with great sovereignty and mighty dominion."[198]

It is unnecessary to recite here all that the Temple is to tell these people, but among the most potent admonitions is a caution against breaking the Covenant of the Báb. They should "fear God" because it is they who benefit from recognizing the Manifestation, not God, for God is self-sufficient. They should also be wary of those who offer up prayers to God yet war against Him by breaking His Covenant. For when they "unsheathed the swords of malice and hatred"[199] against the Manifestation, they are, in fact, warring against God Himself.

Then, in a most powerful exhortation to the people of the Bayán, the Temple cautions that the verses of the Báb were revealed for no purpose other than to lead them to Bahá'u'lláh, and yet they recognize Him not:

Say: Alas for you! How can ye profess yourselves believers, when ye deny the verses of God, the Almighty, the All-Knowing? Say: O people! Turn your faces unto your Lord, the All-Merciful. Beware lest ye be veiled by aught that hath been revealed in the Bayán: It was, in truth, revealed for no other purpose than to make mention of Me, the All-Powerful, the Most High, and had no other object than My Beauty. The whole world hath been filled with My testimony, if ye be of them that judge with fairness.[200]

This admonition continues as the Temple is enjoined by the Holy Spirit to entreat the followers of the Báb to recognize that He (Bahá'u'lláh) is, like the Báb, also the Primal Point, that the Báb longed to be in His presence, and that the Báb Himself would have been among His most faithful followers: "He [the Báb] preceded Me that He might summon the people unto My Kingdom, as it hath been set forth in the Tablets, could ye but perceive it!" The entreaty continues, "O would that men of hearing might be found who could hear the voice of His lamentation in the Bayán bewailing that which hath befallen Me at the hands of these heedless souls, bemoaning His separation from Me and giving utterance to His longing to be united with Me, the Mighty, the Peerless."[201]

Finally, the Temple warns these same Bábís (people of the Bayán) that He is admonishing them not for Himself, but "wholly for the sake of God," because the people possess nothing of value to offer the Manifestation; His reward or "recompense shall be with God, He Who hath brought Me into being, raised Me up by the power of truth, and made Me the Source of His remembrance amidst His creatures."[202] He also powerfully forewarns them about the presence of the "Evil One"[203] and states:

For whoso cherisheth in his heart the love of anyone beside Me, be it to the extent of a grain of mustard seed, shall be unable to gain

admittance into My Kingdom. To this beareth witness that which
adorneth the preamble of the Book of Existence, could ye but perceive it. Say: This is the Day whereon God's most great favour hath
been made manifest. The voice of all who are in the heavens above
and on the earth below proclaimeth My Name, and singeth forth
My praises, could ye but hear it![204]

THE TRUMPET CALL

In the final two paragraphs prior to the five epistles, the Maid of Heaven
commands, "O Temple of Divine Revelation! Sound the trumpet in My
Name! O Temple of Divine mysteries! Raise the clarion call of Thy
Lord, the Unconditioned, the Unconstrained!"[205] Of course, this call is
the second blast mentioned in the Qur'án, the first being the Revelation
of the Báb, signaling the Resurrection, and this second one signaling the
"latter Resurrection."[206]

Then, in a crescendo of Revelation and delight, the Maid commands
the "Maid of Heaven" to "Step forth from the chambers of Paradise and
announce unto the people of the world: By the righteousness of God!
He Who is the Best-Beloved of the worlds—He Who hath ever been the
Desire of every perceiving heart, the Object of the adoration of all that
are in heaven and on earth, and the Cynosure of the former and the latter
generations—is now come!"[207]

Finally, in a warning to all the peoples of the world, the Maid cautions, "Take heed lest ye hesitate in recognizing this resplendent Beauty
when once He hath appeared in the plenitude of His sovereign might
and majesty," for anyone who hesitates, "though it be for less than a
moment, God shall verily bring his works to naught and return him to
the seat of wrath; wretched indeed is the abode of them that tarry!"[208]

Chapter 6

The Letter to Pope Pius IX

Pope Pius IX, 1875
Photograph by Adolphe Braun

When Bahá'u'lláh had the Súriy-i-Haykal reconstructed to include five letters from among those He had already written to various kings and rulers of the world, He obviously had in mind that there was a thematic connection between the tablet in its original form and His purpose in announcing forthrightly both His station and the world-changing impact that His Revelation would have on every aspect of human society. Possibly the most obvious connection He had in mind concerns the delegation of authority from God to humanity: authority emanates from God in the form of the Holy Spirit and subsequently descends to humankind through the intermediary of the Manifestations, Who ordain those teachings and institutions essential for each new era or dispensation—an organic process They instigate in an endless sequence of progressively more encompassing, enlightening, and transformative expressions of the ongoing and endless religion of God.

Consequently, we may well assume that this delegation of authority from the spiritual realm to the physical realm is perhaps the principal symbolic meaning of the *Haykal*, the spiritualization of the human edifice or temple, and, in turn, the collective infusion of that same spirit into the human collective—the social order or body politic. In this context, the letters to the kings and rulers not only inform them of the momentous historical turning point that has occurred with the advent of a new and singularly transformative Revelation from God, but also exhort them to participate in assisting the movement toward a unified planetary governance and a collective system of justice to secure a lasting peace, complemented by the inclusion of the vast panoply of spiritual virtues and attributes into every aspect of daily life.

Whether or not the leaders to whom Bahá'u'lláh writes—both secular and religious—are receptive or even spiritually capable of comprehending what He is saying, the impact of the change that He is foretelling, and their own critical role in this process, one thing is absolutely clear in Bahá'u'lláh's statements to them: they are the ones who bear a weighty burden and divine charge, and their response to His requests and guidance will determine not merely their own spiritual and historical destiny, but the extent of suffering humankind must endure to bring about the inevitable establishment of a global commonwealth.

The theme of delegating authority in this hierarchical manner might call to mind for students of history the theory of the divine right of kings that emerged most prominently in the European Renaissance—the notion that monarchs are God's divinely appointed representatives among His subjects. Of course, the underlying motive of many of the monarchs who endorsed this concept was to sustain supreme and unquestioned authority over the populace—as demonstrated for instance by King Henry VIII, who severed England from the Catholic Church and declared Himself head of the Church of England. And yet, in the Hidden Words of Bahá'u'lláh, we find passages that might seem to echo the nobler aspect of this concept by assigning to kings and rulers the responsibility and honor of carrying out God's plan among their subjects by being just, responsible, and selfless caretakers of those over whom they rule and who are under their guardianship.

For example, Bahá'u'lláh establishes the primacy of the standard of justice in Arabic Hidden Word no. 2:

> O Son of Spirit! The best beloved of all things in My sight is Justice; turn not away therefrom if thou desirest Me, and neglect it not that I may confide in thee. By its aid thou shalt see with thine own eyes and not through the eyes of others, and shalt know of thine own knowledge and not through the knowledge of thy neighbor. Ponder this in thy heart; how it behooveth thee to be. Verily justice is My gift to thee and the sign of My loving-kindness. Set it then before thine eyes.[209]

He later cautions all—and perhaps most especially those in power—that duplicity in this regard shall not be tolerated: "O Son of Spirit! Know thou of a truth: He that biddeth men be just and himself committeth iniquity is not of Me, even though he bear My name."[210] Finally, in Persian Hidden Word no. 64, He warns the unjust rulers of the world, "O oppressors on earth, withdraw your hands from tyranny, for I have pledged Myself not to forgive any man's injustice. This is My covenant which I have irrevocably decreed in the preserved tablet and sealed with My seal."[211]

But there is a second, more obvious theme that Bahá'u'lláh has infused into these epistles: the overt declaration of the variety of insights, advice, and guidance He fashions so carefully to befit the personality, character, and past actions of each of the five recipients. He is, in this act of addressing them individually, carrying out the very actions the Maid of Heaven (the Holy Spirit) has inspired or "commanded" Him to say. That is, if we review the various themes we recounted in the previous chapter that are preceded by the imperative "Say," we will find that every one of them is realized in these five letters, albeit in a tone and through specific allusions that befit the character, personality, and performance of the five recipients.

For example, the letter to Naṣíri'd-Dín Sháh—the most inveterate, relentless, and cruel oppressor of both the Bábís and Bahá'ís—is by far the lengthiest epistle, containing the most substantive discussion of the concept of justice in all its implications. Therefore, we will devote two chapters to examining this document, which is the same length as the other four letters combined and which is about one-third the length of the Súriy-i-Haykal itself.[212]

In this chapter, therefore, let us begin our study of how Bahá'u'lláh has devised each of the other four letters to befit the individual recipient and how, during His discourse, He fulfills the behest of the Maid of Heaven by announcing to each ruler—and thence to those over whom they hold sway—some of the topics we surveyed in the previous chapter. And as we discuss these epistles, the reader might find it useful to refer as needed to the outline of the entire work in the appendix.

As we begin examining the letter to the pope, two points are particularly striking, especially in the context of all that has been told to Bahá'u'lláh by the character or figure of the Maid ("the Holy Spirit") up to this point. The first is the irony with which Bahá'u'lláh advises the pope that he (the pope) is now in exactly the same position as were the Pharisees who disputed with Christ. Even as they were challenged by God to recognize in the lowly son of a carpenter the promised Messiah Who would rule over the House of David, so the pope must now recognize in this Persian prisoner and exile the promised Second Coming of Christ.

Bahá'u'lláh thus notes the parallels between the inability of the highly educated Jews in positions of both religious and governmental authority to recognize in Christ the spiritual fulfillment of the prophecies that the Pharisees, the scribes, and the Sadducees interpreted so literally and the similar inability of Christians who read their own those prophecies about the Second Coming literally to recognize their fulfilment in Bahá'u'lláh.

The second point is that Bahá'u'lláh focuses importantly—and again with superb irony—on the regal pomp and ceremony of the papacy, as well as the massive wealth and worldly possessions that adorn the papal office, in contrast to the meekness and poverty of those circumstances that characterized the life and bearing of Christ, the founder and exemplar of the religion.

Another important observation about this epistle concerns what seems to be the central theme of the Súriy-i-Haykal—the delegation of authority. Bahá'u'lláh instructs the pope what to say to the Christian followers under his guidance and authority. Specifically, the pope is admonished to inform his flock—especially the theologians, the clerics, and monastics, as well as the ordinary believers—that once again the Word has become incarnate or manifest in the form of a human temple, albeit with a new name.

But because there is much more in the epistle worthy of our attention, let us benefit from a more specific examination of the sequence of ideas Bahá'u'lláh unfolds in a relatively linear and straightforward pattern of thought.

THE SECOND COMING

One of the first themes of Bahá'u'lláh's epistle to the pope is that the long-awaited Second Coming has at last occurred. Therefore, Bahá'u'lláh admonishes the pope to command the theologians and clerics to cease writing their treatises, for the Pen of Glory (Bahá'u'lláh) has appeared at the Hour that only God foreknew. This is Bahá'u'lláh's allusion to Mark 13:32, where Christ responds to the question about when the Second Coming will occur: "But of that day and that hour knoweth no man, no, not the angels which are in heaven, neither the Son, but the Father."

In other words, the clerics and divines no longer need dedicate their precious time and energy to studying the scripture in an attempt to ascertain when this dramatic event will occur and when the peoples will be judged, because that very moment is at hand. Bahá'u'lláh commands, "Tear asunder the veils of human learning lest they hinder thee from Him Who is My name, the Self-Subsisting."[213] He then exhorts them to recall what happened to Christ when He appeared so that they will not repeat the same mistake: "Call thou to remembrance Him Who was the Spirit, Who, when He came, the most learned of His age pronounced judgement against Him in His own country, whilst he who was only a fisherman believed in Him. Take heed, then, ye men of understanding heart!"[214]

In this same vein, Bahá'u'lláh exhorts the Christian monks to abandon their seclusion and asceticism and to dedicate themselves to teaching: "Issue forth from your habitations and bid the people enter the

Kingdom of God, the Lord of the Day of Judgement."[215] Then, alluding
to the main theme of the Súriy-i-Haykal, Bahá'u'lláh pronounces to
them, "The Word which the Son concealed is made manifest. It hath
been sent down in the form of the human temple in this day."[216]

After briefly addressing the pope, the theologians, the clerics, and
the monks, Bahá'u'lláh then addresses "the followers of all religions"
regarding the prophecies about this Day, announcing to them that all
"which ye were promised in the Kingdom is fulfilled!" and that "[t]
his is the Word which was preserved behind the veils of grandeur, and
which, when the Promise came to pass, shed its radiance from the horizon of the Divine Will with clear tokens."[217]

Following a descritpion of how He has suffered to bring them this
Revelation, how His "body hath borne imprisonment that your souls
may be released from bondage"[218] and how "[t]he people of the Qur'án
have risen against [Him]," Bahá'u'lláh proclaims that in spite of these
obstacles, nothing will deter Him from His constancy in disclosing the
Word: "Nothing whatsoever can withhold Him from the remembrance
of His Lord."[219] He continues, "Though threatened by the swords of Our
enemies, We summon all mankind unto God, the Fashioner of earth and
heaven, and We render Him such aid as can be hindered by neither the
hosts of tyranny nor the ascendancy of the people of iniquity."[220]

To the Pontiff Himself

After these introductory statements about His advent and its implications for Christians—particularly to those whose professions involve
the institution of the Church—and, briefly, for the followers of all religions, Bahá'u'lláh turns His attention more explicitly to the pope himself, focusing first and foremost on the inappropriateness of the pomp,
ceremony, and riches surrounding the pontiff.

Let Deeds Be Thy Adorning

Bahá'u'lláh's critical advice is not veiled or subtle but rather is a blatant admonition to this spiritual leader to "Sell all the embellished ornaments thou dost possess, and expend them in the path of God. . . .
Abandon thy kingdom unto the kings, and emerge from thy habitation,
with thy face set towards the Kingdom, and, detached from the world,
then speak forth the praises of thy Lord betwixt earth and heaven."[221]

He continues, "Beware lest thou appropriate unto thyself the things of the world and the riches thereof." If the pope is to be a spiritual leader, Bahá'u'lláh continues, he should instead "cleave unto that which hath been enjoined upon thee by Him Who is the Lord of creation" and "refuse to even glance upon" earthly treasures.[222]

A second theme that Bahá'u'lláh proffers in advising the pope has to do with adorning himself with spiritual deeds, rather than with regal robes: "Know that thy true adornment consisteth in the love of God and in thy detachment from all save Him, and not in the luxuries thou dost possess."[223] Perhaps the most touching, poignant, and succinct command by Bahá'u'lláh to the pontiff is His reminder of the simplicity and humble circumstances that characterized the life of Christ: "Be as thy Lord hath been."[224]

He continues by recounting that while Christ spoke in parables that so perplexed the Pharisees and Sadducees, He (Bahá'u'lláh) is speaking directly and without them so that there is no excuse for the pope to misunderstand what He intends.

Bahá'u'lláh concludes this theme by once more advising, in beautiful metaphorical terms, that instead of adorning himself with elaborate vestures and living in luxury, the pontiff should "make My love thy vesture, and thy shield remembrance of Me, and thy provision reliance upon God, the Revealer of all power."[225]

To Christians and People of Other Religions

Bahá'u'lláh then turns His attention to all Christians, though clearly the pope would be included—and, by inference, he is being delegated the authority and responsibility for conveying this information to his own followers. As Bahá'u'lláh draws comparisons between His Revelation and that of Christ, He exhorts Christians in particular to recall the prophecies of the Old and New Testaments, which, if they are attentive, they can now behold fulfilled at long last, but only if they cleanse their eyes and ears of attention to baser matter.

He explains that even as John the Baptist was sent to prepare the people for Christ, so the Báb "hath cried out in the wilderness of the Bayán," proclaiming: "The Day of the advent of the Glorious Lord is at hand! Make ready to enter the Kingdom. Thus hath it been ordained by God, He Who causeth the dawn to break."[226] Bahá'u'lláh further alludes to Christians' own teachings and prophecies by affirming that His own advent fulfills the promise about "that peerless One foretold by Isaiah, and the Comforter[227] concerning Whom the Spirit had covenanted with you [Christians]."[228]

Then, addressing people of all faiths, Bahá'u'lláh warns them not to be like the Pharisees who rejected the Messiah by now rejecting "the Ancient Beauty" Who has appeared to admit all into the kingdom of God. He especially admonishes them to avoid slaying their Redeemer, to emerge from the darkness "by the grace of this Sun" and turn unto God with "with sanctified hearts and assured souls, with seeing eyes and beaming faces," even as the "Supreme Ordainer" has summoned them.[229]

In the concluding paragraphs of the letter, Bahá'u'lláh alludes to the need for all to be faithful to the Eternal Covenant by following Him and not rebelling against Him, for the promised "day of ingathering[230] is come."[231] All will be tested by "the Divine Sifter," and only those who discern the truth will recognize the meaning of "the Day of God" and thereby become sheltered "beneath the shade of His mercy."[232] He particularly admonishes "the concourse of Christians" not to reject Him as they did "on a previous occasion," presumably an allusion to Muḥammad, though the caution is also applicable to the advent of the Báb. In this context, He observes that were they to fail to recognize His advent and the fulfillment of the Promised Day, the failure would be due solely to their own willful choice and to their own "waywardness and ignorance."[233]

Bahá'u'lláh concludes the letter proper by alluding to Christ's promise to His first followers, who were mere fishermen. In a memorable and oft-cited admonition, Bahá'u'lláh tells them: "Thus do We make plain unto you the path of Him Whom the Spirit (Christ) prophesied." But where Christ had promised, "Come ye after Me, and I will make you to become fishers of men," Bahá'u'lláh declares that "[i]n this day, however, We say: 'Come ye after Me, that We may make you to become the quickeners of mankind.'"[234]

With this statement, Bahá'u'lláh has effectively bypassed the authority of the pope as intermediary. Like Christ before Him, Bahá'u'lláh speaks directly to the people, challenging them to realize that it is their own responsibility to recognize and follow Him, even as Christ spoke powerfully to those who gathered to hear His utterances instead of going through the Jewish authorities. An extremely important implication of this circumvention—this direct challenge to the peoples of the world—is that everyone who has access to the Revelation of the

Manifestation is "tested" or "judged" as to whether or not they are capable of discerning the station of the Prophet and are receptive to His teachings, exhortations, and overall guidance. Nevertheless, we should not deemphasize here the extreme weight imposed by Christ on the shoulders of the Jewish authorities to recognize His spiritual station, His Messiahship, and, consequently, their obligation to submit to whatever guidance He might provide regarding social and spiritual laws and governance.

The final paragraph in the letter to the pope is extremely important for the purposes of our assessment of the work as a whole. As we mentioned previously, when Bahá'u'lláh recreates the Súriy-i-Haykal from its original form into a more encompassing and complete expression of how God's guidance becomes manifest (primarily by including the five representative letters), He makes a couple of changes to the original text of the Súriy-i-Haykal itself. This paragraph is the first of these changes, and it demonstrates the care with which Bahá'u'lláh has reforged the tablet as an expanded, continuous whole.

As an important transitional device, this paragraph functions as a segue to the succeeding four letters, and Bahá'u'lláh has included it artfully in this final rendering of the Súriy-i-Haykal so that the following letters are not perceived as afterthoughts or mere appendices, but as representative of the fact that all the rulers of the world need to hear this message in order to respond to its demands upon them.

In this paragraph, the Maid is speaking once again, inspiring Bahá'u'lláh as the "Pen of the Most High" in these terms: "Bestir Thyself in remembrance of other kings in this blessed and luminous Book, that perchance they may rise from the couch of heedlessness and give ear unto that which the Nightingale singeth upon the branches of the Divine Lote-Tree, and hasten towards God in this most wondrous and sublime Revelation."[235] These four "other kings," of course, while already addressed individually serve here in this climactic part of Bahá'u'lláh's public proclamation to represent the totality of all the rulers and ruling bodies of the world.

THE EFFECTS OF THE POPE'S REJECTION OF BAHÁ'U'LLÁH

Each of the five representative letters Bahá'u'lláh thought important to include in this work can be studied out of context—without understanding its external allusions or knowing all the historical circumstances that precede the letter, and without being aware of the events that occur after its revelation in fulfillment of the prophecies contained therein. However, Shoghi Effendi felt it sufficiently important that we be aware of this historical and social context that in his 1941 letter *The Promised Day is Come* he recounted the personal circumstances of each recipient and, more importantly, what happened to those who rejected or, worse, scoffed at or belittled Bahá'u'lláh's claims and cautions. The reader should find this authoritative work fascinating and extremely helpful in understanding how the Súriy-i-Haykal functions as an effective climax to, and summary of, Bahá'u'lláh's proclamation to the worldwide leaders of governments and religions.

As with all the works Shoghi Effendi wrote, *The Promised Day is Come* is highly structured, integrates passages from the works of Bahá'u'lláh relevant to each historical figure or theme, and though only slightly over a hundred pages in length, requires a level of attention and reflection hard to achieve in a single reading. While there are sections devoted to particular figures, for instance, the discourse is structured so that references to particular letters appear throughout the work.

For example, a major portion of the letter to the pope is included,[236] but the aftereffects of the pope's neglect of Bahá'u'lláh's criticisms and admonitions are taken up in the section "Humiliation Immediate and Complete," where the Guardian remarks on the history of what happened to both the pope and the French emperor Napoleon III. Shoghi Effendi observes, "Of all the monarchs of the earth, at the time when Bahá'u'lláh, proclaiming His Message to them, revealed the Súriy-i-Mulúk [Súrih to the Kings] in Adrianople, the most august and influential were the French Emperor and the Supreme Pontiff. In the political and religious spheres they respectively held the foremost rank, and the humiliation both suffered was alike immediate and complete."[237]

After discussing the fall of Napoleon III, Shoghi Effendi then portrays the downfall of Pope Pius IX, whose humiliation was "less spectacular yet historically more significant."[238] Of course, Shoghi Effendi is discussing these figures not only in light of the epistles that Bahá'u'lláh sent to them with His advice, admonitions, warnings, and promises. He is also reviewing the historical context, the theme that the entire panoply of religious orthodoxies and long-standing political dynasties that had dominated the world polity were, as foretold in the scriptures of all the world religions, being eradicated one by one. So also were the now archaic and oppressive systems that these institutions and dynasties had created, and which in turn undergirded them, crumbling in preparation for the "Promised Day," an era in which the "Lesser Peace" would emerge from the fire of ordeal and travail that the world would necessarily undergo, in large part precisely because these world leaders had not recognized Bahá'u'lláh and responded appropriately to His recommendations to disarm and collaborate.

The pope, who "regarded himself as the Vicar of Christ" and the "successor of St. Peter,"[239] was cautioned by Bahá'u'lláh, as we noted before, that this is the "day whereon the Rock [Peter] crieth out and shouteth . . . saying: 'Lo, the Father is come, and that which ye were promised in the Kingdom is fulfilled.'"[240] But heedless of Bahá'u'lláh's lucid guidance, the pope "became the first prisoner of the Vatican" after losing control of the papal states, a consequence explained more completely later.[241]

Prior to detailing some of the disastrous effects that this longest-reigning pope (1846–1878) caused by his actions that diminished the temporal-political authority of the papacy, Shoghi Effendi discusses how the pope introduced a series of logically and theologically baseless doctrines with the *Ubi Primum* (1849), an encyclical increasing what historically is known as the "Mariology" of the Catholic Church. This encyclical asserts that as the "mother of God," Mary was, like Christ, immaculately conceived and, even more theologically strange, that she is the principal intermediary for those wishing to attain salvation.[242] Staunchly against all forms or features of liberalism and modernism, from the separation of church and state to moral relativism, this same pope also introduced the dogma of papal infallibility, a doctrine clearly devoid of any scriptural foundation.

Naturally, how one evaluates the success or failure of Pope Pius IX depends on one's point of view. From the view of those followers of Catholicism who advocate change—less stringent rules, the abolition of celibacy for the priesthood, the ordination of women as priests, the allowance of birth control, and other shifts to befit the changed condition of society and evolving social norms—his lengthy reign might be considered disastrous. On the other hand, from the view of more staunchly conservative Catholics, he might be criticized for losing the temporal powers of the papacy, including through the loss of papal states, while simultaneously being considered extremely successful in his introduction of innovative, if logically spurious, theological dogma that served to tighten the reins of authority over the faithful.

From a Bahá'í perspective, he, of all people, should have had the training and perspective to appreciate the resounding admonitions found in Bahá'u'lláh's epistle, alluding it does to the danger of repeating the failure of the Pharisees to recognize the Messiah—a repetition effected in the pope's failure to recognize the Second Coming, even in light of the convincing arguments contained in the epistle. At the same time, the weightiest test and judgment when a new Manifestation appears does indeed fall upon those who have the most to lose, whether political power, social prestige, or material possessions.

Doubtless from the point of view of the pope, acceptance, or even consideration, of the station of Bahá'u'lláh as fulfilling prophecies of the Old and New Testaments, as well as those of other world religions, was more than he even dared consider. And yet, as anyone can imagine, had he been able and willing to recognize Bahá'u'lláh as fulfilling the promises of Christ regarding the One who would usher in the kingdom of God on earth, the pope's place in history, as well as the immense effect his acceptance might have had on Christianity as a whole, are quite beyond imagination. Most certainly, he would have been considered among the greatest heroes in religious history.

In the end, however, the irreparable decline of papal power in the political realm despoiled whatever doctrinal victories Pope Pius IX might seem to have garnered. Shoghi Effendi states the matter succinctly in the following observation about the last years of the pope's life:

In 1870, after Bahá'u'lláh had revealed His Epistle to Pius IX, King Victor Emmanuel II went to war with the Papal states, and his troops entered Rome and seized it. On the eve of its seizure, the Pope repaired to the Lateran and, despite his age and with his face bathed in tears, ascended on bended knees the Scala Santa. The following morning, as the cannonade began, he ordered the white flag to be hoisted above the dome of St. Peter.[243]

Chapter 7

The Letter to Napoleon III

Napoleon III, ca. 1870
Photograph by Mayer & Pierson

The epistle to Napoleon III included in the Súriy-i-Haykal is Bahá'u'lláh's second letter to a figure who, at the time when he received Bahá'u'lláh's first letter, was one of the "most august and influential" of "all the monarchs of the earth."[244] The first letter was "meek and unprovocative."[245] Praising the emperor's proclamation that "Ours is the responsibility to avenge the oppressed and succor the helpless," Bahá'u'lláh in that letter then humbly beseeches him to "inquire into the condition of such as have been wronged," noting that "there hath not been, nor is there now, on earth any one oppressed as we are, or as helpless as these wanderers," a reference to both Himself and the vigorously oppressed Bahá'ís.[246]

But at the time of the first letter, the emperor was riding the crest of a wave set in motion by a series of apparent successes. He was a popular monarch. He had been elected president in 1848. Then, after seizing power by a coup in 1851 to circumvent the one-term limit imposed on his presidency by the constitution, he became emperor in 1852. Under this "Second Empire," he endeared himself to the French populace by expanding French territories, participating in the defeat of Russia in the Crimean War (1853–1856), and commissioning major reconstruction of parks and gardens in Paris and other major French cities. Additionally, he improved the railway system, modernized the banking system, and fostered the modernization of agriculture. In short, there were legitimate reasons for the emperor to feel great pride in these and other accomplishments; until—and this is surely no coincidence— his fortunes began to change dramatically at roughly the time of his receipt and cavalier rejection of the first letter from Bahá'u'lláh in 1867.

His health began to decline in the 1860s, exacerbated by his distrust of doctors. In the realm of policy, his vast expenditures on public works projects and foreign ventures—especially his failed attempt to establish an empire in Mexico—depleted the treasury. That foolish venture began in 1862 when he sent troops to Mexico, aiming to establish Archduke Ferdinand Maximilian of Austria as Emperor Maximilian I, though governing under French protection.

But the fatal blow to his rule, prosperity, and ultimate reputation occurred in July 1870, a short time after receiving the second letter from Bahá'u'lláh, the one included in the Súriy-i-Haykal that predicts his downfall.

Capitulating to public pressure, the emperor unwisely declared war on Prussia. The subsequent Franco-Prussian War was won swiftly by combined Prussian and German forces superior to the French in numbers, material, and tactics. At the Battle of Sedan, fought on September 1–2, 1870, Napoleon III participated in the fighting himself and was captured. Disgraced, powerless, and unable to secure any sort of restoration of his authority in the rapidly changing political affairs that followed, Napoleon III gathered what funds he could muster from selling jewelry and whatever property remained in his possession, and escaped to England in the spring of 1871. He died there less than two years later at age sixty-four, having fallen like a Greek tragic hero from the heights of power and public acclaim to the depths of ignominy and shame, largely as a result of his overbearing pride, obstinacy, and unquenchable ambition.

By understanding these historical circumstances, we can better appreciate what Bahá'u'lláh says to him in this epistle, written as the critical turning point loomed in the life of an emperor who had, but a couple of years earlier, tossed to the floor the epistle of the Persian prisoner of the Ottoman Empire, reportedly scoffing, "If this man is God, I am two gods!"[247]

Again, it is well worth noting that Napoleon III was not without capacity. Like Pope Pius IX, he had creative ideas about governance and social reform, and he occupied a position from which he could have done immense good for his people. And like the pope, had he but hearkened to the voice of God emanating from that same Persian prisoner, he would likewise have been remembered for ages to come as a heroic figure who assisted in transforming human history.

As mentioned several times already, this is a recurring motif—if not the central theme—that reverberates throughout the Súriy-i-Haykal: that God does not spiritualize a planet directly but rather by conveying His guidance, His wisdom, and His loving assistance through Beings who assume a human form that They might thereby instruct both the leaders of society and the peoples at large, bestowing on them collective enlightenment and prescribing specific paths of action and social reforms. In particular, the Manifestations provide the plans and the means for implementing God's revealed laws, ordinances, and exhortations calibrated to enable humans to govern themselves and, in time, establish a global community characterized by peace and justice—those most prized of all social and political virtues.

Bahá'u'lláh does not begin this epistle by immediately reminding Napoleon III about his failure to heed the humble guidance and requests of the first letter. The voice in this second letter resonates with the tones of omniscience, authority, power, and dire warning. Bahá'u'lláh begins by forthrightly articulating His station as the Word of God become manifest, His purpose to unite the peoples of the world, and the final chance the emperor has to recognize this "Day which God hath exalted above all other days."[248]

THE RETURN OF CHRIST

From the outset, Bahá'u'lláh explains that the promised return of Christ has occurred in His person—the "Most Mighty Bell hath appeared in the form of Him Who is the Most Great Name"—and he invites the emperor to respond befittingly: "the mighty verses of Thy Lord [have] been again sent down unto thee, that thou mayest arise to remember God."[249] He continues, admonishing the emperor to hear the Voice of God calling him, and exhorts him to "[a]rise . . . to serve God and help His Cause," and making an astounding promise as to the glory that awaits the emperor should he do so: "He [God], verily, will assist thee with the hosts of the seen and unseen, and will set thee king over all that whereon the sun riseth."[250]

Bahá'u'lláh then offers a proof of His omniscience that we would think might startle the emperor sufficiently to awaken his consciousness and cause him to take seriously this second epistle from Bahá'u'lláh. Revealing His otherworldly knowledge, Bahá'u'lláh states:

> O King! We heard the words thou didst utter in answer to the Czar of Russia, concerning the decision made regarding the war.[251] Thy Lord, verily, knoweth, is informed of all. Thou didst say: "I lay asleep upon my couch, when the cry of the oppressed, who were drowned in the Black Sea, wakened me." This is what We heard thee say, and, verily, thy Lord is witness unto what I say. We testify that that which wakened thee was not their cry but the promptings of thine own passions, for We tested thee, and found thee wanting.[252]

It is important to note, however, that Bahá'u'lláh implies that the emperor still has the chance to prevent the tragic fall that Bahá'u'lláh foreknows will occur should the emperor again reject this frank caution and underserved offer of grace:

Hadst thou been sincere in thy words, thou wouldst have not cast behind thy back the Book of God, when it was sent unto thee by Him Who is the Almighty, the All-Wise. We have proved[253] thee through it, and found thee other than that which thou didst profess. Arise, and make amends for that which escaped thee. Erelong the world and all that thou possessest will perish, and the kingdom will remain unto God, thy Lord and the Lord of thy fathers of old.[254]

But Bahá'u'lláh's offer of grace or some sort of redemption for the emperor does not mean the emperor will not endure punishment for his former disdainful rejection of Bahá'u'lláh's requests, as well as his other expressions of ambition, avarice, and pride, unless he immediately recognizes his error, accepts the station of Bahá'u'lláh, and implements His guidance. In what may be the most remarkable statement in the letter, Bahá'u'lláh prophetically warns the emperor in no uncertain terms:

For what thou hast done, thy kingdom shall be thrown into confusion, and thine empire shall pass from thine hands, as a punishment for that which thou hast wrought. Then wilt thou know how thou hast plainly erred. Commotions shall seize all the people in that land, unless thou arisest to help this Cause, and followest Him Who is the Spirit of God in this, the Straight Path. Hath thy pomp made thee proud? By My Life! It shall not endure; nay, it shall soon pass away, unless thou holdest fast by this firm Cord.[255]

This assurance that the tribulations foretold by Bahá'u'lláh might still be averted were the emperor to "help this Cause" and hold fast "by this firm Cord" demonstrates to the emperor and to the contemporary reader that God's unrelenting forgiveness is ever available but is contingent on the sincerity of the supplicant in his plea, a sincerity that can be indicated solely through an acknowledgment of his failure, finding expression in a course of action that proves his determination to change. But as before, Napoleon did not heed Bahá'u'lláh's warning, and within the year (1870) he would be captured in the Battle of Sedan.

Nevertheless, Bahá'u'lláh assures the emperor that His purpose in writing this second epistle is *not* to condemn him but rather to forewarn him of what will happen if he does not take advantage of this final opportunity to repent. He thus invites the emperor: "[a]rise, and make amends for that which escaped thee."[256]

Of course, Bahá'u'lláh's caution to the emperor about what will occur should he again ignore Bahá'u'lláh's advice does not necessarily imply a threat of divine intervention resulting from his dismissive behavior toward God's Manifestation. In a more expansive sense, Bahá'u'lláh is actually conveying—as He does to all the royal recipients of His epistles—that downfall, tumult, and failure are the logical consequences of injustice. Or to state a relevant axiom, one does not "break" the laws of God (and nature); rather, one becomes broken by these operant forces, much as one who leaps off a tall building while scoffing at the law of gravity plummets to his death.

REHEARSAL OF THE ORIGINAL MESSAGE

After these cautionary admonitions, Bahá'u'lláh exhorts the emperor once again to listen to His words, and—this time—to heed the plight of the One Who bears the mantle of Prophethood: "It behoveth thee when thou hearest His Voice calling from the seat of glory to cast away all that thou possessest, and cry out: 'Here am I, O Lord of all that is in heaven and all that is on earth!'"[257] Bahá'u'lláh then recites—even as He had done in His first epistle—the dire events that He and His followers have been made to endure in spite of having committed no crime and having had no objective other than the salvation of humankind.

After alluding to His exile from Baghdad to Constantinople and thence to Adrianople, and finally to the Most Great Prison in 'Akká, Bahá'u'lláh remarks ironically, "And if anyone ask them [the persecutors]: 'For what crime were they [the Bahá'ís] imprisoned?' they would answer and say: 'They, verily, sought to supplant the Faith with a new religion!'" Continuing in this vein, Bahá'u'lláh retorts, "If this be My crime, then Muḥammad, the Apostle of God, committed it before Me, and before Him He Who was the Spirit of God [Christ], and yet earlier He Who conversed with God [Moses]." He concludes, "And if My sin be this, that I have exalted the Word of God and revealed His Cause, then indeed am I the greatest of sinners! Such a sin I will not barter for the kingdoms of earth and heaven."[258]

In the succeeding paragraphs, Bahá'u'lláh reminds the emperor how He has already sent "the messages of their Lord" to kings and rulers (including, of course, Napoleon himself). "[Y]et," He states, "We do it once again as a token of God's grace. Perchance they may recognize the Lord, Who hath come down in the clouds with manifest sovereignty."[259]

He concludes the rehearsal to the Emperor by noting that the injustice, oppression, and agony He has undergone and yet endures—"the like of which no other man hath suffered"—is naught but a source of joy and felicity: "I yearn after tribulations in My love for Him [God], and for the sake of His good pleasure."[260]

THE THREE CONCLUDING THEMES

After recalling the same plaint which He had conveyed to the emperor in the first letter, where He humbly requested assistance for Himself and His followers in light of the emperor's promise to assist the downtrodden and the oppressed, Bahá'u'lláh concludes the letter with three major points: the emperor's obligation to protect those over whom he rules, Bahá'u'lláh's advice to the French people themselves about what spiritual principles should govern their daily lives, and a final beneficent and loving entreaty to the emperor to respond appropriately to the wisdom and the spiritual and political guidance of Bahá'u'lláh while time for recompense and rectification of his future actions still remains.

THE OBLIGATIONS OF A RULER

Reiterating a theme He articulates as early as the Hidden Words, Bahá'u'lláh reminds Napoleon that having assumed a position of political leadership, his first obligation is to the people he serves. "Know of a truth," He admonishes the emperor, "that your subjects are God's trust amongst you." It is the emperor's duty, therefore, to watch over them—a duty that he is warned not to disregard: "Beware that ye allow not wolves to become the shepherds of the fold, or pride and conceit to deter you from turning unto the poor and the desolate."[261]

This admonition to act justly towards his subjects is immediately followed by Bahá'u'lláh's explicit counsels to heed the word of God and champion His Cause, perhaps hinting at the reality that the true standard of justice is found nowhere but in the guidance of God for humanity in this day. These spiritual counsels begin with Bahá'u'lláh's promise that were Napoleon to heed God's words and thus "quaff the mystic Wine of everlasting life," he would be "enabled to forsake all that [he] possess[es] and to proclaim [Bahá'u'lláh's] Name before all mankind."[262] Bahá'u'lláh then invites the emperor: "Cleanse then thy soul with the waters of detachment." The monarch should abandon all desire for wealth and esteem and power, and leave such things to those who crave them. If the emperor wishes to retain the burdensome weight of kingship, he should do so "to aid the Cause of [his] Lord."[263] Bahá'u'lláh admonishes Napoleon to arise in His name and announce to the people that "The Day is come, and the fragrances of God have been wafted over the whole of creation."[264] The Manifestation then reiterates His remarkable promise as to what the emperor will receive should he thus arise to teach the Cause: "God will, thereby, exalt thy name among all the kings."[265]

Bahá'u'lláh concludes this advice by telling Napoleon that were He to "show forth His [God's] signs amidst the peoples of the earth," "[b] urn brightly with the flame of this undying Fire which the All-Merciful hath ignited in the midmost heart of creation," and "[f]ollow in My way and enrapture the hearts of men through remembrance of Me," then this would be better for the emperor than all he possesses.[266]

GUIDANCE FOR THIS "DAY" TO THE PEOPLE OF FRANCE AND THE WORLD

Bahá'u'lláh states that anyone in this Day who does not spread the news of this Revelation is unworthy and is of those who have acceded to their own desires and soon shall find themselves "in grievous loss."[267] Therefore, He continues, the peoples of the world should purge themselves from "whatsoever may withhold [them] from drawing nigh unto God," though all are permitted, and even encouraged, to partake of the benefits of this world so long as these are obtained with justice and moderation and do not distract them from the spiritual.

Secondly, Bahá'u'lláh provides the people with a series of specific laws for this new Day. Among these are the following prohibitions: not to let their words differ from their deeds, not to shed the blood of anyone, not to deal unjustly with anyone, and not to cause "disorders in the land after it hath been well ordered."[268] Bahá'u'lláh follows these prohibitions with encouraging, affirmative guidance, including directives to teach the Cause of God, to first adorn themselves with an upright character, to be trustworthy, to be generous with the poor, and to spread the religion with the sword of the tongue, not with coercion, for the "sword of wisdom is hotter than summer heat, and sharper than blades of steel."[269]

Without rehearsing every detail of Bahá'u'lláh's advice, we can summarize the remaining guidance by alluding to some of the other requirements of this "Day of God." Bahá'u'lláh exhorts the rich to accept their responsibility to assist the poor in their midst. He admonishes the priests and monks that the law against eating meat is abrogated except during the period of the nineteen-day fast;[270] He announces that all are to "Regard . . . the world as a man's body, which is afflicted with divers ailments, and the recovery of which dependeth upon the harmonizing of all of its component elements."[271] Perhaps surprisingly, Bahá'u'lláh goes so far as to announce in this same context that new holy days have been established for this new Dispensation, days on which works should be suspended:

> All feasts have attained their consummation in the two Most Great Festivals, and in two other Festivals that fall on the twin days—the first of the Most Great Festivals being those days whereon God shed the effulgent glory of His most excellent Names upon all who are in heaven and on earth [the festival of Ridván and the Declaration of the Báb], and the second being that day on which We raised up the One Who announced unto the people the glad-tidings of this Great Announcement [the Birthdays of the Báb and Bahá'u'lláh].[272]

Bahá'u'lláh Concludes with Final Advice to the Emperor

In spite of the emperor's callous rejection of the first letter from Bahá'u'lláh, and even after the chilling warnings Bahá'u'lláh has specified in this second letter, the epistle closes by emphasizing the vast opportunity that still awaits Napoleon III should he respond appropriately to Bahá'u'lláh's guidance: "We, verily, have desired naught for thee save that which is better for thee than all that is on earth. Unto this testify all created things and beyond them this perspicuous Book."[273]

Bahá'u'lláh then employs what has traditionally been characterized in poetry as the *"ubi sunt"* theme—that is, "Where are those who went before?" The answer to this rhetorical question is ever the same—even those who had amassed empires and acquired massive wealth and power during their lives are today as dead as the lowliest pauper over whom they held sway: "Whither are gone the proud and their palaces? Gaze thou into their tombs, that thou mayest profit by this example, inasmuch as We made it a lesson unto every beholder."[274] Bahá'u'lláh advises the emperor to abandon his desire for earthly ascendancy, which, "in the estimation of the people of Bahá, is worth as much as the black in the eye of a dead ant."[275]

Bahá'u'lláh ends the epistle by observing that "the generality of mankind" risk everything to perpetuate their fame even though "every perceiving soul testifieth that after death one's name shall avail him nothing except insofar as it beareth a relationship unto God, the Almighty, the All-Praised."[276] His last words to the emperor are thus to abandon such folly: "[T]urn thy sight unto God. This is in truth that which beseemeth thee. Hearken then unto the counsel of thy Lord, and say: Lauded art Thou, O God of all who are in heaven and on earth!"[277]

Chapter 8

The Letter to Czar Alexander II

Czar Alexander II, ca. 1880

We have already mentioned, regarding Bahá'u'lláh's choice of letters to kings and rulers to include in the Súriy-i-Haykal, that—with the possible exception of Naṣíri'd-Dín S͟háh[278]—each recipient had demonstrated a degree of capacity to understand the needs of the people and to comprehend some of the measures needed to improve their condition. For while each ultimately rejected, disdained, or ignored the station and claims of Bahá'u'lláh—with the most positive reception being Queen Victoria's seeming acceptance of the possibility that the claims of Bahá'u'lláh might be true—each had also demonstrated the desire for policies that might improve the condition of those over whom they ruled.

We mentioned the attempts of Napoleon III to advance education, especially for women; to upgrade the country's infrastructure; and to modernize agricultural production to reduce poverty and starvation among the populace. And as we briefly examine the public policies of Czar Alexander II, we discover a desire on his part to decrease the massive gulf between the aristocratic royalty and the serfs, who, while not slaves per se, could be bought and sold with the land, though not individually.[279] In fact, his 1861 emancipation of the serfs earned him the epithet "Alexander the Liberator."

Alexander II instigated other reforms that also reflected a concern for improvements in the judicial system and in education, and an intent to diminish some of the exorbitant privileges of the nobility and the aristocratic class. It would seem, then, that, unlike Naṣíri'd-Dín S͟háh, the emperor was not entirely oblivious to the plight of those over whom he ruled.

THE PROPITIOUS POSITION OF THE CZAR

From the outset of this epistle, Bahá'u'lláh informs the czar that he is worthy of a great bounty inasmuch as one of his Russian ministers assisted Bahá'u'lláh when He was imprisoned in the Siyáh-C͟hál: "Wherefore hath God ordained for thee a station which the knowledge of none can comprehend except His knowledge."[280] This allusion recalls the "persistent and decisive intervention of the Russian Minister, Prince Dolgorouki, who left no stone unturned to establish the innocence of Bahá'u'lláh."[281] Shoghi Effendi in *God Passes By* recounts some details regarding how the prince helped instigate Bahá'u'lláh's release:

[T]he public confession of Mullá <u>Sh</u>ay<u>kh</u> 'Aliy-i-Tur<u>sh</u>ízí, surnamed 'Aẓim,[282] who, in the Siyáh-<u>Ch</u>ál, in the presence of the Ḥájibu'd-Dawlih and the Russian Minister's interpreter and of the government's representative, emphatically exonerated Him, and acknowledged his own complicity; the indisputable testimony established by competent tribunals; the unrelaxing efforts exerted by His own brothers, sisters and kindred,—all these combined to effect His [Bahá'u'lláh's] ultimate deliverance from the hands of His rapacious enemies.[283]

However, lest the student of Bahá'í history assign to the prince sole responsibility for Bahá'u'lláh's release, Shoghi Effendi is careful to note that "[a]nother potent if less evident influence which must be acknowledged as having had a share in His liberation was the fate suffered by so large a number of His self-sacrificing fellow-disciples who languished with Him in that same prison."[284] He then cites Nabil's observation that "the blood, shed in the course of that fateful year in Ṭihrán by that heroic band with whom Bahá'u'lláh had been imprisoned, was the ransom paid for His deliverance from the hand of a foe that sought to prevent Him from achieving the purpose for which God had destined Him."[285]

Nevertheless, while in a position to benefit from the actions taken on his behalf to assist the Manifestation—including his Minister's invitation to Bahá'u'lláh to escape persecution altogether by taking up residence in Russia after His release from the Siyáh-Chál—the czar is still exhorted by Bahá'u'lláh to respond to the same challenge He had proffered the pope and Napoleon III. He advises him, "[a]rise thou amongst men in the name of this all-compelling Cause, and summon, then, the nations unto God, the Exalted, the Great. Be thou not of them who called upon God by one of His names, but who, when He Who is the Object of all names appeared, denied Him and turned aside from Him, and, in the end, pronounced sentence against Him with manifest injustice."[286]

To the Czar as a Christian Ruler

In His subsequent advice and guidance, Bahá'u'lláh places great emphasis on the czar's profession of the Christian faith, warning him not to repeat the evil machinations perpetrated by Herod against Christ. Rather, he should acquaint himself "with the things sent down by

[Bahá'u'lláh's] Pen" and become aware of how He has, with patience and forbearance, endured egregious oppression with gladness: "though My body be beneath the swords of My foes, and My limbs be beset with incalculable afflictions, yet My spirit is filled with a gladness with which all the joys of the earth can never compare."[287]

Bahá'u'lláh then affirms that His advent fulfills the prophecies about the "One Whom the tongue of Isaiah hath extolled" and "with Whose name both the Torah and the Evangel were adorned."[288] Bahá'u'lláh then notes, however, that He is not so much concerned with His own suffering as He is with the gift of recognition and salvation He is offering the czar: "We […] desire naught from you except that ye draw nigh unto what shall profit you in both this world and the world to come."[289]

INESCAPABLE PROOF

Bahá'u'lláh provides the czar with salient evidence that this letter is not from some deluded exile who is no more than an obscure prisoner of the Ottoman Empire. Even as Bahá'u'lláh had demonstrated His superhuman knowledge by reciting to Napoleon III the excuse the emperor had given for France's involvement in the Crimean War,[290] so in His letter to Alexander II Bahá'u'lláh similarly shares His intimate and exact knowledge of a prayer that the czar had offered up: "We, verily, have heard the thing for which thou didst supplicate thy Lord, whilst secretly communing with Him. Wherefore, the breeze of My loving-kindness wafted forth, and the sea of My mercy surged, and We answered thee in truth. Thy Lord, verily, is the All-Knowing, the All-Wise."[291]

We can only imagine the stunning impact such knowledge of the czar's inmost thoughts and private supplications must have had, but only if he had been attentive to what lay before him in this astounding message from a Manifestation of God. For even as Bahá'u'lláh's knowledge of Napoleon's private conversation did not serve to sway the response of the French emperor, it would seem that this equally persuasive demonstration of an otherworldly power by Bahá'u'lláh failed to sway the czar sufficiently to move him to investigate further the station, claims, and exhortations contained in this remarkable epistle.

Perhaps relevant to the failure of this proof to convince the czar is the statement by Bahá'u'lláh in *Epistle to the Son of the Wolf* that miracles, while temporarily impressive to those who witness or experience them, are not a sound basis for convincing people of the station or truth of God's Messenger: "We entreat Our loved ones not to besmirch the hem of Our raiment with the dust of falsehood, neither to allow references to what they have regarded as miracles and prodigies to debase Our rank and station, or to mar the purity and sanctity of Our name."[292] For while we can in retrospect appreciate the blatant proof such evidence provides of Bahá'u'lláh's omniscience, we must also take into account how much the czar, together with the other four recipients of epistles included in the Súriy-i-Haykal, had to lose were they publicly to acknowledge the veracity of Bahá'u'lláh's claims and subsequently to heed His call to "[a]rise [...] amongst men in the name of this all-compelling Cause, and summon, then, the nations unto God, the Exalted, the Great."[293]

Of course, we certainly cannot imagine that Bahá'u'lláh was so naïve as to expect that these figures in positions of incredible power and prestige would renounce their religion, wealth, fame, and lofty stations to follow the behests of this "Stranger" from the Orient, as had the simple fishermen who were the first followers of Christ and who, we might suppose, presumed they had nothing much to lose by their receptivity, even though in time all of them would sacrifice their lives for their beliefs. The fact is that even now when people are initially made aware of the Bahá'í Faith, its teachings, and its history, the first question they are likely to ask is, "If all this be true, why haven't I heard about this before? Why isn't it on the news and being shouted from the rooftops?"[294] The answer one might proffer to such an understandable question is, "Now you have heard, and now you do know, and now the test is yours." For this is the judgment imposed upon all the peoples of the world whenever a new Manifestation appears in the course of our collective history. They are forced to confront their own professed beliefs by asking themselves whether the forewarnings, the prophecies, and the explicit promises of their own scripture are merely enigmatic passages to be memorized and recited or whether they forewarn an actual return that has now taken place. They must reflect on the similar challenges and cynicism encountered by the Founder of their own religions Who also appeared in fulfillment of prior expectations—Moses the liberator, Christ the Messiah, Muḥammad the Comforter, the Báb the Qá'im, and Bahá'u'lláh the Promised One of all ages, the Second Coming in this, the Day of Days.

THE MOST GREAT PEACE

But we need not wax homiletic to make the obvious point that while the test for these five rulers was grievous, and none of them responded adequately to it, Bahá'u'lláh's announcement to them was of historic significance if for no other reason than that afterward no one could claim Bahá'u'lláh had withheld the Revelation from the world. Neither could anyone deny the prescience of Bahá'u'lláh's attendant warnings, foreshadowing in most lucid terms the consequences that would follow should these wielders of power ignore His exhortations and, of equal import, fail to heed His explicit guidance about the immediate imperative that they form a pact to institute the "principle of collective security."[295] Had they recognized the station and authority of Bahá'u'lláh and subsequently followed His advice, the world could thereby have foregone the indirect and more arduous path to the "Lesser Peace." As we will observe in Bahá'u'lláh's letter to Queen Victoria, Bahá'u'lláh exhorts thus the rulers who have clearly rejected His claims regarding His station: "Now that ye have refused the Most Great Peace, hold ye fast unto this, the Lesser Peace, that haply ye may in some degree better your own condition and that of your dependents."[296]

In the final paragraphs of the letter to Czar Alexander II, Bahá'u'lláh assures the ruler that nothing He says or requests is for His own benefit, nor can fulfillment of these petitions redound to His own well-being. Rather, everything He is challenging the monarch to recognize, to heed, and to put into action will benefit the totality of humankind, including the czar himself: "It is for the sake of God alone that My tongue counselleth you and that My pen moveth to make mention of you," Bahá'u'lláh assures him, "for neither can the malice and denial of all who dwell on earth harm Me, nor the allegiance of the entire creation profit Me."[297] He concludes, "We, verily, exhort you unto that which We were commanded, and desire naught from you except that ye draw nigh unto what shall profit you in both this world and the world to come."[298]

THE STATION OF THE MONARCH WHO RECOGNIZES BAHÁ'U'LLÁH

In concluding the epistle, Bahá'u'lláh repeats the same *ubi sunt* theme with which He had cautioned Napoleon III: "Think ye that the things ye possess shall profit you? Soon others will possess them and ye will return unto the dust with none to help or succour you. What advantage is there in a life that can be overtaken by death, or in an existence that is doomed to extinction, or in a prosperity that is subject to change?"[299]

And finally, with delicious irony for those students familiar with the history of the Bahá'í Faith and acquainted with the enormous esteem and eternal legacy bequeathed Queen Marie of Romania—the first monarch to respond to exhortations of Bahá'u'lláh and to become a Bahá'í—Bahá'u'lláh asserts: "Blessed be the king whose sovereignty hath withheld him not from his Sovereign, and who hath turned unto God with his heart. He, verily, is accounted of those that have attained unto that which God, the Mighty, the All-Wise, hath willed. Erelong will such a one find himself numbered with the monarchs of the realms of the Kingdom."[300] How exponentially marvelous it is that the monarch "numbered with the monarchs of the realms of the Kingdom" was a woman, thereby reaffirming inferentially Bahá'u'lláh's laws establishing the equality of women and men.

Chapter 9

The Letter to Queen Victoria

Queen Victoria, 1882
Photograph by Alessandro Bassano

The focal point of Bahá'u'lláh's epistle to Queen Victoria, which we cited in our discussion of the letter to Alexander II but which bears repeating, is arguably His poignant and profound historical assessment that, by the time of His writing to the queen, it was clear that the rulers to whom He had written and proclaimed His station had paid Him no heed, an assessment immediately followed by the loving invitation to at least cleave to the remaining path to peace: "Now that ye have refused the Most Great Peace, hold ye fast unto this, the Lesser Peace, that haply ye may in some degree better your own condition and that of your dependents."[301] As we shall see, it is also in this letter that Bahá'u'lláh articulates the basic framework of a pact of collective security that can secure the Lesser Peace.

To the Queen Regarding Governance

If we were to speculate as to why Bahá'u'lláh's most clear articulation to any ruler of the principles of collective security required for the Lesser Peace is given to Queen Victoria, we might suppose that she—and the government over which she presided as constitutional monarch—had done the most to demonstrate a receptivity to the cause of justice. Most notably, the British Parliament had, through successive acts of legislation in the first half of the 19th century, abolished slave trading throughout the British Empire over which Queen Victoria now presided. Bahá'u'lláh specifically praises the ending of this abomination in which England had been a leading participant: "We have been informed that thou hast forbidden the trading in slaves, both men and women. This, verily, is what God hath enjoined in this wondrous Revelation. God hath, truly, destined a reward for thee, because of this."[302]

Bahá'u'lláh also notably praises the queen—and by implication, the English parliamentary form of governance—for delegating governmental authority to representatives elected by universal suffrage; though this was confined at that time to men, it represented a more refined and entrenched model of democratic governance than elsewhere in Europe or the Middle East. He states, "We have also heard that thou hast entrusted the reins of counsel into the hands of the representatives of the people." He then observes, "Thou, indeed, hast done well, for thereby the foundations of the edifice of thine affairs will be strengthened, and the hearts of all that are beneath thy shadow, whether high or low, will be tranquillized."[303]

However, Bahá'u'lláh goes beyond this ostensible advocacy of a form of government in which representatives are elected by the people, and subsequently convene in a consultative forum in which to devise policy and laws and advise a monarch or president. In this same paragraph, Bahá'u'lláh notes that the representational form of government works well only when those elected have as their abiding motive the desire to uphold the well-being of "all that dwell on earth" and the universal principles of justice for all people, something they can achieve only by turning their hearts to God and supplicating Him for guidance:

> It behoveth them, however, to be trustworthy among His servants, and to regard themselves as the representatives of all that dwell on earth. This is what counselleth them, in this Tablet, He Who is the Ruler, the All-Wise. And if any one of them directeth himself towards the Assembly, let him turn his eyes unto the Supreme Horizon, and say: "O my God! I ask Thee, by Thy most glorious Name, to aid me in that which will cause the affairs of Thy servants to prosper, and Thy cities to flourish. Thou, indeed, hast power over all things!"[304]

Bahá'u'lláh concludes this advice with a beatitude to all those who have been elected to positions of power or who are charged with making judiciary decisions: "Blessed is he that entereth the Assembly for the sake of God, and judgeth between men with pure justice. He, indeed, is of the blissful."[305]

In general, then, the letter to Queen Victoria is brief, gentler in tone than the other four epistles, and expressive of serious hope that the queen will combine her nation's noble decision regarding slave trading with recognition and implementation of the other steps needed to bring about universal harmony and lasting peace. As will be explored in more depth later in this chapter, this includes extending the consultative methodology found in a nascent form in the parliamentary assembly to the international arena. He illuminates this crucial and timely advice with a salient medical analogy:

> Regard the world as the human body which, though at its creation whole and perfect, hath been afflicted, through various causes, with grave disorders and maladies. Not for one day did it gain ease, nay its sickness waxed more severe, as it fell under the treatment of

ignorant physicians, who gave full rein to their personal desires and have erred grievously. And if, at one time, through the care of an able physician, a member of that body was healed, the rest remained afflicted as before. Thus informeth you the All-Knowing, the All-Wise.[306]

THE DRAMATIC INTERRUPTION
OF BAHÁ'U'LLÁH'S CAUTIONARY ADMONITIONS

It is at this point that Bahá'u'lláh seems to interrupt His explicit discourse with the queen and shift His attention to the rulers of the world as a group. In this regard, we have noted in our assessment of the previous three letters that the luminaries of power to whom Bahá'u'lláh wrote had each by profession (in the case of the pope) or by advocacy of certain felicitous policies (in the case of Napoleon III and Alexander II) demonstrated some ability to appreciate the advice Bahá'u'lláh proffers.

And yet, it is obvious from the tone as well as from the specific statements in those previous three letters that Bahá'u'lláh is chastising these rulers for their lust for power, their overweening pride in their attainments and possessions, and their failure to appreciate that their only enduring fame or impact on history will be the extent to which they accede to the greater plan of God by complying with Bahá'u'lláh's advice with respect to their rule and the affairs of their people.

He likewise emphasizes in the first three letters the supreme irony that each of these men, though nominally dedicated to serving the Christian religion and its principles, is committing precisely the same grievous error as did the Roman prelates in allowing the Sanhedrin (the governing body of the Jewish community in Jerusalem) to torture and execute the very Messiah Whose advent they professed to anticipate and Whose authority they should have readily accepted. Indeed, Bahá'u'lláh explicitly chastises them for their inability to recognize in Him the return of Christ—the Second Coming—as prophesied in both the Old and New Testaments.

Perhaps due to these very limitations He sees in the other rulers, Bahá'u'lláh reserves for His letter to Queen Victoria a discussion of the specifics of His prescription for the Lesser Peace. It is thus that, curiously and unexpectedly, Bahá'u'lláh suddenly shifts from discussing His pleasure with the queen's policies and form of government to the urgent need for all representatives in every land to become occupied with those policies, principles, and actions that will lead to the security, justice, and well-being of humankind.[307]

For the next nine paragraphs, Bahá'u'lláh addresses not only the queen, but, through her (possibly soliciting her assistance in sharing His guidance), all the rulers of the earth, admonishing them to undertake immediate reforms centered on the theme of unity: "Be united, O kings of the earth, for thereby will the tempest of discord be stilled amongst you, and your peoples find rest."[308]

Of course, the word *tempest* immediately calls to mind the first paragraph of Shoghi Effendi's discussion of these same letters in *The Promised Day is Come*, where the Guardian states that this very same tempest has now begun: "A tempest, unprecedented in its violence, unpredictable in its course, catastrophic in its immediate effects, unimaginably glorious in its ultimate consequences, is at present sweeping the face of the earth. Its driving power is remorselessly gaining in range and momentum."[309]

The fact that Bahá'u'lláh begins this advice by comparing the global body politic to a human body, as discussed earlier, is particularly appropriate given the abiding theme of the Súriy-i-Haykal, God's investiture of the Holy Spirit in a physical human temple. But the symbolic "temple" also applies to the body of humankind that is in the grips of a perilous malady and in desperate need of selfless physicians, a role that the leaders could assume, were they unified in their concern for the betterment of humankind rather than their own individual ascendancy and well-being: "O ye the elected representatives of the people in every land! Take ye counsel together, and let your concern be only for that which profiteth mankind and bettereth the condition thereof, if ye be of them that scan heedfully."[310]

In continuing the human body analogy, Bahá'u'lláh observes that even when a ruler has advocated for policies to improve the condition of the ailing body of humankind, "his motive hath been his own gain, whether confessedly so or not; and the unworthiness of this motive hath limited his power to heal or cure."[311] He then observes that the true remedy for the ills of humankind, the one "which the Lord hath ordained as the sovereign remedy and mightiest instrument for the healing of all the world is the union of all its peoples in one universal Cause, one common Faith," a remedy that can be achieved solely "through the power of a skilled, an all-powerful and inspired Physician."[312] Clearly implicit is that this "Physician" is Bahá'u'lláh Himself, "the Ancient Beauty," the very One Whom the rulers of the world have rejected, imprisoned, denounced, and Whose epistles they have now largely ignored, entirely disregarding the remedies set forth in them.

Bahá'u'lláh concludes His indictment of the rulers by asking on what basis they have remained heedless of His salient guidance when His sole motive has been, and remains that "haply both ye [the rulers] and the poor may attain unto tranquillity and peace."[313] He then recites how they have, one and all, abused their power at the expense of the well-being of their subjects, the very ones who should be their foremost concern. "This, verily, is wholly and grossly unjust," He proclaims, calling them to a higher standard: "Do not rob them [your peoples] to rear palaces for yourselves; nay rather choose for them that which ye choose for yourselves."[314] In forcefully articulating the standard of justice expected of the world's rulers, Bahá'u'lláh highlights the double irony of their actual conduct. Not only is Bahá'u'lláh's counsel, which they continue to ignore, precisely what will profit them, but their ongoing failure to act justly towards their own people ignores the fundamental reality that without them, a ruler has nothing: "By them ye rule, by their means ye subsist, by their aid ye conquer. Yet, how disdainfully ye look upon them! How strange, how very strange!"[315]

THE SUDDEN AND UNEXPECTED SHIFT

It is at this point that Bahá'u'lláh announces the end result of the malfeasance of the rulers of the world, and their inattention to His unambiguous statements regarding His station as a Manifestation of God comparable to Christ. This brings us, as stated at the outset of this chapter, to the arguable core of the letter. Having so callously and cavalierly cast away the opportunity to seize the Most Great Peace, the world's rulers are counseled by Bahá'u'lláh: "hold ye fast unto this, the Lesser Peace, that haply ye may in some degree better your own condition and that of your dependents."[316]

Thus, in spite of their inattention, Bahá'u'lláh does not abandon urging the rulers to take the appropriate measures to instigate the Lesser Peace—perhaps hoping that the queen will discern the wisdom in His guidance and help promote a unified approach to the cessation of war-fare and the wretched toll it imposes on the peoples of the world. "O rulers of the earth! Be reconciled among yourselves," He pleads. "Be united, O kings of the earth, for thereby will the tempest of discord be stilled amongst you, and your peoples find rest, if ye be of them that comprehend. Should any one among you take up arms against another, rise ye all against him, for this is naught but manifest justice."[317]

Here it is well worth noting that Bahá'u'lláh has the wisdom and om-niscience to realize that His pleas and selfless admonitions will go un-heeded. He gives ample testimony to His foreknowledge that the rulers of His time—and those who will follow them—will ignore His council, perhaps most famously in His allusion to the looming catastrophe of the World Wars found in a passage of the Kitáb-i-Aqdas addressed to Kaiser William I:

> Think deeply, O King, concerning him [Napoleon III], and con-cerning them who, like unto thee, have conquered cities and ruled over men. The All-Merciful brought them down from their palaces to their graves. Be warned, be of them who reflect . . . O banks of the Rhine! We have seen you covered with gore, inasmuch as the swords of retribution were drawn against you; and you shall have another turn. And We hear the lamentations of Berlin, though she be today in conspicuous glory.[318]

By now, the reader should understand that these letters are not in-tended solely for the benefit of the rulers and peoples of the time the epistles were revealed. Rather, they are supremely important historical documentation of the fact that Bahá'u'lláh as Manifestation provided a pathway to peace that would have avoided all the war, massive loss of life, and privations that have afflicted such a substantial portion of the earth's population since His time, and that even now abides. In addition, it is our duty to study this history and teach it to our descendants so that this same unfortunate pattern of response does not recur in the future, either when the next Manifestation appears, or, more pressingly, at this very moment when the guidance, plans, and laws of the Universal House of Justice provide humankind with infallible guidance delineating the most propitious pathway to the felicitous future heralded by Bahá'u'lláh.

Returning to the letter, we find that suddenly, in the penultimate para-graph, Bahá'u'lláh halts, as if the Holy Spirit operating through Him has made Him aware of the futility of any further admonitions, inasmuch as He has already clearly articulated these same admonitions in the Súriy-i-Mulúk, the Tablet to the Kings revealed in 1867: "Rein in Thy pen, O Pen of the Ancient of Days, and leave them to themselves, for they are immersed in their idle fancies," advises the voice within Him, that same voice emanating from the persona of the Maid.[319] Instead, He should turn His attention to the queen, for whom there still may be hope that she will heed His guidance and promote the cause of justice.

The letter thus closes with a prayer that, we may confidently presume, Bahá'u'lláh has revealed especially for the queen to recite. One clue that the identity of the supplicant is the queen resides in the verse alluding to other "handmaidens who have believed in Thee": "Deprive me not, O my Lord, of the fragrances of the Robe of Thy mercy in Thy days, and write down for me that which Thou hast written down for Thy handmaidens who have believed in Thee and in Thy signs, and have recognized Thee, and set their hearts towards the horizon of Thy Cause."[320]

Of course, we cannot conclude our review of this letter and its relationship to the theme of the Súriy-i-Haykal—the investiture of the power of the Holy Spirit in the world of being by means of establishing a spiritually based commonwealth of nations—without mentioning the queen's reported response after reading the letter, so unlike the disdain of the other recipients: "If this is of God, it will endure; if not, it can do no harm."[321] Perhaps this response is hardly a ringing endorsement, and yet, compared to that of the other recipients, and most especially in light of the actions of Naṣíri'd-Dín Sháh upon receiving Bahá'u'lláh's epistle, the axiom in her benign observation—an allusion to Acts 5:39[322]—holds a nugget of marvelous truth inasmuch as the very Cause of the prisoner Whose letter she perused has indeed endured!

Even more lovely in its irony is the fact that the first World Congress of the Bahá'í Faith in 1963 to announce the election of the Universal House of Justice—and, thus, celebrate the completion of the "Crowning Feature"[323] of the Administrative Order of the Bahá'í Faith—was held in Royal Albert Hall. The hall, which was named after Queen Victoria's beloved husband, was opened by her in 1871, about the same time the Súriy-i-Haykal was being composed in its final form. It is also well worth noting that the only monarchy that remained intact after the tribulations and revolutions Bahá'u'lláh cautioned would soon arrive was that of England, though, as Bahá'u'lláh notes, it is a parliamentary form of government and not an absolute monarchy.

Chapter 10

The Letter to Naṣíri'd-Dín S̱h̲áh
Part One: Background and Initial Considerations

Naṣíri'd-Dín S̱h̲áh, ca. 1880
Photograph by Gaspard-Félix Tournachon (Nadar)

We begin our examination of the climactic letter Bahá'u'lláh saw fit to include in the pentacle design of the Súriy-i-Haykal by providing background and context so essential to appreciating both the tone and substance of this, the most lengthy of the five epistles. More than any of the other letters, the letter to the king of Persia—also titled the "Lawḥ-i-Sulṭán"— symbolizes the transfer of governance from the Creator to His creation, the investiture of power into the hands of the sovereigns, the elected representatives, and the spiritual leaders—they who, as recipients of the call of the Ancient of Days, were largely oblivious to the potential for greatness that they so brashly and casually dismissed. Once this context is properly studied and understood, one can begin to appreciate why the letter to Naṣíri'd-Dín Sháh, among all the other announcements Bahá'u'lláh made to the kings, rulers, governmental institutions, and religious leaders of the world, should rightly be chosen to conclude the representative epistles in the Súriy-i-Haykal.

As we have noted earlier in our examination of the Súriy-i-Haykal, these letters were not *proforma*, as if Bahá'u'lláh could not reasonably have expected the recipients to discern in these messages some signs of the station, the sagacity, and the otherworldly knowledge of the Most Great Pen. Not only are these epistles fashioned explicitly with the background and, in some cases, personalities and experiences of the recipients in mind, but Bahá'u'lláh has carefully included moral and political verities, as well as allusions to personal circumstances, that, by all rights, should have alerted the recipients to the fact that this was a voice of empathy, wisdom, and authority, and hardly the aimless or fanciful pleadings of some fanatic, some deranged stranger.

But the letter to Naṣíri'd-Dín Sháh is distinctive in so many ways because this monarch was well aware of the Composer of this epistle. After all, the king had previously done everything in his power to see that Bahá'u'lláh was imprisoned, tortured, and—so he had thought— exiled to a prison so remote from Persia and so dire in its conditions that surely the very name of Bahá'u'lláh, let alone those of His Cause and its followers, would never again be voiced within his hearing.

And yet, here He was again: Bahá'u'lláh, this same Prisoner the king had tried to destroy, daring to address him in a lengthy and magnificent formal instruction—indeed, a mandate. What was doubtless even more disturbing to the king was that this unwelcome and totally unexpected document was delivered into his hands, not by some dignitary or person of rank or import, but by a mere lad of seventeen—the youth whom his Lord had titled "Badíʻ"[324] ("wonderful") and who was prepared to fearlessly defy whatever consequence the startled despot and his myrmidons would most certainly devise—and devise them they did. But here again we would do well to note how Bahá'u'lláh has delegated the honor and authority of carrying out this historically important mission—a demonstration of heroism that will endure through the ages—to one whom many outside observers might consider the most ordinary and menial servant among His followers. In addition, the inspiration the figure and story of Badíʻ have provided for Bahá'í youth ever since demonstrates the fathomless wisdom and foresight that only a Manifestation of God could possess.

IMPORTANT BACKGROUND INFORMATION UNDERLYING
THE CONTEXT OF THE LETTER

In a section of *The Promised Day is Come* titled "Divine Retribution on the Qájár Dynasty," Shoghi Effendi traces the origins of the Qájár dynasty and the tumultuous and disastrous reigns of its successive Sháhs, but focuses most specifically on the relentless oppression that occurred under the authority of Naṣíri'd-Dín Sháh: the execution of the Báb and thousands of His followers, the imprisonment of Bahá'u'lláh in the Siyáh-Chál, the further exile of Bahá'u'lláh to Baghdad, and finally the king's petitions to Sulṭán 'Abdu'l-Azíz to have Bahá'u'lláh exiled further away from Persia to Constantinople, to Adrianople, and eventually to 'Akká, where the Sháh reasonably presumed Bahá'u'lláh and the Bahá'í religion would die out and never again disrupt his tyrannical rule.[325]

Because of this history and the length and tone of the letter to Naṣíri'd-Dín Sháh, Bahá'u'lláh foreknew that whosoever would deliver this epistle to the king would most surely meet with dire consequences—that they would certainly be tortured and executed. After all, in addition to being "omniscient at will,"[326] Bahá'u'lláh understood the king's character and temperament all too well. And though many believers had petitioned Bahá'u'lláh to have the honor of carrying the Lawḥ-i-Sulṭán to the king, Bahá'u'lláh entrusted the task to the young Badíʻ, "in whom, as affirmed by Bahá'u'lláh, 'the spirit of might and power was breathed.'"[327]

While Badíʻ and the details of his heroism merit a volume of their own, for our present purposes we can do no better than cite Shoghi Effendi's synopsis of Badíʻ's venture in conveying the epistle:

A four months' journey had taken him [Badí'] to that city [Tehran], and, after passing three days in fasting and vigilance, he had met the Sháh proceeding on a hunting expedition to Shimírán. He had calmly and respectfully approached His Majesty, calling out, "O King! I have come to thee from Sheba with a weighty message"; whereupon at the Sovereign's order, the Tablet was taken from him and delivered to the mujtahids of Ṭihrán who were commanded to reply to that Epistle—a command which they evaded, recommending instead that the messenger should be put to death.[328]

As a consequence of this decision, the young Badí', "surnamed the 'Pride of Martyrs' . . . was arrested, branded for three successive days, his head beaten to a pulp with the butt of a rifle, after which his body was thrown into a pit and earth and stones heaped upon it."[329]

THE TONE OF THE LETTER

The historical context may inform us as to why the Sháh and the religious authorities in league with his tyrannical rule reacted so harshly and so vehemently to the letter—as opposed to the kings and rulers included in the Súriy-i-Haykal already discussed, who either totally ignored their own letter from Bahá'u'lláh or else disdained it as having no important significance relevant to the success of their endeavors. But what we might not expect from the letter, especially since this is hardly the beginning of the relationship between the Sender and the recipient, is the remarkably benign and loving tone contained in a message to the very one under whose authority the Primal Point had been executed, and who had been the most inveterate oppressor of the Bábís, and subsequently Bahá'u'lláh and the Bahá'ís. Indeed, the reader might instead expect a tone at least as harsh and remonstrative as that found in the letters to the pope or to Napoleon III. But such is not the case. Instead, He begins with humility, explaining to the "King of the Earth" (the Sháh) that Bahá'u'lláh is but a "Vassal": "Verily, I am a Servant Who hath believed in God and in His signs, and have sacrificed Myself in His path."[330]

While the kindness and sincerity of Bahá'u'lláh's lengthy discourse to Naṣíri'd-Dín Sháh are evident throughout, there are, of course, warnings, cautions, and prophetic allusions, even as there are in the previous four letters. In this final letter, however, these are couched in the most kindly and understanding words, a language reminiscent of Bahá'u'lláh's advice in the Lawḥ-i-Maqṣúd about teaching others: "Therefore an enlightened man of wisdom should primarily speak with words as mild as milk, that the children of men may be nurtured and edified thereby and may attain the ultimate goal of human existence which is the station of true understanding and nobility."[331]

We can imagine, however, that this conciliatory language, together with the lengthy advice and tone of deference, instead of soothing the troubled monarch, would instead have rankled him beyond all bounds. For not only was the One he might have presumed to be at long last silenced, deceased, or at the very least, banished from his presence, still alive, but He was also thriving, albeit in a dank prison city, and possessed of followers who, like Badí', would readily and happily sacrifice their lives to carry out such a perilous mission. The bewildered and angered king may well have wondered whether he himself could command any similar sort of loyalty from the minions and sycophants with whom he surrounded himself during the entirety of his reign.

SIMILAR TO HIS TREATMENT OF MÍRZÁ YAHYÁ

As we ponder the tone of this lengthy epistle, we might recall that it was five years later, in 1873, that Bahá'u'lláh revealed His Most Holy Book—the Kitáb-i-Aqdas—where He similarly, and perhaps equally unexpectedly for most readers, demonstrated forgiveness and hope for His brother Mírzá Yaḥyá, who had been the source of untold suffering for Bahá'u'lláh. Even so, Bahá'u'lláh in the Kitáb-i-Aqdas exhorts Mírzá Yaḥyá to repent of his actions while there is yet time, to realize that no matter how grievous his sins, God's forgivingness is endless.

In most touching terms, Bahá'u'lláh recalls how He raised His brother—"remember how We nurtured thee by day and by night for service to the Cause"—and then exhorts him: "Fear God, and be thou of the truly repentant. [...] Beware lest the fire of thy presumptuousness debar thee from attaining to God's Holy Court. Turn unto Him, and fear not because of thy deeds. He, in truth, forgiveth whomsoever He desireth as a bounty on His part; no God is there but Him, the Ever-Forgiving, the All-Bounteous."[332]

We might also find remarkable the understanding that Bahá'u'lláh expresses about how Mírzá Yaḥyá might have allowed his appointment by the Báb as His "nominee" to tempt him to make his spurious claims to successorship, even as other Bábís were not exactly sure what this appellation meant or what authority it conferred upon Mírzá Yaḥyá: "Granted that the people were confused about thy station, is it conceivable that thou thyself art similarly confused?"[333]

Of course, as we have noted repeatedly, Bahá'u'lláh is hardly naïve about Mírzá Yaḥyá or human nature in general. He is fully aware that Mírzá Yaḥyá committed his atrocities in full knowledge of what he was doing, however much he might have been encouraged in his abominable acts by Siyyid Muḥammad-i-Isfahaní, who tempted him to undermine Bahá'u'lláh's station. Thus, Bahá'u'lláh concludes His advice in a more somber and sober tone, reminding Mírzá Yaḥyá, "We admonish thee solely for the sake of God. Shouldst thou accept this counsel, thou wilt have acted to thine own behoof; and shouldst thou reject it, thy Lord, verily, can well dispense with thee, and with all those who, in manifest delusion, have followed thee."[334]

Finally, after reminding Mírzá Yaḥyá (who at this time resided on the island of Cyprus, where he had been exiled) that the evil influence of Siyyid Muḥammad-i-Iṣfáhání has now been removed—"God hath laid hold on him who led thee astray"[335]—Bahá'u'lláh concludes His counsel to Mírzá Yaḥyá thus: "Return unto God, humble, submissive and lowly; verily, He will put away from thee thy sins, for thy Lord, of a certainty, is the Forgiving, the Mighty, the All-Merciful."[336]

WHY ATTEMPT TO REASON WITH THE SHÁH?
FOREKNOWLEDGE AND MERCY

A question may arise, both with respect to Bahá'u'lláh's address to Mírzá Yaḥyá in the Kitáb-i-Aqdas and His letter to the Sháh: given His foreknowledge of how these men will respond—or rather, utterly fail to respond—why bother to address them at all, let alone in loving tones? The question may especially apply to the letter to the Sháh, given Bahá'u'lláh's clear understanding that the youthful messenger who bore it would meet with death; indeed, He assured Badí' that he would suffer martyrdom.

One reason, of course, has already been suggested: each letter written by Bahá'u'lláh has wider significance for humanity as a whole, regardless of who its direct recipient may be. Not only are the words of each epistle possessed of the same fathomless layers of import inherent in all of Bahá'u'lláh's Writings but, as suggested in the first chapter, some of these meanings are only accessible once we understand the historical context in which they were revealed. In other words, it is precisely in knowing that this was a letter to the Sháh—and in further understanding something of the actions of the Sháh which form a context for the letter's content—that we unlock some of the significance and important lessons that it holds for us today. We, in other words, would be deprived of a portion of the Revelation that Bahá'u'lláh deems significant for *us* had He not written this letter. Likewise, had it not been delivered in the tragic yet awe-inspiring circumstances that we have reviewed, we would be deprived of this further context to the letter, and of the example of the heroic, joyful sacrifice of Badí' that stands out even within the annals of the illustrious martyrs of Bahá'í history.

A further significance of Bahá'u'lláh's decision to send a letter that He knows the Sháh will not even deign to read emerges when we consider again its kindly and gentle approach and tone. Through this tone, Bahá'u'lláh is demonstrating for all time to future readers who examine the epistle with an open mind and consider its historical context that He provides for every soul a pathway to salvation and understanding, that He tests no one beyond their capacity to comprehend the truth, and that, as He emphasizes in His message to Mírzá Yaḥyá in the Kitáb-i-Aqdas, the salvation and redemption of every soul lies in their own freely chosen response. Bahá'u'lláh's foreknowledge of rejection, in other words, in no way constrains or causes the actions of the Sháh, who—like each of us—is presented with tests that are not beyond his capacity to bear, and chooses his response to them. Bahá'u'lláh's infinite mercy means that the Sháh must be given his chance; the fact that he refused to take it lessens neither the magnitude and significance of the mercy shown to him, nor the power of the lesson provided to us about the individual's responsibility towards the truth. Ultimately—and simultaneously with the letter's importance as a lesson for us—every exhortation is solely for the benefit of the recipient: the Cause of God will endure and succeed with or without their assistance.

THE SYMPHONIC STRUCTURE OF THE EPISTLE

Having discussed the tone of the epistle to the Sháh, we can now begin to consider its content. It would require a volume to examine this letter sufficiently, to elucidate every subtle twist and turn in this masterpiece of epistolary composition. And for the purposes of this study of the overall meaning and impact of the Súriy-i-Haykal, such an examination is not necessary. But by beginning from a wide perspective, we can attempt to appreciate the overall structure of the work, and see how Bahá'u'lláh interweaves many of the same themes He has shared in the previous letters to the other kings and rulers yet adds nuance that only the Sháh can understand and appreciate—if, indeed, he can muster the will and receptivity to consider the letter at all.

Yet, while the Sháh proved impervious to its salutary purposes, we, with our historical objectivity, can perhaps discern in retrospect its foundational structure, its abiding theme, and the leitmotifs that Bahá'u'lláh has so artfully compressed into the longest and most profound of the five letters, thereby making it a fitting climax to one of the major works penned by the Manifestation for this dispensation.

We might find the term "symphonic" useful in relation to the structure of the epistle. The work does not progress in an obviously linear manner: intermixed with admonitions and homilies about the need to exchange the desire for power and lust after possessions for a dedication to the will of God are narratives about Bahá'u'lláh's personal history and suffering, together with prayers, challenges to the clergy, and forewarnings to the Sháh about whom he should and should not trust. And yet, underlying and harmonizing this admixture of diverse narrative forms and developments is one abiding theme reverberating throughout like a musical motif—the theme of justice in all its ramifications.

Of course, the concept of justice is not a simple one; it cannot be easily defined or encompassed. Plato required the whole of *The Republic* to attempt it, and the Bahá'í writings make absolutely clear that justice is always in a state of relative understanding and application, whether one considers the individual's attempt to be just—a theme Bahá'u'lláh repeatedly calls to the monarchs' attention—or the collective charge that God through His Manifestations has given humankind to fashion a just society by degrees so that this earthly realm will ever more expansively and completely replicate in metaphorical expression the celestial kingdom of heaven.

If we consider the complex structure of this letter in light of the symphonic conceit, we can imagine this background or underlying theme—i.e., justice as a spiritual concept touching on all things—being carried by the lower tones of percussion and base strings, while at the forefront of this artful composition the more ephemeral but brighter voices of the violins articulate the theme of justice in all its varied and specific applications, which include the king's relationship to his people as God's shadow among them, and his treatment of Bahá'u'lláh as God's emissary tasked with fostering a unified social order and world peace among the nations of the world.

With this symphonic structure in mind, we may find it useful to spot the markers in this work that set off the appearances of these themes, rather than merely listing a pastiche of diverse and seemingly disconnected elements, however beautiful and empowering those elements might be individually. For while the entire panoply of ingredients is what "the Pen of the Most High" is inspiring Bahá'u'lláh ("the Most Great Pen") to convey to the king—and thence to humankind as a whole—we can better appreciate the composition as a coherent work by discerning these underlying themes and motifs that bind the various parts into an artistic whole.

A MAN LIKE OTHERS, ASLEEP UPON MY COUCH

The first crucial theme of this letter that merits our attention is the nature of the Manifestation and His Revelation. One of the more subtle tasks the Manifestations of God must undertake is to explain to those who have known Them prior to Their declaration that They have now assumed the lofty station and powers of God's Vicegerent on earth, the Promised One of the prior religions whose advent will set in motion the transformation of human society. A few "get it," as this new understanding makes sense of the loftiness they may have suspected was there all along, but most do not recognize the complete implications of the station, nor do they see why this same individual Whom they have known as a companion or associate should suddenly assume such a grandiose status and thence command their obeisance and obedience.

We have noted how, in the previous letters Bahá'u'lláh has included in the Súriy-i-Haykal, He forthrightly announces His station. Since most recipients of these letters may not have heard of Bahá'u'lláh before, they have no need to understand His ostensible transformation. But the Sháh knows full well Bahá'u'lláh's prior identity as a member of the nobility Who became a follower of the Báb and an important leader in the Bábí Faith. As already noted, the Sháh had been responsible for the execution of the Báb, the egregious assault on the Bábí community throughout Persia, and the imprisonment and exile of Bahá'u'lláh.

It is in this context that Bahá'u'lláh speaks to the king respectfully,

as a law-abiding citizen of his realm, Who, while imprisoned, became
an intermediary imbued by the Holy Spirit with special knowledge
and powers. By speaking to the king as God's Intermediary—and
as God's Intercessor on the king's behalf—Bahá'u'lláh maintains a
humble and loving tone, while also making clear that the counsel He
is about to impart at great length should not be presumed by the king
to be advice from a mere subject, but rather divinely inspired guidance from God.

Bahá'u'lláh conveys this information in one of the most well-
known—and sometimes misunderstood—passages regarding His
experience in the Siyáh-Chál: "O King! I was but a man like others, asleep upon My couch, when lo, the breezes of the All-Glorious
were wafted over Me, and taught Me the knowledge of all that hath
been. This thing is not from Me, but from One Who is Almighty and
All-Knowing. And He bade Me lift up My voice between earth and
heaven, and for this there befell Me what hath caused the tears of
every man of understanding to flow."[337]

He then assures the Sháh that His knowledge is bestowed by God—
"[t]he learning current amongst men I studied not; their schools I entered not"—and that the king can inquire in cities where Bahá'u'lláh
dwelt to confirm this fact. He explains that He acts as commanded by
God: "His all-compelling summons hath reached Me, and caused Me
to speak His praise amidst all people. I was indeed as one dead when
His behest was uttered. The hand of the will of thy Lord, the Compassionate, the Merciful, transformed Me."[338]

'Abdu'l-Bahá's Authoritative Interpretation
and Explication of This Statement

On the one hand, we can appreciate the need for Bahá'u'lláh to conceal at this point the complete nature of His station, purpose, and
power. To one familiar with the life of Muḥammad, the statement
will resonate with how the Prophet describes His own station to His
followers, who believe He is a Prophet, but most of whom accept as
infallible and authoritative only the words He utters when He is in His
trancelike state, presumably while He is receiving the Word of God
through the Angel Gabriel.

But 'Abdu'l-Bahá explains that this passage in the letter to the
Sháh is not intended to imply that Bahá'u'lláh was an ordinary,

albeit immaculate man, Who suddenly became transformed through the epiphany He describes as having taken place in the Siyáh-Chál. To begin with, as we have previously noted, there were no couches in the Siyáh-Chál. Bahá'u'lláh, like His fellow prisoners, had his neck weighted down with chains and his feet in stocks in the pitch dark and dank stench of a prison that originally had been built as an underground cistern.

'Abdu'l-Bahá explains that this statement to the Sháh is a metaphor, a figure of speech—Bahá'u'lláh was *like* an ordinary man sleeping on a couch when He received the first intimations of His Revelation in this dream vision:

> We come to the explanation of the words of Bahá'u'lláh when He says: "O King! I was but a man like others, asleep upon My couch, when lo, the breezes of the All-Glorious were wafted over Me, and taught Me the knowledge of all that hath been. This thing is not from Me, but from One Who is Almighty and All-Knowing." This is the station of divine revelation. It is not a sensible, but an intelligible reality. It is sanctified from and transcendent above past, present, and future. It is a comparison and an analogy—a metaphor and not a literal truth.[339]

'Abdu'l-Bahá then explains the metaphorical meaning of the state of being asleep in this passage in three different ways: "For example, sleeping is the state of repose, and wakefulness is the state of motion. Sleeping is the state of silence, and wakefulness is the state of utterance. Sleeping is the state of concealment, and wakefulness is that of manifestation."[340]

For our purposes, possibly the most relevant part of 'Abdu'l-Bahá's authoritative interpretation of this passage from the letter to the king is His conclusion that "the Manifestations of God have ever been and will ever be luminous Realities, and no change or alteration ever takes place in Their essence. At most, before Their revelation They are still and silent, like one who is asleep, and after Their revelation They are eloquent and effulgent, like one who is awake."[341] In other words, no essential change or transformation takes place when They receive the intimation from God through the Holy Spirit indicating that it is now time for Them to reveal those utterances that are intended to guide humankind through the next dispensation.

THE BACKGROUND THEME OF BAHÁ'U'LLÁH'S LIFE

Bahá'u'lláh's experience in the S͟háh's dungeon, while of particular significance, is not the only episode from His life that He describes in this
letter. Bahá'u'lláh rehearses for the king how He was delivered from the
Siyáh-C͟hál and how, after being exiled to Baghdad, He demonstrated
through His deeds that He was not among the "sowers of sedition":
"We, verily, are clear of them, and We beseech God not to associate Us
with them."[342] Then, in three relatively brief paragraphs, Bahá'u'lláh
notes how those who turn toward God must distinguish themselves by
deeds and not "cast behind their backs the commandments of God" or
follow "the prompting of their own desires,"[343] a possible allusion to the
response of Napoleon III to Bahá'u'lláh's first letter.

However, Bahá'u'lláh casts no aspersions on Naṣíri'd-Dín S͟háh
himself in this regard but simply adjures him to act befittingly going
forward: "I adjure thee by thy Lord, the All-Merciful, to look upon thy
servants with the glances of the eye of thy favour, and to treat them with
justice, that God may treat thee with mercy."[344] Following this gentle request, Bahá'u'lláh asserts the unsurpassed power and authority of God
to do as He sees fit and, "through the power of His sovereign might," to
reveal "what He pleaseth," for God "is supreme over His servants and
exerciseth undisputed dominion over His creation."[345]

Bahá'u'lláh does not narrate the trials that have befallen Him to elicit
pity from the S͟háh—whom Bahá'u'lláh knows full well to be "pitiless
as the sun"[346]—but rather He recounts these tribulations at the behest
of the Holy Spirit: "The Pen of the Most High addresseth Me, saying:
Fear not. Relate unto His Majesty the S͟háh that which befell thee. His
heart, verily, is between the fingers of thy Lord, the God of Mercy, that
haply the sun of justice and bounty may shine forth above the horizon
of his heart. Thus hath the decree been sent down by Him Who is the
All-Wise."[347]

Here we observe the theme of the trials of Bahá'u'lláh and the theme
of justice intertwined—the story of what befell Bahá'u'lláh will be revealed to the S͟háh "that haply the sun of justice and bounty may shine
forth above the horizon of his heart," or if not the heart of the S͟háh, then
most certainly the hearts and minds of those reading this text hereafter.

Thus, in the next paragraph, the connection between the theme of
justice and the need for the king to consider what has happened to the
One he has banished is explicitly set forth: "Look upon this Youth, O

King, with the eyes of justice; judge thou, then, with truth concerning what hath befallen Him."[348] Bahá'u'lláh then states what could well be considered His specific charge or challenge to the king regarding everything else that follows: "Of a verity, God hath made thee His shadow amongst men, and the sign of His power unto all that dwell on earth. Judge thou between Us and them that have wronged Us without proof and without an enlightening Book."[349]

Having already alluded to what befell Him while imprisoned in the Siyáh-Chál, Bahá'u'lláh next describes His subsequent exile to Baghdad, albeit in the most benign terms: "By the leave and permission of the King of the Age, this Servant journeyed from the Seat of Sovereignty [Tehran] to 'Iráq, and dwelt for twelve years in that land."[350] Bahá'u'lláh then reminds the Sháh that His trust has always been placed wholly in God: "[t]hroughout the entire course of this period no account of Our condition was submitted to the court of thy presence, and no representation ever made to foreign powers." He notes that He resided in Baghdad until such time as successive petitions to the Ottoman Sultán 'Abdu'l-Azíz from Persian representatives eventually coerced the governor of Baghdad to comply with the order that Bahá'u'lláh be sent to Constantinople. There, as Bahá'u'lláh mentions, He did not seek an audience with, or assistance from, 'Abdu'l-Azíz or his officials—a characteristic refusal to act as a petitioner, let alone demonstrate the humility and complete obeisance that might have been expected from a political exile before one who was sultan of the Ottoman Empire and caliph of Sunni Islam: "Later this Servant was summoned to Constantinople, whither We arrived accompanied by a poor band of exiles. At no time thereafter did We seek to meet with anyone, as We had no request to make and no aim in view but to demonstrate unto all that this Servant had no mischief in mind and had never associated with the sowers of sedition."[351] Following this paragraph, we find a passage that relates again to the major theme of justice as it applies to the duty of monarchs. Once again, Bahá'u'lláh employs the figurative image of a monarch being "God's shadow," except here He qualifies this epithet as alluding solely to a "just" king: "A just king is the shadow of God on earth. All should seek shelter under the shadow of his justice, and rest in the shade of his favour."[352]

The final part of the letter details the exiles of Bahá'u'lláh and relates to the Sháh that He is about to be sent to the most desolate of prisons, the prison city of 'Akká: "Erelong shall the exponents of wealth and power banish Us from the land of Adrianople to the city of ʻAkká."[353] Of course, it is important to realize that while the epistle itself was revealed shortly before the exile took place—August 1868—the letter was not delivered by Badíʻ until a year later in July 1869, after the exile had taken place.

Bahá'u'lláh then describes the nature of that city, stating, "it is the most desolate of the cities of the world, the most unsightly of them in appearance, the most detestable in climate, and the foulest in water." He continues, "[i]t is as though it were the metropolis of the owl, within whose precincts naught can be heard save the echo of its cry," and concludes, "[t]herein have they resolved to imprison this Youth, to shut against our faces the doors of ease and comfort, and to deprive us of every worldly benefit throughout the remainder of our days."[354]

PRAYERS AND THEIR THEMES

While ultimately the theme of justice, especially as it relates to the treatment of the Manifestation and His faithful adherents, permeates every part of this exquisitely arranged letter, it is valuable to examine a few of the letter's ingredients that can also stand alone. Most prominent among these are several prayers and expositions on religious and philosophical matters. While the latter merit a chapter of their own, we can conclude this chapter by considering the prayers. A brief assessment of these may provide the reader with an even more ample sense of precisely how bountiful the Lawḥ-i-Sulṭán is.

THE FIRST PRAYER

The first prayer begins in paragraph 200 but is preceded by Bahá'u'lláh's reminder to the Sháh of how the Prophet Muḥammad was similarly rejected by the learned and divines of His time, while the then-Christian king of Ethiopia, upon hearing but a single Súrih of the Qur'án, recognized in these verses the same truth that Jesus had brought. Bahá'u'lláh then admonishes that were the Sháh himself to be similarly attentive, he, too, would dedicate his powers and possessions to the service of God. Bahá'u'lláh concludes this prologue to the prayer with the following assurance of His goodwill towards the Sháh: "We beseech God to aid thy Majesty to hearken unto that Word whose radiance hath enveloped the whole world, and to protect thee from such as have strayed far from the court of His presence."[355]

It is not clear where the first prayer stops. Thematically, there is a shift between paragraphs 200 and 201, and another, more marked, shift between 201 and 202, which warrant considering each of paragraphs 200 and 201 as distinct prayers, as I do here. Further, at the end of paragraph 201 we encounter words with which Bahá'u'lláh often concludes His revealed prayers, which suggests that this may be the conclusion of a prayer: "No God is there but Thee, the Ever-Forgiving, the Most Compassionate."[356] Then again, there are prayers of Bahá'u'lláh that have such passages between sections of a single prayer, a structure that He may be employing here inasmuch as the next paragraph is also a prayer that does not end until the completion of paragraph 205: "Thou art, in truth, the God of power, of glory and wisdom."[357] For our purposes of analyzing the text, I here describe paragraph 200 as the "first prayer" and paragraph 201 as the "second prayer," while the "third prayer" runs from paragraphs 201 to 205.

The entreaty in the first prayer is a powerful appeal to God that is extremely relevant to the themes of the letter as a whole and clearly intended to evoke in the king the sense that the sole intent of Bahá'u'lláh in writing this epistle is to benefit him and his subjects and not to gain any profit or recompense for Bahá'u'lláh Himself. Paragraph 200 focuses on reciting to God the sacrifices made by those dedicated believers who have given their lives in serving God and in propagating His Cause, and includes a possible allusion to the atrocities in Nayríz, where, after surrendering with the promise of freedom, the Bábí defenders, including the outstanding Vaḥíd, were slaughtered and, in a macabre echo of the martyrdom of the Imam Husayn, their severed heads were "raised aloft on spears in [God's] path." The same paragraph then implores God: "remove the veils that have come in between Thee and Thy creatures and debarred them from turning unto the horizon of Thy Revelation."[358]

THE SECOND PRAYER

The second prayer, or else the second part of the first prayer, focuses entirely on the infinite grace and bounty of God. "Withhold not Thy servants," Bahá'u'lláh implores, "from the most mighty Ocean, which Thou hast made the repository of the pearls of Thy knowledge and Thy wisdom"—an obvious allusion to Bahá'u'lláh's own Revelation. He further entreats: "Cast upon [thy servants], O My God, the glances of the eye of Thy favour and bounty, and deliver them from self and passion." Maintaining this same theme, the supplication concludes, "From everlasting Thy bounty hath embraced the entire creation and Thy mercy hath surpassed all things. No God is there but Thee, the Ever-Forgiving, the Most Compassionate."[359]

THE THIRD PRAYER

What seems clearly to be a third prayer with a distinctly different theme follows immediately beginning in paragraph 202 and continues to the end of paragraph 205. Focusing on the fact that God is well aware of the purity of Bahá'u'lláh's motive, both in all He has done and in all He is attempting to accomplish on behalf of the peoples of the world, this lengthy prayer, while meaningful to all who peruse it, obviously is intended as yet another of the many proofs in the letter that Bahá'u'lláh has no ulterior motive, no desire for power, and no aspiration to undermine the king's authority nor to seek retribution for all the horrendous actions the Sháh has thus far perpetrated against the Bábís and Bahá'ís—beginning with his presence, as crown prince, at the gathering of clerics in Tabríz that condemned the Báb to the bastinado, until the present time (1868, almost twenty years later) when he is assisting in perpetrating the oppression of the Bahá'ís in general and Bahá'u'lláh in particular.

This is a theme Bahá'u'lláh will emphasize later in the letter when, in one of His frank assessments of the king's injustice, He notes, "For more than twenty years this people have, day and night, been subjected to the fury of the Sovereign's wrath, and have been scattered by the tempestuous gales of his displeasure, each to a different land."[360] Bahá'u'lláh continues to recount the suffering of the followers and, in paragraph 204, focuses on His own suffering, even though He notes that every minute of His life has been spent serving God: "I have embraced all that is with Thee, and forsaken all that might lead Me away from the retreats of Thy nearness and the heights of Thy glory."[361]

Possibly the weightiest portion of this particular prayer occurs in the third paragraph, where Bahá'u'lláh states to God His motive in writing this epistle, a statement that, if the king ever bothered to read carefully this epistle—or read it at all—would most surely have caught his attention and elicited amazement. For here, well into the letter, is a concise statement of the precise theme of this, the lengthiest and most complex of all the epistles Bahá'u'lláh wrote to the kings and rulers of the world: "This is an Epistle, O My God, which I have purposed to send unto the King," Bahá'u'lláh begins this concluding paragraph. He continues, "Thou knowest that I have wished of him naught but that he should show forth justice to Thy servants and extend his favours unto the people of Thy kingdom."[362]

The concluding sentence in this prayer, which maintains Bahá'u'lláh's magnanimous and selfless tone, might well be considered a concise articulation of the main theme and purpose of both this epistle and, as we will discuss in depth later, the Súriy-i-Haykal as a whole: "Assist Thou, O My God, His Majesty the Sháh to keep Thy statutes amidst Thy servants and to manifest Thy justice amongst Thy creatures, that he may treat this people as he treateth others. Thou art, in truth, the God of power, of glory and wisdom."[363]

THE FOURTH PRAYER

The fourth prayer included in the epistle occurs much later, beginning with paragraph 250 and continuing through paragraph 251. Appearing in the midst of an ongoing discourse with the Sháh, this supplication by Bahá'u'lláh expresses two related concerns. The first is contained in a relatively elaborate conceit, while the second is less imagistic, but both beseech God to strengthen and protect Bahá'u'lláh and to enable Him to endure constant rejection—"the blasts of denial from those who remain heedless of the mysteries of Thy name."[364]

Situated in the midst of Bahá'u'lláh's narration to the Sháh about how His utterance has been ignored, the prayer is an unexpected interruption, but extremely effective in demonstrating that even the Manifestation is not impervious to the effects of denial and tests, and that He—like ordinary human beings—must constantly seek assistance from God to sustain Him throughout the trials He must endure.

This observation might well remind us of those pictures of 'Abdu'l-Bahá where He is holding prayer beads, thus indicating that although He is the perfect Exemplar of what it means to be a true Bahá'í, He is able to undertake His tasks and endure a life of tests without respite only because He is in a sustained, daily dialogue with God. Implicit in this same image is a reminder to those who would aspire to follow His example that we also must maintain this same regimen if we are to fulfill whatever destiny God through His Manifestation has designated for us.

In this vein, Bahá'u'lláh Himself expresses His constant reliance upon God in this prayer, which begins with a supplication for protection, expressed through the conceit of the lamp that is used a number of times in the Bahá'í writings. Here the figurative image is quite elaborate: "I ask Thee by Thy Name, through which Thou hast subdued all who are in the heavens and all who are on the earth, to protect the lamp of Thy Cause within the globe of Thine omnipotence and Thy bountiful favour, lest it be exposed to the blasts of denial from those who remain heedless of the mysteries of Thy name, the Unconstrained. Increase, then, by the oil of Thy wisdom, the radiance of its light."[365]

The Cause of God is thus likened to a lamp providing light, or enlightenment, to the world of humanity, but its flame is protected by the globe of God's "omnipotence" and "bountiful favour" from the winds or blasts of those who deny the Revelation and who would, were it not for that globe, possibly be capable of extinguishing the illumination derived from the flame of the Revealed Word, the radiance of whose light is fueled by the "oil of [God's] wisdom."

The second paragraph of the prayer is much more personal and demonstrates for us as readers—or as believers—the fact reiterated throughout the revealed works of Bahá'u'lláh that He happily endures whatever befalls Him in His mission to impart a Revelation so profound that it will transform the diverse peoples of the world into a single, peaceful, and unified global community. At the same time, He is able to endure and persevere solely because of God's unfailing response to His supplications for assistance and protection: "Lift Me up, then, unto Thyself, cause Me to enter beneath the shadow of Thy mercy, and give Me to drink of the pure wine of Thy providence, that I may dwell within the tabernacle of Thy majesty and beneath the canopy of Thy favour."[366]

We might think that the Manifestations of God would not need to rely so heavily and frequently on prayer, but clearly They do. Furthermore, we might infer from Bahá'u'lláh's statements throughout His revealed works that He is in constant communication with God. However, we can also be sure that an ancillary reason for Bahá'u'lláh's interweaving of prayers within His tablets—a reason also reflected in the emphasis in the Bahá'í Faith on translating, disseminating and sharing the prayers of Bahá'u'lláh to God (especially those that Shoghi Effendi saw fit to include in the collection *Prayers and Meditations of Bahá'u'lláh)*—is that being aware of these prayers benefit *us*, in at least two ways. First, they demonstrate to us our own need to be in a state of constant and unwavering communion with the realm of the spirit if we are to fulfill our own tasks as believers. Second, they serve as yet another reminder of the fact that however lofty the station of the Manifestations may be, They are totally subservient to God.

In other words, the multitude of prayers revealed by Bahá'u'lláh and the Báb—and 'Abdu'l-Bahá, for that matter, since He too is an extraordinary Being with capacity beyond our reckoning—demonstrates that no created being, whether an ordinary human or a celestial spirit of whatever spiritual rank or purity of soul, is autonomous or able to subsist without the constant support of the Creator. The state of being that we are thus called to recognize—this condition of dependency and "nearness," of striving to be in the presence of God, while not neglecting our need for action—is connected to the very reason for our creation as revealed by Bahá'u'lláh in the Short Obligatory Prayer: "Thou has created me to know Thee and to worship Thee."[367]

Chapter 11

The Letter to Nasíri'd-Dín Sháh
Part Two: Bahá'u'lláh's Guidance to the Sháh

We have reviewed some of the diverse components of Bahá'u'lláh's lengthy and complex letter to the Sháh. And were our purpose simply to provide an overview of this concluding epistle, what we have noted thus far would suffice. But in addition to being the lengthiest missive Bahá'u'lláh sent to any of the kings, rulers, and dignitaries, the letter also contains important information that is particularly relevant to the Sháh as a Shí'ih Muslim. These portions of the letter discuss the arrival of the "Day of Days," the Second Coming, as well as the long-awaited emergence of a global peace based on justice and human fulfillment in all its ramifications. This letter also contains running throughout a continuous narrative that, while specialized for the Sháh, consolidates the various insights we examined in the previous chapter while also leading the Súriy-i-Haykal as a whole to its climax.

The Major Themes of the Súriy-i-Haykal in the Letter to the Sháh

As we have mentioned previously, to a certain extent the foundational theme of the Súriy-i-Haykal can be discerned in its symbolic title and the symbolic arrangement of the work into the form of a *haykal*, a "temple" or pentacle representing the human body as the seat, in this physical life, of the soul, which is our essential reality, our true "self," our "inmost heart." It is of course no coincidence that the word *temple* also alludes to a physical edifice in which we go to worship or, symbolically, a physical space where God abides and in which we can gain access to the presence of God through prayer and reflection. These functions are concisely and poetically specified in the term used to designate the structure that functions as a temple in the Bahá'í Faith: the Mashriqu'l-Adhkár, the "Dawning Place of the Worship of God."

As we discussed at some length in the first chapter, the Maid's guidance for constructing the Temple (symbolizing the Manifestation's preparation for His mission) constitutes a major part of the work prior to the inclusion of the letters. On both the symbolic and literal levels, the Holy Spirit (as personified in the voice of the Maid of Heaven Who has appeared to Bahá'u'lláh in a dream vision in the Síyáh-Chál) discusses those attributes and powers that must characterize the human personage that the spirit or soul of Bahá'u'lláh will inhabit (or, more accurately, with which it will associate) in order for Him to carry out His arduous, challenging, but climactic mission, which marks the decisive turning point in the development of the "ever-advancing civilization" of humankind on planet Earth.[368]

Of course, God's delegation of authority to Bahá'u'lláh in order to fulfill the divine purpose of human creation is not confined to the Manifestation's earthly life. Shoghi Effendi cites 'Abdu'l-Bahá as observing that after His passing, Bahá'u'lláh continues to assist the progress of His Faith, and in fact does so even more powerfully after His release from the constraints of having to operate through a physical temple:

> Yet, as the appointed Center of Bahá'u'lláh's Covenant and the authorized Interpreter of His teaching had Himself later explained, the dissolution of the tabernacle wherein the soul of the Manifestation of God had chosen temporarily to abide signalized its release from the restrictions which an earthly life had, of necessity, imposed upon it. Its influence no longer circumscribed by any physical limitations, its radiance no longer beclouded by its human temple, that soul could henceforth energize the whole world to a degree unapproached at any stage in the course of its existence on this planet.[369]

The passage is illuminating; not only does it employ the terms "tabernacle" and "human temple" to allude to the physical station of Bahá'u'lláh's existence, but it also specifies that Bahá'u'lláh "had chosen temporarily to abide" in this edifice. The idea that the Manifestation, prior to His incarnation, plays some part in "choosing" the persona with which He will associate, as well as where that persona will reside, is confirmed elsewhere by Shoghi Effendi, who provides insight into the very factors that weigh in this choice:

[T]he primary reason why the Báb and Bahá'u'lláh chose to appear in Persia, and to make it the first repository of their Revelation, was because, of all the peoples and nations of the civilized world, that race and nation had, as so often depicted by 'Abdu'l-Bahá, sunk to such ignominious depths, and manifested so great a perversity, as to find no parallel among its contemporaries.[370]

Further insight into the Manifestation's continued—indeed, in-creased—power to assist humanity once no longer constrained by His earthly persona and material circumstances can be found in statements in *Light of the World: Selected Tablets of 'Abdu'l-Bahá*, a recently re-leased collection of authoritative translations. It is likely that Shoghi Effendi in the above-cited passage is referencing, if not these very state-ments, ones similar in theme and content. For example, in the following excerpt from tablet 43, 'Abdu'l-Bahá observes the following about the passing of Bahá'u'lláh:

Although the Sun of Truth may outwardly be veiled by the clouds of concealment, were one to look with a perceiving eye, listen with a hearing ear, and ponder with an awakened heart, it would become evident that the splendours of the Most Great Light have grown stronger and the rays of the lamp of God waxed brighter, that the waves of His most mighty Ocean have surged higher and the out-pourings of the heaven of His bounty have become more abun-dant and manifest. For, until now, the veil of the human temple hath been an impediment to beholding the Sun of Truth. But now, wholly sanctified from all earthly things, that resplendent Orb and Day-Star of the highest heaven shineth forth above the Supreme Horizon and beameth bright from the all-glorious Realm. This is His explicit text: "Verily, We behold you from Our realm of glory, and shall aid whosoever will arise for the triumph of Our Cause with the hosts of the Concourse on high and a company of Our favoured angels."[371]

Here, too, the term "human temple" echoes one of the themes of the Súriy-i-Haykal discussed earlier, that the human temple is actually a veil, "an impediment" to our ability to appreciate the true reality or nature of the Manifestation. Implicit in this same passage is what our study of the history of the life of any of the Manifestations makes obvious—that the Manifestation is required to struggle to fulfil His mission while operating within the constraints of a human persona that must act in the context of a decadent social environment.

THE DELEGATION OF AUTHORITY

The construction of the temple as a symbolic representation of Bahá'u'lláh's willingness to become incarnate in order to fulfill His tremendously important but unimaginably burdensome task is perhaps the major unifying theme of the Súriy-i-Haykal, at least at the first level of meaning. This delegation of God's divine authority, attributes, and powers to a Being from the spiritual realm, and the subsequent need for that Messenger-Teacher to take on a human persona, prefigures and parallels the authority which Bahá'u'lláh, as God's Vicegerent, subsequently conveys to those figures in charge of human governance, regardless of what political structure is presently operant in their particular country or territory.

Again, this idea might remind us of the medieval and Renaissance notion of "the divine right of kings" as mentioned in our examination of the letter to the pope—a political-metaphysical theory justifying absolute monarchy by theorizing that the monarch as God's representative on earth is not subject to nor dependent on the consent of the governed. While some systems of government that operated according to this theory of political authority also included a parliament—appointed or elected—these representatives or councils were, more often than not, merely advisory and did not have the power to overturn or alter the decisions of the monarch.

The four monarchs[372] who received the epistles included in the Súriy-i-Haykal each had varying degrees of autonomy in this regard. But when we consider all that Bahá'u'lláh has to say to those in power, both in this work and elsewhere, it is clear that the theme of delegation of authority to rulers by God is relevant to each of these letters' recipients, regardless of the particular constitutional arrangement within which they operate.

Put another way, Bahá'u'lláh is not, at the time of the construction of the Súriy-i-Haykal in its final form, advocating a particular form of government, even though we noted His praise of Queen Victoria for her reliance on parliamentary advisors. Rather, Bahá'u'lláh is stating that the authority delegated to any ruler carries with it certain inescapable obligations. The most important of these is justice, and Bahá'u'lláh's conception of "justice" includes a variety of safeguards and rights for the people whom the rulers serve; these go beyond merely ensuring the subsistence of the people and include, for instance, the right to education and, perhaps most important of all, freedom of religion.

THE ATTENDANT THEME OF JUSTICE

We have observed Bahá'u'lláh's admonitions to the rulers regarding the delegation of this divine authority and those duties and obligations that result from their appointment, regardless of how their authority was obtained or how it was exercised by those who preceded them. And this concept of justice—from its broadest sense of equity and righteousness to its more mundane application in the creation and application of the laws of the land and the treatment of those who abide under the care of these rulers—is perhaps the major recurring theme that echoes and resounds throughout these letters.

For it is in the specific advice Bahá'u'lláh imparts that we glimpse time and again this unified picture of what the delegation of authority from God to man entails. And with the advent of this Revelation—the main effect of which will be to create a unified and just global community from the diverse peoples, beliefs, and cultures of the world—the delegation of authority from God to humankind via His Prophets reaches its stage of completion. That is not to say that the planetary system devised by Bahá'u'lláh represents a static condition in need of no further *refinement*—there is no end to the perfectibility of the system as it adapts to the changing capacities and requirements of humanity. However, it is reasonable to assert that with the advent of the Most Great Peace promised by Bahá'u'lláh, God will have officially and completely delegated the authority for just human governance and social order to the peoples of the world, albeit ever under the oversight and inspiration of Bahá'u'lláh, under the guidance of the global commonwealth for which He provides the blueprint, and, in successive dispensations, subject to the guidance of future Manifestations in the Bahá'í Cycle and in cycles yet to be born.

THE SPECIFIC ADVICE AND ADMONITIONS TO THE SHÁH

Without assuming that this survey of Bahá'u'lláh's guidance to the shah is exacting or complete, we can usefully observe a number of successive sections or topics addressed by Bahá'u'lláh, excluding the prayers and the other matters already discussed in the previous chapter.

JUDGE US FAIRLY

We can start this assessment by observing that—beginning with paragraph 194 and concluding in paragraph 199—Bahá'u'lláh first adjures the shah to judge Him fairly and not rely on the opinion of those advisors who have ulterior motives. Accordingly, in a most touching challenge, Bahá'u'lláh beseeches the king to compare the motives of his advisors, who seek their own benefit, to the motives of Bahá'u'lláh, Who desires nothing but the king's own well-being: "They that surround thee love thee for their own sakes, whereas this Youth loveth thee for thine own sake, and hath had no desire except to draw thee nigh unto the seat of grace, and to turn thee toward the right hand of justice."[373]

As we noted in the previous chapter, included in this request that the king apply the standards of justice in his treatment of Bahá'u'lláh and His followers is an allusion to the treatment of Muḥammad and His followers by those deemed to be the learned of His day, and a reminder that when believers showed but a single súrih to the king of Ethiopia, the wise monarch immediately discerned in those verses the same accents and spirit that distinguish the words of Christ.

Bahá'u'lláh thus challenges the Sháh to act accordingly, not to judge Bahá'u'lláh by what others might say but to examine His revealed utterances for himself. "O King! Wert thou to incline thine ear unto the shrill of the Pen of Glory and the cooing of the Dove of Eternity," Bahá'u'lláh assures him, "thou wouldst attain unto a station from which thou wouldst behold in the world of being naught save the effulgence of the Adored One, and wouldst regard thy sovereignty as the most contemptible of thy possessions."[374]

Bahá'u'lláh then addresses the spurious accusations with which He has been assailed—allegations that He wishes "to perpetuate His name" or that He aspires to "the vanities of the world."[375] The utter baselessness for such assertions, Bahá'u'lláh points out, is made apparent by the fact that during His entire ministry, He has been "immersed in an ocean of tribulations" and that since He "expecteth to lose His life at any moment," how could He be said to "seek after worldly vanities?" Bahá'u'lláh affirms that those who perpetrate such falsehoods will ultimately "be called upon to account for their words."[376]

Another accusation Bahá'u'lláh responds to is that "He hath disbelieved in God," to which Bahá'u'lláh responds by reciting with wonderful eloquence the testimony of His belief in God, in the Manifestations of God, and that "there is none other God but Him, that from everlasting He was alone with none else besides Him, and that He shall be unto everlasting what He hath ever been."[377]

Bahá'u'lláh subsequently reminds the Sháh of the execrations Muḥammad, like Bahá'u'lláh, endured at the hands of "the divines of that age," how they "turned away from Him" and "contended with Him," so that haply the Sháh may "apprehend that which, in this day, remaineth concealed behind the veils of glory."[378]

Finally, in this same vein and as another vindication of His intentions, Bahá'u'lláh testifies that if the Sháh were "to incline [his] ear to the melodies of that Nightingale which warbleth in manifold accents upon the mystic bough as bidden by [his] Lord," he would cast aside concerns for the things of this world. Then he would instead dedicate himself to God and find himself "raised up to the summit of exaltation and glory, and elevated to the pinnacle of majesty and independence."[379]

ACCUSATIONS AGAINST THE FRIENDS OF GOD

After the first prayer, and toward the end of His narration about His successive exiles, Bahá'u'lláh takes up the defense of His followers, "the friends of God," explaining what has befallen them, and how they have endured and demonstrated the sincerity of their motives.

One obvious and undeniable proof of the sincerity of His followers, Bahá'u'lláh notes, has been their willingness, even their eagerness, to lay down their lives rather than recant their beliefs. Akin to this observation is Bahá'u'lláh's statement in this same section that the sincerity of His followers is demonstrated by the manner in which the deeds of these faithful souls "are in conformity with their words."[380] In addition, the comportment of the Bahá'ís testifies to the sincerity and nobility of their faith by the degree to which they have disdained the things of this world—whether physical comfort or personal safety—to uphold their belief in the advent of this new Revelation from God: "The friends of

God have not, nor will they ever, set their hopes upon the world and its ephemeral possessions."[381]

Bahá'u'lláh simultaneously appeals to the S̲h̲áh's own duty to be just with all his subjects and not to let his concerns be "restricted to one or another person" inasmuch as justice demands that all his subjects should be able to "seek shelter under the shadow of his justice, and rest in the shade of his favour."[382] Bahá'u'lláh makes a succinct but profound argument for the basic human right of the Bahá'ís to be treated with justice. He begins by stating that "whether this Cause be seen as right or wrong by the people," it is apparent from their actions that the Bahá'ís "have forsaken their all in their eagerness to partake of the things of God."[383] It would be patently absurd, Bahá'u'lláh points out, to think "that a man of sound judgement should sacrifice his life without cause or reason" as the Bahá'ís have shown themselves willing to do.[384] And as for the possibility that the Bahá'ís "have taken leave of their senses," this is "highly improbable" since not merely one or two individuals have followed this Cause, but "a vast multitude of every class" have "hastened with heart and soul to the field of sacrifice in the way of the Beloved."[385]

The last paragraphs of this part of His discourse focus not only on the willing sacrifices made by the Bahá'ís in demonstrating the depth and staunchness of their beliefs, but also on the length of time during which they have remained faithful despite being continually harassed, oppressed, and persecuted. It is here that Bahá'u'lláh writes, as noted earlier: "For more than twenty years this people have, day and night, been subjected to the fury of the Sovereign's wrath, and have been scattered by the tempestuous gales of his displeasure, each to a different land."[386] Bahá'u'lláh describes "the children who have been left fatherless," "the fathers who have lost their sons," noting: "No land is there whose soil hath not been tinged with their blood, nor reach of heaven unto which their sighs have not ascended."[387] And yet throughout this entire period of relentless affliction and "despite all these calamities and tribulations, the flame of divine love hath so blazed in their hearts that even should their bodies be torn asunder they would not forsake their love of Him Who is the Best-Beloved of the worlds, but would welcome with heart and soul whatever might befall them in the path of God."[388]

There is more of the same evidence in the paragraphs that follow. In fact, the tone becomes even more intense, more severe, building to a crescendo as Bahá'u'lláh cites passages from the Hidden Words focused on the odiousness of those who are in positions of authority or who have "a name to be wise"[389] yet are bent on injustice, falsehoods, and self-aggrandizement; those who are "seeming fair yet inwardly foul . . . like clear but bitter water"[390]; he who is the "essence of desire"[391]; and he who is the "bondslave of the world" lying "upon the bed of heedlessness fast asleep."[392]

Bahá'u'lláh then reminds the king of the justifiable expectations of "these refugees" who—though they turn to God, assured that "these tribulations will be followed by the outpourings of a supreme mercy, and these dire adversities will be succeeded by an overflowing prosperity,"—should, as the Sháh's subjects, be able to rely on this same outcome from him: "We fain would hope, however, that His Majesty the Sháh will himself examine these matters and bring hope to the hearts."[393]

Bahá'u'lláh continues this theme by reiterating the standards that should be maintained by the truly learned, especially in this long-awaited period of the "Latter Days." Bahá'u'lláh cites a ḥadíth from Sádiq, the Sixth Imam, regarding the duplicity and mischief that the religious leaders shall perpetrate in this time: "The religious doctors of that age shall be the most wicked of the divines beneath the shadow of heaven. Out of them hath mischief proceeded, and unto them it shall return."[394] For while a few have "showed forth kindness" in the past,[395] at the present time "all have lost sight of every other consideration, and are bent upon the persecution of this people."[396]

Finally, Bahá'u'lláh reminds the king that if people of many different religions "abide peacefully beneath the shadow of thy sovereignty," why should the Bábís and the Bahá'ís not be treated the same way? After all, Bahá'u'lláh explains, the king and his servants "should be animated by such lofty aims and sublime intentions as to continually strive to bring all religions beneath the shelter of his shadow, and to rule over them with perfect justice."[397] Bahá'u'lláh further reminds the king that it is specifically contrary to justice "that for the trespass of a single soul a whole group of people should be subjected to the scourge of [the king's] wrath," for "in every community there have been, and will ever be, the learned and the ignorant, the wise and the heedless, the profligate and the pious," making it unjust to condemn an entire community for the wrong actions of a misguided few.[398] This is likely a reference to the attempted assassination of the Sháh by a small group of misguided Bábís in 1852, an attempt which, though on its face the project of a deranged few too ignorant to even arm themselves appropriately for their heinous task, was the justification for the unleashing of anti-Bábí pogrom of unbridled cruelty throughout Iran, in the course of which Bahá'u'lláh Himself was imprisoned in the Síyáh-Chál.[399]

A New Revelation from God

The next theme, closely related to the previous one—even as the entire discourse to the king dwells on the duty of the "shadow of God" to be a just, fair, and equitable guardian for all those under his care—focuses on the specific fact that Bahá'u'lláh and His followers have suffered mistreatment simply because they believe that God has sent a new Messenger.

Bahá'u'lláh observes that Bahá'í belief is in no way contrary to the Qur'án. Based on their acceptance of the Qur'ánic verities that God is "unconstrained"[400] and "doeth as He willeth"[401] and "ordaineth as He pleaseth,"[402] Bahá'ís believe that God has indeed sent another Prophet. Bahá'u'lláh then explains that "the essential requirement for whoso advanceth a claim" is to produce proofs of His station; it is these proofs, rather than the opinion of the peoples, whether "learned or ignorant,"[403] that each soul must then use to determine if such a claim is valid.

Bahá'u'lláh subsequently recites verses from the Qur'án in which Muḥammad remarks how every Manifestation of God met with repudiation and cruelty, even as did Muḥammad Himself when "the divines of that age, both Christian and Jewish, turned away from that Daystar of the heaven of glory."[404] When they could not repress His teaching, they schemed to kill Him; "so they schemed, and God schemed, and God, verily, is the best of schemers."[405] As another example of how the Prophets of God are consistently rejected by the very ones whom we would think might be the most receptive and attentive in recognizing Their station—the religious leaders and divines who, supposedly, are the most the learned in and familiar with their own scripture—Bahá'u'lláh then cites the treatment that Jesus received, and how "all the divines charged that Quintessence of faith with impiety and rebellion."[406]

Bahá'u'lláh then points out the recurring pattern by which the divines and followers of a given religion hold that no further revelation will occur. He thus notes, for example, that even though Christ forewarned His followers in the Gospel of John that He would return, and also promised that a Comforter would come, the Christian divines failed to understand these verses. Bahá'u'lláh leaves unstated—but the Sháh would be well aware—that therefore virtually none of the Christian divines recognized Muḥammad when He appeared, even as most of the divines of all faiths do not now recognize the Báb and Bahá'u'lláh as the fulfillment of their own prophecies, whether in the Old Testament, the New Testament, the Qur'án, or the authoritative ḥadíth.

Next, Bahá'u'lláh challenges the Sháh regarding His own claim to Prophethood. He begins, "permit Me, O Sháh, to send unto thee that which would cheer the eyes, and tranquillize the souls, and persuade every fair-minded person that with Him is the knowledge of the Book."[407] He concludes this theme with a statement of His understanding that such a thing cannot happen until the time is ready for God to unseal the station and utterances of Bahá'u'lláh for all to behold.

In a delightfully lucid conceit, Bahá'u'lláh employs the image of the Word of God as a choice wine that will be unsealed when the time is right: "For the present, however, since the season is not ripe, the tongue of My utterance hath been stilled and the wine of exposition sealed up until such time as God, through the power of His might, shall please to unseal it. He, verily, is the Almighty, the Most Powerful."[408] The Kitáb-i-Aqdas—revealed a few years later in 1873—represents the unsealing of that wine: "Think not that We have revealed unto you a mere code of laws. Nay, rather, We have unsealed the choice Wine with the fingers of might and power."[409]

THE PARALLELS TO THE TREATMENT OF THE FOURTH IMÁM

Doubtlessly relying on the fact that Násiri'd-Dín Sháh as an Ithná-'Asharíyyih (twelver) Shí'ih is familiar with the history of the Imams of his faith, the first eleven of whom were each persecuted and martyred, Bahá'u'lláh calls to mind a parallel between the treatment of His followers and those of Zaynu'l-'Ábidín, the Fourth Imam.

The fact that Bahá'u'lláh's own followers have been led as captives from Baghdad to Mosul, Bahá'u'lláh says to the Sháh, should remind the king of what happened to the Fourth Imam when he and his followers were brought to Damascus. Bahá'u'lláh recounts those events in succession, beginning with how the Imam and his followers were asked if they were Kharijites—a faction opposed to both the Imams and the Umayyad state. Zaynu'l-'Ábidín replied on their behalf that they were faithful followers of Muḥammad and believers in His verses. Then they were asked if they had disobeyed the laws of Islam, to which he replied that they "were the first to follow the divine commandments" and were "the sign of the Ancient of Days and the source of His remembrance amongst the nations."[410]

When asked if they had "forsaken the Qur'án," the Imam answered that it was revealed "[i]n our House,"[7411] and that they (the Imams) are "the streams that have branched out from the Most Great Ocean, through which God hath revived the earth, and through which He shall revive it again after it hath died." The Imam continued, "Through us His signs have been diffused, His proofs revealed, and His tokens disclosed. With us is the knowledge of His hidden meanings and His untold mysteries."[412] Finally, when they were asked, "For what crime have ye been punished?" the Imam Zaynu'l-Ábidín replied, "For our love of God . . . and for our detachment from aught else save Him."[413]

Bahá'u'lláh concludes this analogous anecdote by noting that while He has not recited the exact words the Imam uttered, He has provided the sense of the conversations that took place because precisely the same spurious taunts and questions have been directed against Him and His followers, even as their oppressors acknowledge the injustices that were perpetrated against followers of their own religion. In short, those who condemn the injustices of the past are now committing even worse offenses but are totally unaware of and indifferent to this pitiful irony.[414]

THE PURITY OF MOTIVE, THE VALUE OF BAHÁ'U'LLÁH'S SUFFERING, AND THE URGENCY OF THE MOMENT

In what is effectively the final theme of the epistle, Bahá'u'lláh focuses on two related subjects—the purity of His motive, as well as that of His followers—and the fact that suffering is an inherent and expected test for those who follow in the path of God.

THE PURITY OF HIS MOTIVE

Having related the experience of the Fourth Imam, Bahá'u'lláh says that His purpose in all He has done and said is not to "foment sedition" but to "purify His servants from whatsoever hath prevented them from drawing nigh unto Him, the Lord of the Day of Reckoning."[415] He then reiterates a portion of the account of what happened in the Síyáh-Chál, something He has discussed in full earlier (beginning in paragraph

192), emphasizing that His sole purpose in revealing His teachings is to accede to the promptings of the Holy Spirit: "This thing is not from Me, but from God." He then reaffirms in a beautiful poetic image that "the breezes of My Lord, the All-Merciful, passed over Me, awoke Me from My slumber, and bade Me lift up My voice betwixt earth and heaven."[416]

As an obvious proof of this purity of motive, Bahá'u'lláh reiterates that all the suffering He has endured has not deterred Him from His mission but instead only confirms His purpose: "By Him Who is the Truth!" He attests, "I fear no tribulation in His path, nor any affliction in My love for Him and in the way of His good pleasure." In yet another metaphoric verse, He compares adversity in the path of God to "a morning dew upon His green pasture, and a wick for His lamp which lighteth earth and heaven."[417] Bahá'u'lláh then employs as further proof of His motive the *ubi sunt* theme we previously noted in our examination of the epistle to Napoleon III (paragraph 156 and following) and to the czar (paragraph 158).

Here again we see the utility of considering the Súriy-i-Haykal as symphonic in structure. This third allusion to the *ubi sunt* theme serves as a reminder to the Sháh, but perhaps even more so to the reader who can now recognize it as a repeated motif or melody in the Súriy-i-Haykal as a whole, of the brevity, impermanence, and illusory nature of all we possess or attain in the ephemeral physical phase of our existence. In yet another wonderfully ironic and poetic rhetorical question, Bahá'u'lláh entreats the Sháh to consider whether or not we can distinguish the deceased from each other, and discern any difference between "the sovereign's crumbling skull" and "the subject's mouldering bones."[418]

The next three paragraphs continue this theme explicitly, emulating again the original Latin rhetorical question *Ubi sunt qui ante nos fuerunt?*—"Where are those who were before us?" The obvious answer is that all are deceased; their mortal frames have turned to dust; and whatever fame, riches, or accomplishments they might have achieved are most probably lost to the collective memory of humankind. "Naught can now be seen but their deserted haunts, their roofless dwellings, their uprooted tree-trunks, and their faded splendour."[419] "Alas for them!" He laments. "All have perished and are gone to rest beneath a canopy of dust. Of them one heareth neither name nor mention; none knoweth of their affairs, and naught remaineth of their signs."[420]

THE URGENCY OF THE MOMENT

Bahá'u'lláh then moves from the rhetorical *ubi sunt* to the larger question of how the human being should respond to this fact—the inevitability of physical death, and the erasure of all that we possess in this life—that all people of common sense know to be true. The answer lies in the realization that our only enduring efforts and accomplishments are those done on behalf of God's plan, especially in this long-awaited Day of Days:

> Blessed is he who hath said, or now shall say, "Yea, by my Lord! The time is come and the hour hath struck!", and who, thereafter, shall detach himself from all that hath been, and deliver himself up entirely unto Him Who is the Possessor of the universe and the Lord of all creation.[421]

Yet even for such devoted souls as recognize the truth and dedicate themselves to divine service, the merit of their efforts is still contingent on God's acceptance of the purity of their motive, "[f]or naught is reaped save that which hath been sown, and naught is taken up save that which hath been laid down, unless it be through the grace and bestowal of the Lord."[422] Therefore, we must "beseech God to deal with us according to His bounty, and not His justice, and to grant that we may be of those who have turned their faces unto their Lord and severed themselves from all else."[423]

BAHÁ'U'LLÁH'S FINAL WORDS TO THE SHÁH

As with the conclusion to any well-wrought symphony, the ending of this lengthiest and most complex among all the epistles Bahá'u'lláh sent to the governmental and religious leaders of the age repeats previous themes, then blends them all in a crescendo—one final plaintive entreaty to the Sháh, made in spite of Bahá'u'lláh's awareness that His soul-stirring verses are falling on deaf ears. For while Bahá'u'lláh (as well as the heroic Badí') was fully cognizant that the implacable heart of the king was proof against even this magnificent treatise, this epistolary masterpiece, He is writing not solely to the Sháh but to the totality of humankind, including us here and now, with lessons still relevant, axioms and guidance that will remain salient throughout this present period of turmoil and strife as we await the glorious reformation of human society.

In the final paragraphs, Bahá'u'lláh reiterates that He is not concerned about His own wellbeing, even though the "fount of well-being hath run dry, and the bower of ease hath withered": "I advance with My face set towards Him Who is the Almighty, the All-Bounteous."[424] He expresses this determination in one of His best known statements about how little concern He has for this life: "By God! Mine head yearneth for the spear out of love for its Lord. I never passed a tree, but Mine heart addressed it saying: 'O would that thou wert cut down in My name, and My body crucified upon thee, in the path of My Lord!', for I see the people wandering distraught and unconscious in their drunken stupor."[425]

After alluding to the further exile to 'Akká He is about to endure, Bahá'u'lláh makes a weighty observation about the theme of the Súriy-i-Haykal as a whole: "We further beseech Him [God] to make of this darksome tribulation a shield for the Temple of His Cause, and to protect it from the assault of sharpened swords and pointed daggers."[426] He explains the meaning of this enigmatic and symbolic statement by noting, "Adversity hath ever given rise to the exaltation of His Cause and the glorification of His Name. Such hath been God's method carried into effect in centuries and ages past. That which the people now fail to apprehend they shall erelong discover, on that day when their steeds shall stumble and their finery be folded up, their blades blunted and their feet made to falter."[427]

After rehearsing once more the tribulations He is about to endure, Bahá'u'lláh returns to this same theme—that despite the present turmoil and persecution of the Cause of God, and the ostensibly continuing failure of world governments to accede to the obvious needs of the peoples over whom they hold sway, the time is nigh when all of this will suddenly change, when the presently veiled truth will come to light: "Erelong shall the snow-white hand of God rend an opening through the darkness of this night and unlock a mighty portal unto His City." "On that Day," He continues, "shall the people enter therein by troops, uttering what the blamers aforetime exclaimed,[428] that there shall be made manifest in the end that which appeared in the beginning."[429]

Finally, prior to the paragraph added by Bahá'u'lláh to conclude the entirety of the Súriy-i-Haykal in the final rendering of this tablet—a paragraph we will discuss in the next and final chapter of this study—Bahá'u'lláh pens a series of verses unsurpassed in eloquence, power, and poetic beauty. To the contemptuous divines who, in their blindness, have perpetrated on Him such oppression, Bahá'u'lláh triumphantly proclaims:

> Though they now rejoice in the adversity that hath befallen Us, soon shall come a day whereon they shall lament and weep. By My Lord! Were I given the choice between, on the one hand, the wealth and opulence, the ease and comfort, the honour and glory which they enjoy, and, on the other, the adversities and trials which are Mine, I would unhesitatingly choose My present condition and would refuse to barter a single atom of these hardships for all that hath been created in the world of being.[430]

He concludes this assessment of His life with the well-known passage: "But for the tribulations that have touched Me in the path of God, life would have held no sweetness for Me, and Mine existence would have profited Me nothing."[431]

In His final words to the Sháh, Bahá'u'lláh offers the following two supplications, however assured He may be that the king will not be moved. First, He says, "We pray God, moreover, to graciously aid the King to do His will and pleasure, and to confirm him in that which shall draw him nigh unto the Dayspring of God's most excellent names, so that he may not give countenance to the injustice he witnesseth, may look upon his subjects with the eye of loving-kindness, and shield them from oppression."[432] Lastly, He concludes the letter proper with a second supplication regarding the Sháh: "And finally We beseech God, exalted be His glory, to enable thee to aid His Faith and turn towards His justice, that thou mayest judge between the people even as thou wouldst judge between thine own kindred, and mayest choose for them that which thou choosest for thine own self. He, verily, is the All-Powerful, the Most Exalted, the Help in Peril, the Self-Subsisting."[433]

Chapter 12

The Contemporary Relevance of the Súriy-i-Haykal

As we noted previously, both Bahá'u'lláh and Badí' were well aware that the message to the Sháh and the historical act of its delivery were intended primarily for us today and for future ages; there was no expectation of changing the mind of a potentate who had already demonstrated his malignancy toward the Bábís, the Bahá'ís, and anyone else whom he deemed a threat to what he considered his supreme authority to do as he pleased. For unlike Queen Victoria, Alexander II, and Napoleon III, who had demonstrated at least some interest in improving the conditions of their subjects, Naṣíri'd-Dín Sháh—and, indeed, the Qájár dynasty as a whole—had consistently focused solely on their own self-interest.

Thus, as foreshadowed in Bahá'u'lláh's epistle, after disdaining the letter and having Badí' tortured to death, Násiri'd-Dín Sháh continued in his efforts to maintain his ineffectual monarchical rule. His absolutism and resistance to reform were both increasingly antiquated in an age of rapid global political change in the wake of the Industrial Revolution. Concomitant with radical material transformation brought on by industrialization in many societies was the ascent of the voice and power of an oppressed and discontented working class. So revolutionary and encompassing were these changes, especially in the West, that by the end of the "long nineteenth century," marked by the outbreak of the First World War, empires and monarchies were in relentless decline.

Political dissatisfaction did not leave Persia untouched, and only four years after the ascension of Bahá'u'lláh, Násiri'd Dín Sháh was assassinated by Mirza Reza Kermani on May 1, 1896. Thus ended a reign of stark injustice; but popular demand for drastic reform only grew, ultimately culminating in the Constitutional Revolution that took place between 1905 and 1911, during which a parliament was established. While the political trajectory of Iran during the twentieth century would be tortuous, the Qajar dynasty itself continued to decline until its final end in 1925.

But as we noted in the previous chapter, the supplications by Bahá'u'lláh to God that the S̲h̲áh might reform his conduct and bring about justice for both the Bahá'ís and the generality of his subjects do not constitute the end of the Súriy-i-Haykal as a whole. There remains one critical paragraph (¶ 276) that Bahá'u'lláh added to the work after it had been revised to incorporate the five letters to the kings and rulers.

The significance of this addition is great, for several reasons. The most obvious of these is that the final paragraph effectively encapsulates the five letters by returning again to the voice of the Maid of Heaven. More importantly, the Maid's final statement demonstrates that these very epistles are themselves an integral part of the means by which the future of humankind will be brought about—regardless of the response of those rulers to whom they are addressed, and whom Bahá'u'lláh explicitly charges with carrying out His guidance. Before seeing how this is so, however, we can first explore how this brief paragraph also alludes once again to some of the key layers of significance of the symbol of the temple—and even hints, in its very final words, to yet further such layers.

THE BODY OF GOD

The Maid begins this final paragraph by acknowledging, "Thus have We built the Temple with the hands of power and might, could ye but know it."[434] As we have repeatedly noted, at the first level of interpretation, the symbol of the Temple represents the physical persona employed by the Holy Spirit through which the Revelation from God—the Word made flesh—is conveyed to humankind. As we have also noted, Bahá'u'lláh's declaration of this Revelation occurred by degrees, first to family and close followers at the garden of Riḍván in Baghdad and subsequently to the world at large via the epistles to representative world leaders and their governments.

But the final paragraph, in addition to returning to the overarching structure of the work—the internal dialogue between the conscious mind of Bahá'u'lláh and the Holy Spirit operating through Him—can also be interpreted as an allusion to the increasingly expansive expression of God and Godliness in a physical edifice. This allusion operates on a number of levels.

First, by harking back to the building of the Temple, this conclusion reemphasizes the major symbolic meaning of the work as a whole: the spiritual preparation by which the Manifestation fashions His "temple" to function in a symbolic or figurative sense as the body of God among us. Therefore, it is useful to repeat here perhaps the best known and most memorable passage that alludes directly to this relationship between God and the Manifestation:

> Say: Naught is seen in My temple but the Temple of God, and in My beauty but His Beauty, and in My being but His Being, and in My self but His Self, and in My movement but His Movement, and in My acquiescence but His Acquiescence, and in My pen but His Pen, the Mighty, the All-Praised. There hath not been in My soul but the Truth, and in Myself naught could be seen but God.[435]

This succinct encapsulation of the main theme of the Súriy-i-Haykal calls to mind two other important statements confirming the sense in which the appearance of the Manifestation among us is tantamount to the appearance of God in human form.

The first of these is Bahá'u'lláh's explanation that the unity of the Manifestations, and their collective unity with the Holy Spirit, requires us to equate all that the Manifestations say and do as identical with the words and actions of God Himself, an axiom we cited in the very first chapter: "The essence of belief in Divine unity consisteth in regarding Him Who is the Manifestation of God and Him Who is the invisible, the inaccessible, the unknowable Essence as one and the same."[436] Again, the ability of the Manifestation to incarnate perfectly all the attributes of God implies that these Beings are ontologically distinct from us ordinary human beings, however enlightened and spiritual we may become. For while we have the potential for infinite development and spiritualization, we will forever remain human souls, whereas the Manifestations are another order of being and appear among us inherently perfected.

Consequently, as Shoghi Effendi states quite clearly in a passage we also cited in the first chapter, the Manifestations represent the most refined and perfect access we have to God, whether in this life or in the afterlife:

"We will have experience of God's spirit through His Prophets in the next world, but God, is too great for us to know without this Intermediary. The Prophets know God, but how is more than our human minds can grasp. We believe we attain in the next world to seeing the Prophets."[437]

At a second level of allusion, this final paragraph speaks to our own role in contributing to the increasing expression of the divine in creation over time. As discussed earlier in this book, we can understand the narrative apparatus devised by Bahá'u'lláh in the Súriy-i-Haykal as a means by which we can reflect on how best to implement our part in carrying out the plan of God for this era. Thus, we are reminded here at the end of the Súriy-i-Haykal that the core attitude required in this effort is one of orientation towards the Manifestation Himself, the Temple in which we find our nearest access to God. The Maid proclaims that we can follow no more perfect course for our lives than to direct ourselves to this Temple: "Draw ye nigh unto it," the Maid invites us, an exhortation followed by a rhetorical question: "Be fair, O peoples of the earth! Which is preferable, this [Temple], or a temple which is built of clay?" She then issues the imperative, "Set your faces towards it. Thus have ye been commanded by God, the Help in Peril, the Self-Subsisting. Follow ye His bidding, and praise ye God, your Lord, for that which He hath bestowed upon you."[438]

But there may be a third level at which this allusion operates. Bearing in mind the levels of meaning and various relationships emanating from the symbolism of the Temple, we can be alert to yet another, broader meaning implicit in the "Temple": the physical universe in its entirety as the means through which the presence of God is attained and His powers and attributes apprehended by all humankind on every inhabited planet.

This significance is suggested by the distinctive way in which the Maid concludes the entire Súriy-i-Haykal, declaring: "He, verily, is the Truth. No God is there but He. He revealeth what He pleaseth, through His words 'Be and it is.'"[439] This final sentence is an allusion to a familiar Qur'ánic axiom found in verses 2:117; 3: 47; 3:59; and 6:73. It is a translation of *Kun fa yakúnu* (كن فيكون): "Be and it is." This elliptical phrase is a concise but abstruse representation of the process by which God has but to wish or will creation to be, and it is destined to come into being. From a Bahá'í perspective, it is clear that on one level, that which God wills comes into being through an indirect process whereby God delegates power to the Manifestations who then instigate the various stages of the creative process, through Their utterance and through the example of Their immaculate character.

But this cryptic statement can also be understood as alluding to the universe as a whole: as explained in the notes to the Kitáb-i-Aqdas, the Arabic *kun* "has been used in the Qur'án as God's bidding calling creation into being."[440] In this context, 'Abdu'l-Bahá helps us see how the universe too can best be understood in terms of a single body, organic in structure and coherent in its operation. Far from being a disorganized morass of heavenly bodies interacting in some random fashion, He affirms, the totality of creation is devised with precision, functions according to discernible laws, and constitutes a single, unified, organic image of the powers and attributes of God expressed in material form—what we might well think of as the Body of God:

> [T]his endless universe is like the human body, and that all its parts are connected one with another and are linked together in the utmost perfection. That is, in the same way that the parts, members, and organs of the human body are interconnected, and that they mutually assist, reinforce, and influence each other, so too are the parts and members of this endless universe connected with, and spiritually and materially influenced by, one another. For example, the eye sees and the entire body is affected; the ear hears and every limb and member is stirred. Of this there is no doubt, for the world of existence is also like a living person. Thus, the interconnection that exists between the various parts of the universe requires mutual influences and effects, whether material or spiritual.[441]

In this sense, the totality of creation might well be considered the most expansive application of the symbolic meaning of the temple. That is, while the physical appearance of the Manifestation of God in human form conveys to us Godliness as expressed perfectly in human terms, creation itself is the necessary environment for bringing into being an evolving human social order in which the Manifestation can usefully appear and thereby fulfill the wish of God expressed in the ḥadíth of the Hidden Treasure discussed later in this chapter—the desire to be known and thence loved. Similarly, since the universe itself is usefully likened to the human body, as the above quotation from 'Abdu'l-Bahá highlights, even the pentacle arrangement of the Súriy-i-Haykal resonates with this broadest of interpretations of the Temple. In brief, the entirety of physical reality as an expression of the divine rationale underlying creation can be usefully understood as the Body of God, something students and lovers of the endlessly wondrous beauty of the natural world experience daily, whether in pondering the innerworkings of life at the quantum level or marveling at the seemingly endless expanse of structures at the cosmic level.

HOW THE SÚRIY-I-HAYKAL CLARIFIES MISUNDERSTANDINGS IN PRIOR REVELATIONS

Despite these and other layers of symbolic meaning we might derive from, or perceive expressed in, the Súriy-i-Haykal, the central focus of this final paragraph is undeniably the Manifestation, Who, unlike the mysteries of creation that we are only beginning to understand, whether at the quantum or cosmic levels, speaks directly to us, explains how best we can presently relate to the material world, and provides us with the perfect example of how we should conduct ourselves in carrying out His guidance for this age.

It is worth reflecting here on why the station, function, or nature of the Manifestation should receive this final emphasis, as well as being a central theme in the text overall, and indeed in so many of Bahá'u'lláh's Writings. We may begin to appreciate the wisdom behind this when we recall the conflicting understandings prior religions have reached on the all-important question of the ontology of the Prophet, two examples of which were briefly reviewed in Chapter 2. Given the proximity or accessibility to the Creator that the Manifestation as the "Temple" of God provides, we can perhaps appreciate why the Christian clerics and divines, after much conflict and consultation, determined to their satisfaction that Christ and God are one essence, in spite of Christ's clear statements in which He distinguishes between His essential reality and that of His "Heavenly Faither" who sent Him, Who informs Him what to reveal, and to Whom, He affirms to His disciples, He is soon to return: "For I came down from heaven, not to do mine own will, but the will of him that sent me."[442] And yet the early Church patriarchs also had to account for those statements where Christ seems to indicate that His body is the body of God: "If ye had known me, ye should have known my Father also: and from henceforth ye know him, and have seen him"[443] and "he that hath seen me hath seen the Father."[444]

We can also appreciate how important and significant it was, some three centuries after Christian authorities had deified Christ, for Muḥammad to refute the literalist inference drawn from these and other passages by explaining that Christ's station was that of a Messenger, an Intermediary, and not that of the literal incarnation of God Himself:

> They do blaspheme who say: Allah is one of three in a Trinity: for there is no God except One Allah. If they desist not from their word [of blasphemy], verily a grievous penalty will befall the blasphemers among them. Why turn they not to Allah, and seek His forgiveness? For Allah is Oft-Forgiving, Most Merciful. Christ the son of Mary was no more than a Messenger; many were the Messengers that passed away before him. His mother was a woman of truth. They had both to eat their [daily] food. See how Allah doth makes His Signs clear to them; yet see in what ways they are deluded away from the truth![445]

The *Haykal* or Temple thus serves to clarify in a single conceit the ontology of the Manifestations while simultaneously distinguishing between the Manifestation and God. The Temple is the means by which we gain access to God, or at least as much nearness as it is possible for us to attain. And yet by no means do we confuse the Temple (whether as the physical persona of the Manifestation or as a House of Worship) with the essential reality that is God. Furthermore, by taking the symbol of the Temple—a physical edifice—and recasting it as primarily signifying the Manifestation, Bahá'u'lláh helps us see that turning towards and approaching the Temple is not a process that has an end in the way that entering a building and performing specified acts of worship does. The journey towards the Manifestation, which for our purposes is the journey to God, is essentially spiritual, and is thus eternal in degree, with each degree providing increasing knowledge and joy. Or stated succinctly, the joy is in the journey itself; it does not await some end point, final victory over ourselves, or some ultimate stage of attainment.

THE DELEGATION OF AUTHORITY TO HUMANKIND THROUGH "THE BODY OF GOD"

We have alluded to the theme of the delegation of authority throughout our discussion of the Súriy-i-Haykal, especially as it applies to the Creator's delegation of His authority to the Manifestation through the power of the Holy Spirit—symbolized by the construction of the Temple—and to that authority and guidance delegated in turn by Bahá'u'lláh to the recipients of His epistles. As our examination of this important work draws to a close, we would do well to revisit this theme, and consider how it elucidates our understanding of God's plan for the construction on earth of a global polity that emulates the spiritual principles of the celestial realm—the "kingdom of God on earth"[446] alluded to by Christ. This will also help us to see the specific role that the Súriy-i-Haykal itself has to play in bringing God's purpose in this regard into effect.

THE PURPOSE OF CREATION

To understand why precisely the theme of God's delegation of authority to humankind through the Manifestation is of such importance to His overall plan for His creation, it is helpful to take a step back, and begin with the most fundamental principles relating to the nature of human existence. What, in other words, is the high-level concept of human purpose in the Bahá'í Faith, within which the concept of delegation can then be situated?

In *The Purpose of Physical Reality*, I focus on these fundamentals by examining the paradox that arises from an initial survey of the Bahá'í teachings that relate to the field of theodicy—the attempt to "justify the ways of God to man," as Milton so aptly puts it.[447] The paradox is this: If God intends for us to be spiritually refined, and if, as the Bahá'í writings repeatedly assert, we are already "essentially" spiritual beings (human souls) temporarily associating with, or operating through, the intermediary of physical temples, then why did the Creator—Who is cable of devising whatsoever He wishes—not fashion us already in the precise refined spiritual condition He desires for us to attain? Why are the majority of us—those of us who do not die prematurely in infancy or childhood—made to experience the illusion that we are physical beings, then tempted at every turn to aspire to physical or sensual indulgences, while also being made to endure the hardships that a physical life ultimately imposes? This enigma seems especially perplexing as we approach the end of our physical lives: many of us discover that all we have struggled so hard to achieve seems to diminish or disappear by degrees as we experience the deterioration of the very physical temple that has been the instrument for our spiritual education. Why, even before the death of the body, are most of us destined to reach a point where that divinely fashioned temple can no longer serve to house or channel our spirit, or at least cannot do it well?

There are at least two obvious answers to this question, neither one of which is particularly satisfying or complete. We can respond that since God as Creator thinks this arrangement is a good idea, then it must have some spiritual purpose or value, because, by definition, God's plan is benign and perfect. But this answer only leaves us asking *why* He thinks this to be true. The second response is no less incomplete: only by experiencing the ultimate pain and suffering that physical life inevitably entails can we appreciate fully the bounties of an afterlife where love and justice are no longer veiled, nor alloyed with baser concerns.

Of course, even these two justifications are contingent on the actual existence of an altruistic Creator, an afterlife, and an abundance of love and forgiveness on the part of the Creator to offset our many failures. That is, the afterlife itself—especially if we have not been entirely good people—might not necessarily promise to be a completely positive experience. Even the Bahá'í teachings, logical and satisfying as they may be in responding to our queries about the spiritual purpose of existence, affirm that we may undergo some sort of retributive experience if we have done poorly in executing our principal moral obligation in this life: the exercise of our free will to become good people, to treat others with love and justice, and to recognize the Manifestation and then follow His laws and exhortations.

Additionally, even if such negative or retributive experiences are temporary and are not physical, even if they are devised by a loving God solely to teach us and elevate us as we continue our growth and development in the next stage of our existence, there still might be much to fear. For as anyone who has experienced severe emotional distress knows, experiences of extreme guilt, clinical depression, anxiety disorders, panic attacks and grievous despair can be at least as horrific as any physical pain.

THE HADÍTH OF THE HIDDEN TREASURE

Fortunately, the Bahá'í Writings point us to a particularly powerful lens through which to consider the reason for our physical existence, in our quest to then situate the concept of delegation in its proper context. This lens is the Islamic hadíth of the Hidden Treasure, a brief and beautiful gem that is taken up in many places in the Bahá'í Writings: in passages and entire texts Bahá'u'lláh and 'Abdu'l-Bahá shine the light of Their divine insight through this gem, casting its facets into brilliant relief.

The ḥadíth contains the Creator's explanation for why He creates: "I was a Hidden Treasure," He affirms. "I wished to be made known, and thus I called creation into being in order that I might be known."[448] As is explained in a note to the Kitáb-i-Aqdas, Bahá'u'lláh revealed several verses that reiterate in similar terms precisely this same axiomatic verity. One well known allusion to the theme of this ḥadíth can be found in the Arabic Hidden Words, where the voice of the Creator articulates the purpose of creation: "O Son of Man! I loved thy creation, hence I created thee. Wherefore, do thou love Me, that I may name thy name and fill thy soul with the spirit of life."[449] In other places, the reference to God as a Hidden Treasure is even more explicit. Thus, in one prayer revealed by Bahá'u'lláh, we find the following statement that testifies to God's desire to create a means by which He—infinite and essentially unknowable though He be—can be comprehended and subsequently loved and cherished for His beneficence, magnanimity, and unfailing love for us: "Lauded be Thy name, O Lord my God! I testify that Thou wast a hidden Treasure wrapped within Thine immemorial Being and an impenetrable Mystery enshrined in Thine own Essence."[450] The prayer continues by observing that physical reality has been devised as a means whereby human beings can gain access to the attributes of a Creator whose essential reality remains unknowable: "Wishing to reveal Thyself, Thou didst call into being the Greater and the Lesser Worlds, and didst choose Man above all Thy creatures, and didst make Him a sign of both of these worlds, O Thou Who art our Lord, the Most Compassionate!"[451]

These statements certainly seem to confirm our previous observations that in addition to the Manifestation as our primary and most perfectly designed access or "way"[452] to God, creation as a whole can also be considered as having the sole purpose of preparing this "way"—functioning, as we suggested earlier, as the Body of God writ large. Indeed, in the context of the prayer as a whole—which clarifies that the "Man" chosen "above all [God's] creatures" is the Manifestation—it seems that the Manifestation provides us access to God by being a "sign" of both the human soul and creation itself (the "Lesser" and "Greater Worlds").[453] These two are of course intimately linked. As we saw in the first chapter, physical and metaphysical, or spiritual, reality are in an organic unity, to the extent that "[t]hey are the exact counterpart of each other."[454]

Similarly, there are tantalizing hints scattered through the Writings that, no matter how awe-inspiring and unfathomable the natural world in its immeasurable vastness may seem, the human soul is, in some sense, not only its acme and apotheosis, but its summation: "Dost thou deem thyself a small and puny form, / When thou foldest within thyself the greater world?"[113] As we have mentioned in the first chapter, the physical universe is a means by which God teaches us indirectly, engaging us in our own learning process. Employing our God-given knowledge and free will, we can come to discern metaphysical or spiritual attributes as expressed in physical-social experiences, and then manifest those same spiritual virtues by giving dramatic expression to our understanding of the relationship between the two realms, the spiritual and the physical. And of course, integral to this systematically designed classroom is the perfect Teacher—the Manifestation—and the guidance He provides by means of which we are shown how to perceive our own spiritual reality veiled in the illusory and temporary physical experience. In the same prayer just cited, Bahá'u'lláh describes God's delegation of this educative function to the Manifestation in these terms: "Thou didst enable Him to unravel Thy mysteries, and to shine with the lights of Thine inspiration and Thy Revelation, and to manifest Thy names and Thine attributes."[455]

Perhaps no work among the Bahá'í writings focuses so precisely on responding to the enigmas of human purpose than does 'Abdu'l-Bahá's *Tafsír-i-Hadíth-i-Kuntu Kanzan Makhfíyyan* ("Commentary on the Islamic Tradition 'I was a Hidden Treasure'"). In an authoritatively translated passage from this commentary, 'Abdu'l-Bahá explains both the nature of the "wish" of the Creator as well as how that wish becomes fulfilled through the successive appearances of the Manifestations: "O wayfarer in the path of the Beloved!" 'Abdu'l-Bahá begins, "Know thou that the main purpose of this holy tradition is to make mention of the stages of God's concealment and manifestation within the Embodiments of Truth, They who are the Dawning-places of His All-Glorious Being."[456] Then, explaining this concept in metaphorical terms, 'Abdu'l-Bahá says, "For example, before the flame of the undying Fire is lit and manifest, it existeth by itself within itself in the hidden identity of the universal Manifestations, and this is the stage of the 'Hidden Treasure.'"[457]

However, the "Treasure"—the evidence of Divine Revelation by means of which we learn to know God—becomes apparent and perceivable once the Manifestation reveals Himself: "And when the blessed Tree is kindled by itself within itself, and that Divine Fire burneth by its essence within its essence, this is the stage of 'I wished to be made known.'"[458] 'Abdu'l-Bahá then continues to explain the next stage in the process: "when it [the Divine Fire] shineth forth from the Horizon of the universe with infinite Divine Names and Attributes upon the contingent and placeless worlds, this constituteth the emergence of a new and wondrous creation which correspondeth to the stage of 'Thus I called creation into being.'"[459]

As physical reality continually emanates from God without beginning or end, the wish of the Creator to be known is promoted by the appearance of the Manifestations, a process we can presume occurs on each and every planet capable of bringing forth and sustaining "human" life. And with the appearance of these Vicegerents of God, certain individuals—"the sanctified souls"—become able to "rend asunder the veils of all earthly attachments and worldly conditions, and hasten to the stage of gazing on the beauty of the Divine Presence and are honoured by recognizing the Manifestation and are able to witness the splendour of God's Most Great Sign in their hearts;" and "then will the purpose of creation, which is the knowledge of Him Who is the Eternal Truth, become manifest."[460]

Stated in terms of our study of the Súriy-i-Haykal, we become enamored with the Creator through our love of the Manifestation as the Temple of God—the perfect embodiment of all God's attributes and powers expressed through the vehicle of this human persona among us—in order that we might apprehend these abstruse metaphysical realities as they become accessible to us in His human comportment, daily actions and interactions, and explicit guidance contained in laws, ordinances, and exhortations.

THE SOCIAL IMPERATIVE IN SPIRITUAL DEVELOPMENT

Thus, implicit in the ḥadíth of the Hidden Treasure, as unfolded for us by Bahá'u'lláh and 'Abdu'l-Bahá, is an educational system, in which we are provided with a perfect classroom (physical reality) and perfect teachers (the Manifestations). However, even with these two components, the system would be incomplete without the social dimension of human existence. As I have explored in *The Arc of Ascent* and *The Ascent of Society*, we cannot pursue our inherent objective of learning to know and love God alone. Stated in the simplest of terms, to know and then to worship requires a social context, within which we can first perceive divine virtues as manifest in human action and interaction and then, by participating in social practices, learn an increasing amount about spiritual virtues. The logic underlying this reciprocity between knowing and doing as it relates to our relationship with others is easy to comprehend: most human virtues— love, justice, kindness, truthfulness, selflessness, and so on—deal with our relationships with others.

To explain the necessity of this social component of individual spiritual development we can consider the underlying flaw in the ascetic view of spiritualization. The major premise of the ascetic or monastic life is that spirituality is best achieved when one becomes isolated as much as possible from the comforts, distractions, and temptations of the flesh—distancing oneself as much as possible from all forms of material reality as a whole. However, such a solitary existence, no matter how sincere and dedicated to prayer, meditation, and purity of thought, is forbidden by Bahá'u'lláh in this Day. For this is the Day when the oneness of humankind must not only be acknowledged, but acted upon: there is an urgent need for each of us to recognize our common humanity and personally take part in collective action to respond adequately, to the extent possible, to the challenges facing our families and our communities, our species and our planet—challenges that will, in the final analysis, leave humankind with no choice other than to create a unified response to global crises.

THE SÚRIY-I-HAYKAL AND THE PATH TO THE LESSER PEACE

This logical conclusion—that personal spiritual development is necessarily a social pursuit—brings us back to Bahá'u'lláh's admonishments to the kings and rulers regarding their obligation to help foster and fashion a collective social edifice to accommodate and secure the material and spiritual aspirations of all the peoples of the world. In His letters to those rulers, He invites them to take the first step in this project by creating a global pact of collective security—the seed that will ultimately germinate into a global commonwealth. And while it is unnecessary for us to recount in detail here the historical events and movements that have taken place since Bahá'u'lláh's letters to the kings and rulers— events moving us ever closer to a universal recognition of the obvious need for the remedies Bahá'u'lláh proposes in the five epistles we have reviewed—the contemporary relevance and efficacy of His admonitions and guidance to world leaders are becoming increasingly apparent to anyone whose vision is not obscured by bias, by a desire for personal or group ascendancy, or by the misinformation that proliferates in a fractured body politic, in which essentially every problem we face is made a battlefield fought over by opposing camps.

Humanity has, step by painful step, begun to see the indispensability of measures akin to those prescribed by Bahá'u'lláh for the reorganization of its collective life. However, following the failure of the leaders to whom He wrote to proactively initiate such measures, these have instead largely occurred in reaction to global calamities, and have represented only partial executions of the prescribed design. Thus, in the wake of the failure of the League of Nations and the horrors of the Second World War, another attempt was made to establish some form of collective security in the form of the United Nations. The architects of the UN aspired to address threats to global peace, and to ensure the overall stability of a world increasingly requiring unified international responses to safeguard human rights. Since its founding, the UN has also sought to create international consensus and action around securing education, women's rights, child welfare, responsible use of natural resources and environmental stewardship, health care, and other essential concerns.

In response to these same challenges, there have also emerged myriad Non-Governmental Organizations, many of which came about in direct response to the inadequacy of efforts by world governments: Doctors without Borders, the Environmental Defense Fund, and the Organization for Poverty Alleviation and Development, to name a few.

Daily, the urgent need for the realization of Bahá'u'lláh's vision of planetary unity and collaboration becomes increasingly evident. To describe the unvarnished truth of our present condition, we can do no better than to return to Bahá'u'lláh's portrayal of the world community as a patient suffering from a mortal illness. We have as a world community "pushed the envelope" with regard to a plethora of shared problems that threaten to destabilize, or worse, make uninhabitable our increasingly fragile planetary home. Consequently, it is becoming ever more obvious that as Bahá'u'lláh so forthrightly foretold, sheer necessity will, sooner or later, bring about a unified global response.

And yet, however obvious this truth may be from a dispassionate perspective, it is perhaps the most insidious characteristic of the state of social disorder prevalent in the world today that we seem collectively unable to see, and act, on the imperative of unity. For, as alluded to above, disunity and conflict are not merely the substantive problems we face; they infect the very ways in which we try to address our collective challenges. In such a climate, logical discourse, grounded in the scientific search for reasonable solutions, struggles to counter denials of the imperative to advance towards global unity, or attempts to retain or else regress to some narrower vision of nationalism, sectarianism, or even tribalism; for social discourse has become fractured, and science itself portrayed by so many as untrustworthy.

The result is that rants, jargon, and political cant, which periodically spill over into physical acts aimed at the subversion of social order, have rendered inadequate or inoperable intelligent and collaborative responses to our myriad problems—including natural disasters that channel forces quite impervious to rhetoric or personal opinion. Daily, it seems, the time lessens in which to deter, or at least to ameliorate to some degree, the "tempest" Bahá'u'lláh has described—that conflagration that will ultimately bring about the unity that present-day world leaders seem sadly unable or unwilling to instigate through collective international action, the very remedy our planetary community so desperately needs.

THE COVID-19 PANDEMIC

The COVID-19 pandemic, the likes of which the world has not experienced since the influenza pandemic of 1918–1919 that infected one-third of the world's population,[461] has provided stark proof of the pressing need for collective and collaborative action. Indeed, while at the time of writing the pandemic may be abating after afflicting the peoples of the world for over two years, this disease has taken more lives in the United States alone (over one million) than the 1918 epidemic or even the gruesome slaughter that was the American Civil War, which accounted for more American causalities than all other wars combined.

It seems, therefore, superbly fitting that the eighth and final leader of the once aggressive and fearsome Soviet Union, Mikhail Gorbachev—having gained much wisdom as he helped steer humanity away from the dangers of nuclear warfare by playing a central role in ending the Cold War—offered the following view of what we must learn from our present crisis. On April 15, 2020—early in the unfolding of this global catastrophe—Gorbachev observed, "During the first months of this year, we have seen once again how fragile is our global world, how great the danger of sliding into chaos. The COVID-19 pandemic is facing all countries with a common threat, and no country can cope with it alone."[462] He went on to relate the present crisis to the threat of nuclear war during the 1980s, highlighting the shift in mindset that led to breakthrough in that case:

> I recall how in the mid-1980s, we addressed the nuclear threat. The breakthrough came when we understood that it is our common enemy, a threat to all of us. The leaders of the Soviet Union and the U.S. declared that a nuclear war cannot be won and must never be fought. Then came Reykjavik and the first treaties eliminating nuclear weapons. But even though by now 85% of those arsenals have been destroyed, the threat is still there.[463]

He then noted that "other global challenges remain and have even become more urgent: poverty and inequality, the degradation of the environment, the depletion of the earth and the oceans, the migration crisis." And then, turning his attention to the undeniable interdependence of the peoples and nations of the world, Gorbachev stated, "And now, a grim reminder of another threat: diseases and epidemics that in a global, interconnected world can spread with unprecedented speed."[464]

He concludes with several axiomatic observations that seem increasingly relevant with each passing day. Paralleling the guidance in Bahá'u'lláh's exhortations to the world leaders regarding the reduction of arms,[465] Gorbachev cautions, "What we urgently need now is a rethinking of the entire concept of security. Even after the end of the Cold War, it has been envisioned mostly in military terms. Over the past few years, all we've been hearing is talk about weapons, missiles and airstrikes. . . . Is it not clear by now that wars and the arms race cannot solve today's global problems? War is a sign of defeat, a failure of politics."[466]

Then, echoing Bahá'u'lláh's admonition about the weighty burden that the amassing of arms and perpetration of aggression against other nations impose on the populace, Gorbachev asserts, "The overriding goal must be human security: providing food, water and a clean environment and caring for people's health. To achieve it, we need to develop strategies, make preparations, plan and create reserves. But all efforts will fail

if governments continue to waste money by fueling the arms race."⁴⁶⁷
He ends his cogent and penetrating assessment of world affairs with a
plea—one that could well have been plucked from the Bahá'í texts—
about the contraction of our world community into a single country:

> To address this at the highest international level, I am calling on
> world leaders to convene an emergency special session of the U.N.
> General Assembly, to be held as soon as the situation is stabilized.
> It should be about nothing less than revising the entire global agen-
> da. Specifically, I call upon them to cut military spending by 10%
> to 15%. This is the least they should do now, as a first step toward
> a new consciousness, a new civilization.⁴⁶⁸

JUSTICE AND THE TWIN PILLARS OF REWARD AND PUNISHMENT

Let us consider an even more recent demonstration of the toll we continue to pay for ignoring Bahá'u'lláh's guidance in the Súriy-i-Haykal
regarding the need to establish a pact among nations to secure collective
justice. On February 24, 2022, the Russian Federation—having already
annexed Crimea in March 2014, thereby re-establishing Russian rule
of the peninsula⁴⁶⁹—launched an unprovoked invasion of the sovereign
nation of Ukraine. Without regard to the damage incurred by cities,
infrastructure, or the citizenry, the vast Russian war machine merciless-
ly attacked strategic and civilian targets alike. At time of writing, the
invasion continues despite protestations from virtually every country,
from the European Union and the United Nations; stringent sanctions
from the United States and numerous other countries have also failed to
deter the aggressor.

As already alluded to in our examination of the Súriy-i-Haykal,
Bahá'u'lláh stresses that the most immediate cure or remedy for the
ailing human body politic is an international pact of collective security.
Bahá'u'lláh repeatedly alludes to the critical need to implement this
remedy in His letters to the world leaders, and later makes it an explicit
ordinance in His blueprint for a world society as outlined in the Kitáb-i-
Aqdas, the Most Holy Book, which establishes a framework of law and
principle to undergird the moral, social, and governmental infrastructure of a global commonwealth.

At the heart of this pact is mutual agreement among the signatories
that should one nation arise against another, a combined force consisting

of combatants from all member states would immediately quell the conflict, and restrain the aggressor state and hold its government accountable. The notes to the Kitáb-i-Aqdas, in consolidating guidance from Bahá'u'lláh and elaborations by Shoghi Effendi on this subject, clarify that "the principle of collective security enunciated by Bahá'u'lláh . . . does not presuppose the abolition of the use of force, but prescribes 'a system in which Force is made the servant of Justice,' and which provides for the existence of an international peace-keeping force that 'will safeguard the organic unity of the whole commonwealth.'"[470]

Underlying this principle of collective security as enunciated by Bahá'u'lláh are the "twin pillars" of reward and punishment—principles equally applicable to the training of the individual as to the maintenance of international peace and accord within society and among states. In the tablet titled "Bishárát" (Glad-Tidings), Bahá'u'lláh states this axiom succinctly: "O people of God! That which traineth the world is Justice, for it is upheld by two pillars, reward and punishment. These two pillars are the sources of life to the world."[471] Similarly, in the Tablet of Maqsud, Bahá'u'lláh observes, "The Great Being saith: The structure of world stability and order hath been reared upon, and will continue to be sustained by, the twin pillars of reward and punishment."[472]

As we have noted above, since Bahá'u'lláh's repeated articulation, in His epistles to world governments and later in His specific laws governing the society that has yet to be born, of the need for a collective security pact backed by a world force capable of sustaining a just and enduring peace, humankind throughout the world has come to clearly recognize this need. But thus far each attempt has fallen short of the universal participation and support required to create and legitimize a pact and a force capable of maintaining the collective security of our global community. Had such a pact been secured—as was the initial vision for the United Nations—and had such a collective force been fashioned, the current invasion by Russia would not have occurred: if the aggressor had not been deterred months earlier once the signs of its intentions were made clear, as is likely, it would have been immediately repulsed once hostilities broke out.

The question thus arises as to what sort of crisis or vitiation of the basic tenets of justice must take place before the need for collective action to sustain survival on our planet supersedes the power of self-seeking individuals to undermine what the peoples of the world require and deserve—simply to lead a decent life where family life is secured, individual enlightenment is encouraged and enabled, and local communities in every clime can establish the peaceful and just environment that each of us can envision but that we can only achieve collectively.

The Unfortunate Retrenchment from a Global Outlook

Three decades ago, increasing global unity and international collaboration seemed possible, even imminent. This attitude caused many, most especially within the Bahá'í community, to rejoice, to hope that, perchance, the need for some catastrophic "tempest" to coalesce the collective will of the peoples of the world to usher in the Lesser Peace might be circumvented after all—in spite of the unqualified forewarnings in the words of Bahá'u'lláh, confirmed by Shoghi Effendi in the letters contained in *Citadel of Faith*.[473]

I recall one globally impactful speech during this time period as a particular source of optimism. On September 11, 1990, President George H. W. Bush spoke before a joint session of Congress, in the midst of the Persian Gulf crisis precipitated by Iraqi dictator Saddam Hussein's invasion of the sovereign nation of Kuwait. In his address, President Bush presented a vision of a "new world order." His use of this salient phrase and his proposal for creating a form of collective security naturally excited and encouraged the worldwide Bahá'í community. Indeed, seven months later, in its 1991 Riḍván letter to the Bahá'ís of the World, the Universal House of Justice acknowledged the efficacy of this approach to international disputes:

The forces which united the remedial reactions of so many nations to the sudden crisis in this region demonstrated beyond any doubt the necessity of the principle of collective security prescribed by Bahá'u'lláh more than a century ago as a means of resolving conflict. While the international arrangement envisioned by Him for the full application of this principle is far from having been adopted by the rulers of mankind, a long step towards the behavior outlined for the nations by the Lord of the Age has thus been taken. How illuminating are Bahá'u'lláh's words foreshadowing the future reorientation of the nations: "Be united, O concourse of the sovereigns of the world," He wrote, "for thereby will the tempest of discord be stilled amongst you, and your peoples find rest. Should any one among you take up arms against another, rise ye all against him, for this is naught but manifest justice."[474]

President Bush's invocation of the phrase "new world order" echoed the precise words of Bahá'u'lláh regarding the future world commonwealth: "The world's equilibrium hath been upset through the vibrating influence of this most great, this new World Order. Mankind's ordered life hath been revolutionized through the agency of this unique, this wondrous System—the like of which mortal eyes have never witnessed."[475]

The speech itself seemed to be animated by President Bush's realization that a form of collective security could provide an essential component of an enduring world peace, just as Bahá'u'lláh had advised the kings and rulers. Of course, as we have noted, Bahá'u'lláh states in His letter to Queen Victoria that by the time He is writing to her, the Most Great Peace that Bahá'u'lláh had set before the rulers in His first epistles had already been soundly rejected, the chance for its immediate attainment lost by their refusal to recognize in Bahá'u'lláh the Promised One of all ages. But, as we also emphasized, this failure did not absolve the rulers of any further responsibility, even as Bahá'u'lláh notes in the Lawḥ-i-Ra'ís: "It behoveth everyone to traverse this brief span of life with sincerity and fairness. Should one fail to attain unto the recognition of Him Who is the Eternal Truth, let him at least conduct himself with reason and justice."[476] The principle of collective security, which Bahá'u'lláh prescribes as the pathway to the Lesser Peace, was no less operant at that time than it is today; and this Lesser Peace is destined over the course of time and through successive stages of political evolution to bring about the Most Great Peace after all.

"We stand today at a unique and extraordinary moment," President Bush's speech begins. "The crisis in the Persian Gulf, as grave as it is, also offers a rare opportunity to move toward an historic period of cooperation."[477] He then describes the possible outcome of such collaboration: "Out of these troubled times, our fifth objective—a new world order—can emerge: a new era—freer from the threat of terror, stronger in the pursuit of justice, and more secure in the quest for peace. An era in which the nations of the world, East and West, North and South, can prosper and live in harmony." He hints at the details of such a collective security with the following words, which, not coincidentally, allude to his prior meeting with President Gorbachev, whose worldview regarding a global accord we have cited above:

A hundred generations have searched for this elusive path to peace, while a thousand wars raged across the span of human endeavor. Today that new world is struggling to be born, a world quite different from the one we've known. A world where the rule of law supplants the rule of the jungle. A world in which nations recognize the shared responsibility for freedom and justice. A world where the strong respect the rights of the weak. This is the vision that I shared with President Gorbachev in Helsinki. He and other leaders from Europe, the Gulf, and around the world understand that how we manage this crisis today could shape the future for generations to come.[478]

Needless to say, the hope and contagious optimism of this brief period in which the principles of a collective security advocated by Bahá'u'lláh were articulated and temporarily implemented have not only dissipated; they have virtually disappeared, even though the obvious need for such a collective enterprise increases exponentially with each passing day.

THE BIRTH OF A NEW VISION

Since the milestone international response to Iraq's aggression against Kuwait, year by year and decade by decade global cooperation has degenerated, coinciding with the rebirth and reinvigoration of a type of nationalism that rides the crest of a vast and mounting wave of divisiveness, populism, and international rivalry.

But as the wider world sinks into pessimism, sectarianism, and the inflaming of what many thought to be discarded prejudices—deriving in no small part from the surge of migration impelled by natural catastrophes, revitalized jihadism in the Middle East, and the destabilization of various national governments—the worldwide Bahá'í community is giving birth to an entirely new and innovative methodology to prepare the way for the Lesser Peace.

A NEW PLAN TO HELP USHER IN A NEW AGE

When I first became a Bahá'í in the spring of 1960, three years after the death of the Guardian and three years prior to the election of the Universal House of Justice, there was to a certain extent in the Bahá'í community a benumbing sort of attitude about the advent of the Lesser Peace. While enthusiastically teaching and informing others about the news of the advent of Bahá'u'lláh and the promise of world peace and a world commonwealth, we were simultaneously largely passive in considering what role we might be able to play in bringing about the transformation of human society in the meantime.

We were, most of us, waiting for those calamitous events that we knew must occur in order to awaken the minds and hearts of humankind to the dire need for the transformation of the world from a loosely assembled collection of nation states to a unified and collaborative commonwealth. We could, of course, increase our numbers to the extent possible so that, once such an event or series of events occurred, there would be sufficient Bahá'ís around to explain how to establish world peace and to participate in its construction. In fact, Bahá'ís around the world were in the midst of completing the Ten-Year World Crusade designed by Shoghi Effendi, the central goal of which was to establish as many National Spiritual Assemblies as possible, since they would be the "pillars," the electorate, that would establish the Universal House of Justice in 1963, the final step in erecting the Bahá'í administrative order.

But with each emerging catastrophe or sudden threat of a world-engulfing holocaust, we found ourselves gathering to pray, waiting to see if, at last, the transformative crisis was at hand. Such events as the Cuban Missile Crisis were thus viewed with mixed emotions—perhaps the Lesser Peace was here at last, and yet we knew that the Bahá'í community itself would be tested and chastened along with the rest of humanity, and the prospects of stark disorder and chaos portended in the Bahá'í writings regarding such a crisis could hardly be contemplated with joy or eagerness or assuaged by Bahá'u'lláh's assurance that the "tempest" would be "glorious in its ultimate consequences."[479]

But the Universal House of Justice in its wisdom and infallible guidance—while obviously attentive to and cognizant of not only the level of understanding within the Bahá'í community, but also of the radical shifts in attitudes in a wider society that has lurched from passive anticipation of calamity to warranted hope, followed by the present trend to pessimism and division—seems to have determined that the institution created by Bahá'u'lláh to establish the foundation for this "New World Order" should not formulate guidance for the Bahá'í community based solely on present conditions. The state of secular governance, the divisiveness prevalent among the peoples of the world, the emotional roller-coaster wrought by successive changes in increasingly destabilized global community—while these must be seen clearly and taken into account, they would not dictate the plans devised for the continuing realization of the design for human redemption set out by Bahá'u'lláh.

It was thus but a few years after this remarkable speech by President Bush that the Universal House of Justice gradually instituted a total reformation of how the Bahá'í community would take part in helping shape the future of world polity.

AN ACTIVE APPROACH TO THE LESSER PEACE

It must be understood that this reformation was in no way a rupture with what had come before. In many organic systems, periods of steady growth and development along certain lines lead to sudden, and, to the novice observer, unprecedented change: a flower bursts from the bud; a caterpillar goes from the routine of gathering food to a sudden total focus on weaving a cocoon. The specific focus that the worldwide Bahá'í community embarked on in the mid 1990s, under the direction of the Universal House of Justice, may be viewed in such a light: a new course, but one that organically built on—and indeed, fulfilled—what had come before.

It would require volumes to describe what had come before—the history of the progress and worldwide emergence of the Bahá'í Faith since Bahá'u'lláh first revealed and then reconfigured the Súriy-i-Haykal. I have attempted to provide a bare outline of that progress in *God's Plan for Planet Earth and for Your Neighborhood*. The work begins by describing the evolution of the Bahá'í administrative order until the election of its crowning institution—the Universal House of Justice—in 1963, and it concludes by examining the global plans for development devised by that body, which, at the time of its writing, culminated with the four Five Year Plans from April 2001 to April 2021.[480]

This is not the place to review these developments in any detail. However, I think it is important to conclude this study of the Súriy-i-Haykal, and its relation to the events that have occurred since its revelation, by highlighting how the plans and actions that the Universal House of Justice has set in motion shed light on the central themes of the tablet, and on Bahá'u'lláh's foreshadowing of the future, not only regarding the Bahá'í Faith, but also concerning the progress of our planetary community as a whole.

In a most general sense, these plans seem to have derived from the fact that a massive change in our worldview—especially at the global level—will rarely if ever be successfully imposed from the top down. Kings, emperors, dictators, and religious leaders through the ages have tried and ultimately failed to impose such changes. Put simply, meaningful, thoughtful, benign, and lasting change of attitude is best achieved when the impetus derives from education and discourse at the level of the family and the community—what might usefully be described as the "elementary particles" of civilization.

For while we do well to think globally—even as Bahá'u'lláh exhorts world leaders to do in the Súriy-i-Haykal—we live locally. It would seem, then, that this is one major rationale underlying the sequence of plans and attendant guidance to the Bahá'í community—and to the world at large—emanating from the Universal House of Justice since the inception of the sequence of Five Year Plans in 2001 and now continuing with the Nine Year Plan (2022–2031). Therefore, let us briefly review how and when the plan to implement transformation at the level of the neighborhood and the community emerged. Ultimately, then, we will discern how the delegation of authority we have discussed—from God to the Manifestations, from the Manifestations to governments—finally devolves on the grassroots level of us ordinary folks working together with friends and neighbors in our respective communities.

Beginning in 1996, the Universal House of Justice instituted two radical but thoroughly logical changes in the relationship between the Bahá'í community and the secular community, setting in motion the only effective way by which the Bahá'í community could help the global body politic focus not on catastrophe, but rather on creating a global network anchored at the community level to embrace and sustain humankind through any and all present and future exigencies.

First, the Universal House of Justice set about constructing a method whereby the Bahá'í community could work alongside and be integrated with the community at large—again, a process based on the rationale that real and lasting change must be initiated at the level of the grassroots, at the foundation of social order. Clearly such change can and should be exhorted, assisted, and monitored from the top if it is to succeed. But as already mentioned, while we think globally and speak hopefully of change at the global level, as did President Bush, we live locally, and it is solely the pattern of life we establish and model in our daily lives that can bring about transformation at the territorial, national, or global levels. The local communities, the neighborhoods, are inevitably the pillars upholding the social order as a whole.

The second change created and instituted by the Universal House of Justice was, as I discuss at some length in *God's Plan for Planet Earth*, to create by degrees agencies and methodologies whereby transformation delegated to the community level could be initiated, monitored, and assisted. And throughout the twenty years of four Five Year Plans, this methodology of delegating responsibility for establishing a framework for change at the community level became increasingly sophisticated, flexible, and adaptive; obviously, not every neighborhood within a community, or community within a territory, or country within a continent could or would progress in this community-building program at the same pace.

Consequently, the systems that evolved over the sequence of Five Year Plans from 2001 to 2021 became increasingly flexible and innovative to befit the conditions that obtained in every conceivable state of growth, in locations ranging from remote villages to urban neighborhoods. But because the system—this framework for action involving core activities of devotional gatherings, children's classes, junior youth spiritual animation programs, and a sequence of graduated study circles for youth and adults—has been applied in neighborhoods in every country, this same framework has transformed a sort of passivity, a collective waiting for some calamity to bring about change, into an active process of building a New World Order from the ground up.

Inasmuch as information about the nature and function of these institutions is everywhere available and accessible, it is unnecessary here to reiterate the details of these plans, the exact nature of the institutions and agencies created, or the sequence of actions that have emerged from this endeavor since the mid-1990s. Likewise, as mentioned above, the Universal House of Justice of the Bahá'í Faith has now devised a continuation of this framework for action with a Nine Year Plan (from 2022 to 2031) that is further advancing and refining this innovative response for the individual, the family, and the community in such a way that no one need await change at the level of secular governance—the framework within which we can act is already in place, and each individual is encouraged to decide how he or she can most effectively become involved.

In light of these plans, the Súriy-i-Haykal holds an arguably greater relevance for each of us today than at any prior point in the history of the Bahá'í Faith. The numerous passages in the letters to the rulers in which Bahá'u'lláh speaks past them to the people—these call to us with more urgency than ever before; and in the framework for action developed over the past decades under the guidance of His Universal House of Justice, we find a context within which we can respond to His admonitions with greater clarity and certainty than ever before. Further, with respect to His admonitions to the rulers themselves, we are no longer passive witnesses to a conversation between the Manifestation and the rulers to whom He delegates authority to govern—if ever we were. No; for the requirements and principles of justice that He presents to them are a guide for us as well, standards against which we can measure each action that we contribute to the building up of a new world order, from the grassroots.

THE ABIDING RELEVANCE OF THE SÚRIY-I-HAYKAL

Let us conclude by noting that a study of the Súriy-i-Haykal is relevant not merely because of its strategic place in religious history—whether as the culmination of Bahá'u'lláh's declaration of His Revelation to the world at large or as a poignant, dramatic exploration of how the appearance of the Manifestation presents us with our best access to the presence of God. Rather, the work is enduringly relevant precisely because the overriding themes of delegation of authority to the peoples of the world and the imperative of securing a just and lasting peace through a system of collective security are perhaps even more pertinent now than they were during the time the Súriy-i-Haykal was revealed.

As we reflect on these themes in the work, we see that Bahá'u'lláh has effectively addressed and challenged three distinct entities: Himself, the rulers of the world, and the peoples of the world. Baha'u'llah, of course, fulfilled His own mandate bestowed upon Him by the Maid—the Holy Spirit working within Him and through Him—by constructing perfectly "the Temple" of His own appearance among us, replete with every attribute and power assigned to Him in this tablet.

As we have noted, the second entity He addresses—the secular kings and rulers, as well as the religious authorities of the time—failed utterly, even as they continue to falter. They "threw behind their backs" the one chance to attain the Most Great Peace without the needless strife and "tempests" that must now occur to compel humankind to respond appropriately to the guidance of Bahá'u'lláh. They also ignored—and largely continue to ignore—His counsels about those processes and patterns of action necessary to establish the foundation for the Lesser Peace.

Unexpectedly, however, the third entity, the rank and file of the peoples of the world, *is* responding. Furthermore, as has been noted by Shoghi Effendi, the degree to which our work at the grassroots level, as implemented today by the programs devised by the Universal House of Justice, demonstrates the efficacy of the solutions articulated by Bahá'u'lláh, is the degree to which we can help mitigate the suffering humankind must endure before it realizes that the sole resolution for every major crisis we presently face lies in the guidance from the Temple of God among us: "No doubt to the degree we Bahá'ís the world over strive to spread the Cause and live up to its teachings, there will be some mitigation to the suffering of the peoples of the world. But it seems apparent that the great failure to respond to Bahá'u'lláh's instructions, appeals and warnings issued in the 19th century, has now sent the world along a path, or released forces, which must culminate in a still more violent upheaval and agony. The thing is out of hand, so to speak, and it is too late to avert catastrophic trials."[481]

More than ever before, then, the very themes and cautions so eloquently and powerfully set forth in the Súriy-i-Haykal have now become fully apparent; and the challenge they set before us is clear. The body of humankind on planet Earth must, like the Temple of the Manifestation Himself, be constructed from the ground up, with feet of iron to "stand firm and demonstrate such constancy as to cause the feet of every severed soul to be strengthened in the path of God,"[482] eyes "that will contemplate the manifold signs of their Creator,"[483] ears that will "hearken unto the melodies of your Lord,"[484] tongues that "will praise and extol Me amongst the Concourse of eternity,"[485] breasts cleansed so that "the light of My beauty may appear therein,"[486] and inmost hearts which become "the dawning-place of Our knowledge and the dayspring of Our wisdom unto all who are in heaven and on earth."[487]

Appendix

A Structural Outline of the Complete Súriy-i-Haykal

1. As prelude, **Bahá'u'lláh reveals a series of beatitudes in praise of God**:

1.1. Glorified is He (¶ 1–2)

    1.1.1. Who Hath revealed verses to those who understand

    1.1.2. Who revealeth verses to those who perceive

    1.1.3. Who guideth whomsoever He pleaseth unto His path

        1.1.3.1. Verily, I am the Path.

        1.1.3.2. Well is it with them that hasten thereunto (¶ 1)

    1.1.4. Who sendeth down His verses to those who comprehend

    1.1.5. Who speaketh forth from the Kingdom of His Revelation

    1.1.6. Who remaineth unknown to all save His honored servants

    1.1.7. Who quickeneth whomsoever He willeth by virtue of His word "Be," and it is!

    1.1.8. Who causeth whomsoever He willeth to ascend unto the heaven of grace

    1.1.9. Who sendeth down therefrom whatsoever He desireth to a prescribed measure (*Qadar*)

1.2. Blessed is He (¶ 3)

    1.2.1. Who doeth as He willeth by a word of His command

    1.2.2. Who inspireth whomsoever He willeth with whatsoever He desireth through His irresistible and inscrutable command

    1.2.3. Who aideth whomsoever He desireth with the hosts of the unseen

1.2.4.   Who exalteth whomsoever He willeth by the power of His sovereign might

1.2.5.   Who confirmeth whomsoever He chooseth in accordance with His good pleasure

1.3.   Blessed is He (¶ 4)

1.3.1.   Who, in a well-guarded tablet, hath prescribed a fixed measure unto all things

1.3.2.   Who hath revealed unto His Servant that which shall illumine the hearts and minds of men

1.3.3.   Who hath sent down upon His Servant such tribulations as have melted

1.3.3.1.   The hearts of them that dwell within the Tabernacle of eternity

1.3.3.2.   And the souls of those who have drawn nigh unto their Lord

1.3.4.   Who hath showered upon His Servant, from the clouds of His decree, the darts of affliction

1.3.5.   Who beholdeth Me enduring them with patience and fortitude

1.3.6.   Who hath ordained for His Servant that which He hath destined for no other soul

1.4.   Blessed is He (¶ 5)

1.4.1.   Who hath caused to rain down upon His Servant, from the clouds of enmity, and at the hands of the people of denial, the shafts of tribulation and trialFrom the clouds of enmity

1.4.1.1.   And yet seeth Our heart filled with gratitude

1.4.2.   Who hath laid upon the shoulders of His Servant the burden of the heavens and of the earth

1.4.2.1.   A burden for which We yield Him every praise, though none may grasp this save them that are endued with understanding

1.5.   Glorified is He

1.5.1.   Who hath surrendered the embodiment of His Beauty to the clutches of the envious and the wicked. A fate unto which We are fully resigned, though none may perceive this save those who are endued with insight

1.5.2.   Who hath left Ḥusayn to make His dwelling amidst the hosts of His enemies

      1.5.2.1.   And exposed His body with every breath to the spears of hatred and anger

  1.6.   Yet do We yield Him thanks for all that He hath destined to befall His Servant Who repaireth unto Him in His affliction and grief

THE DIALOGUE BETWEEN BAHÁ'U'LLÁH AND THE MAIDEN BEGINS

1.   The beginning of Bahá'u'lláh's description of His vision in the Siyáh-Chál and the dialogue that followed. He recalls how He "beheld a Maiden—the embodiment of the remembrance of the name of My Lord—suspended in the air before Me" who "was raising a call which captivated the hearts and minds of men. She was imparting to both My inward and outer being tidings which rejoiced My soul, and the souls of God's honoured servants" (¶ 6). Pointing her finger at the head of Bahá'u'lláh, the Maiden exalts His station with a series of lofty epithets, saying This is

  1.1.   The Best-Beloved of the worlds

  1.2.   The Beauty of God amongst you

  1.3.   The power of His sovereignty within you

  1.4.   The Mystery of God and His Treasure

  1.5.   The Cause of God and His glory

  1.6.   He Whose Presence is the ardent desire of

      1.6.1.   The denizens of the Realm of eternity

      1.6.2.   And of them that dwell within the Tabernacle of glor And yet from His Beauty do ye turn aside

2.   The Maid of Heaven addresses the "people of the Bayán" (¶ 8–11)

  2.1.   Chastises them for refusing to recognize Bahá'u'lláh

3.   The Maid of Heaven speaks to Bahá'u'lláh as Pen of the Most High telling Him to

  3.1.   Raise up from this Temple the temples of the Oneness of God that they may tell out the tidings of their Lord (¶ 12)Speaks to and about Bahá'u'lláh

      3.1.1.   We have ordained this Temple to be the source of all existence in the new creation, and will raise up beneath the shadow of every letter of this Temple a people (¶ 13)

3.1.1.1.   Whose number none can reckon save God

3.1.1.2.   Who will remain unswayed by the insinuations of the rebellious

3.1.1.3.   Whom God has exalted above the rest of His creation (¶ 14)

3.1.1.4.   Who are the Protectors of the Cause on earth (¶ 16)

4.   The Maid of Heaven speaks to the Temple about what He must accomplish (¶ 17)

4.1.   Arise by the power of Thy Self

4.2.   Aid, then, Thy Lord

4.3.   Take heed lest Thou falter

4.4.   Assist Thy Lord

5.   Quaff the water of life in My name, She tells the Temple: through Thee have We gathered together all created things (¶ 18)

6.   She begins to address certain components of the Temple

6.1.   She addresses the "Eyes of this Temple" (¶ 19)

6.1.1.   Look not upon the heavens… nor upon the earth… for We have created you to behold Our own Beauty

6.1.2.   Through you We will bring into being keen and penetrating eyes that will contemplate the manifold signs of their Creator

6.2.   She Addresses the Ears of the Temple (¶ 20)

6.2.1.   Hearken unto the melodies of your Lord and not idle clamor

6.2.2.   Through you, ears of the faithful heed the Word of God

6.3.   She Addresses the Tongue of the Temple (¶ 21)

6.3.1.   We have taught thee whatsoever had remained concealed in the Bayán and have bestowed upon thee the power of utterance

6.3.2.   Through you We shall bring into being eloquent tongues that will praise and extol Me

6.3.3.   None shall speak "unless they be inspired by this Tongue"

6.3.3.1.   "Few, however, are they who understand!"

7.   Maid of Heaven speaks to "Maid of inner meanings" (¶ 22)

7.1.   Reveal thyself so that people may arise and extol "this Youth"

7.2.   Grieve not if people don't accept "the crimson wine" because there are a people not yet revealed who will understand and praise Me (¶ 23). Through these faithful ones God "shall exalt His name, diffuse His signs, uphold His words, and proclaim His verses, in spite of those that have repudiated His truth, gainsaid His sovereignty, and caviled at His signs" (¶ 24)

8.   Bahá'u'lláh addresses the Maid of Heaven about what He has been made to endure

8.1.   If you encounter these receptive souls, recount what "this Youth" has suffered.

8.2.   Recount how we chose a brother (Mírzá Yaḥyá), taught him, exalted his station, and protected him.

    8.2.1.   We then taught the Cause of God, but My brother became jealous when the fame of the Cause was spread, disputed My words, repudiated my signs, "Nor would his hunger be appeased unless he were to devour My flesh and drink My blood" (¶ 26).

8.3.   This brother attempted to win one of My servants over to his own designs [allusion to Mirzá Yahyá's attempt to persuade Ustád Muhammad-'Alíy-i-Salmání to kill Bahá'u'lláh]. When Our companions learned this, they were angered, but we "enjoined upon them patience", took up residence in another house and did not oppose him. But when he realized his plan had been exposed, he accused Me of what he had himself committed. "His purpose was none other than to inspire mischief and to instill hatred into the hearts of those who had believed in God, the All-Glorious, the All-Loving" (¶ 27–28)

8.4.   We were bewildered by his actions, and then "he had committed that which no pen dare describe, and by which he disgraced the dignity of My station and profaned the sanctity of God" (¶ 29).

9.   The Maid of Heaven Comforts Bahá'u'lláh addressing Him first with the epithet "Pen of Eternity," and telling Him not to grieve, "for erelong shall God raise up a people who will see with their own eyes and will recall Thy tribulations"[488] (¶ 30)

9.1.   Don't waste Your time writing about these enemies; God has recorded their names and deeds. Instead, recount what You have purposed for this Temple, that its signs and tokens may become manifest on earth

9.2.   "Living Temple,"[489] stretch forth Thy hand over all in heaven and earth, and seize the reins of command. "Do as Thou willest, and fear not the ignorant." "Through the upraising of Thy hand to the heaven of My grace, the hands of all created things shall be lifted up to their Lord" (¶ 31)

10.   The Maid of Heaven tells Bahá'u'lláh as "Living Temple" what advice to give to the people (¶ 32)

10.1.   Forsake all that you possess

10.2.   Fear God

10.3.   Don't alter or pervert the text of the Word of God

10.4.   This is the Hand of God that holds all the good of the heavens and the earth (¶ 33)

10.5.   Soon God will raise up hands to win victory for this Youth by subduing the peoples and kindreds of the earth, demonstrating the might of God (¶ 34)

10.6.   These hands will assuredly prevail through the ascendancy of My Will against all the hosts of creation (¶ 35)

10.7.   These hands shall rejoice at all times in the signs and verses of their Lord while those who disbelieve shall incur His wrath

11.   The Maid of heaven tells Bahá'u'lláh as "Living Temple": "**We have . . . appointed Thee to be the sign of My majesty amidst all that hath been** and all that shall be, and have ordained Thee to be the emblem of My Cause betwixt the heavens and the earth, through My word 'Be', and it is!" (¶ 36)[490]

12.   She then addresses the four letters that comprise the word "Temple," each of which has a symbolic meaning regarding some divine attribute or power with which the Temple is endowed

12.1.   The First Letter "betokens" the Essence of Divinity

12.2.   The Second Letter symbolizes My name, the Almighty (*Qadir*) (¶ 38)

12.3.   The Third Letter symbolizes My name, the All-Bountiful (*Karím*) (¶ 39). This Letter is told:

12.3.1.   Send down that which shall enrich all created things, and gather Thy servants beneath Thy shade (¶ 40)

12.3.2.   Soon God will raise up through Thee hands of indomitable strength and arms of invincible might whose ascendancy will cause consternation and dismay to seize all the dwellers of the earth (¶ 41)

12.3.3. Sword Imagery: "Beware lest ye shed the blood of anyone. Unsheathe the sword of your tongue from the scabbard of utterance, for therewith ye can conquer the citadels of men's hearts." "Aid ye your Lord, the God of Mercy, with the sword of understanding" (¶ 42)

12.3.4. Tell of the significance of this Tablet, upon which God hath inscribed that which the wisest of men cannot fathom. "Blessed be the one who readeth it, who pondereth its contents, and who is numbered with them that comprehend!"[491]

12.3.5. The letter is told to speak perhaps the most well-known passage of the Súriy-i-Haykal, part of which reads, "Naught is seen in My temple but the Temple of God, and in My beauty but His Beauty, and in My being but His Being, and in My self but His Self" (¶ 44)[492]

12.3.6. Do not speak of duality in regard to God. God is single and sanctified above His names, of which He has created manifestations in the world of being (¶ 45) [taken together with the previous paragraph, this seems to be a reminder that Though the Manifestation is our best access to God, and can thus rightly claim that "Naught is seen in my temple but the Temple of God," God nevertheless remains a distinct Essence]

12.4. The Fourth Letter symbolizes *Fadl* or "Grace." From this source of grace emanate all the evidences of grace in the world (¶ 46). This Fourth Letter is instructed to say that:

12.4.1. In this day, all created things have been endowed with all the potentialities they can carry, out of the grace of God: "[t]he whole creation hath been made the recipient of the revelation of the All-Merciful, and the earth the repository of things inscrutable to all except God, the Truth, the Knower of things unseen" (¶ 47)

12.4.2. The whole earth hath been created anew

12.4.3. This grace can never be "adequately understood," how much less the Essential Reality of God Himself

12.5. Transitioning back to addressing the Temple as a whole, the Maid of Heaven continues the theme of grace, telling the Temple to not be troubled if none seem ready to receive His gifts: "for erelong shall He raise up sanctified hearts and illumined eyes who shall flee from every quarter unto Thine all-encompassing and boundless grace" (¶ 48)

13.   The Maid of Heaven explains to the Temple some points about the revealed Word (¶ 49)

13.1.   The Word's reception: when Revelation occurs, "unbelievers seek to remedy the sickness of their hearts" by denying: "These are not clear verses from God, nor do they proceed from an innate and untaught nature"

13.2.   The Word's relationship to the Holy Spirit and Most Great Spirit: "Say: the Holy Spirit Itself hath been generated through the agency of a single letter revealed by this Most Great Spirit [...] And that innate and untaught nature in its essence is called into being by the verses of God" (¶ 50)

13.3.   The modes in which the Word is revealed: We have revealed Our verses in nine different modes; one would suffice as a proof. We could reveal verses in countless other modes. (¶ 51)

13.4.   The universality with which the Word is bestowed: "Verily, there is naught from which Our favour hath been withheld, inasmuch as We have dealt equitably in the fashioning of each and all, and by a word of Our mouth presented unto them the trust of Our love" [in context, this seems to signify that God has revealed His Word equally to all]. Some accept it, some reject it (¶ 52)

13.5.   The uniqueness of the Word of God: it cannot be confounded with the words of ordinary people, and should not become a source of dissention (¶ 53)

13.6.   The nature of rejection of the Word: some claim the divine verses are contrived (i.e. by an ordinary human). When they behold the power these verses exercise in the world, they attribute it to sorcery (¶ 54)

13.6.1.   The "followers of the Qur'án" did this with the Báb; now another people [implied to be the Bábís, as they are distinguished from the people fo the Qur'án here] are doing the same thing with the Ancient Beauty, particularly "He who is incapable of speaking in Our presence" (i.e. Mirzá Yahyá)

13.6.2.   This kind of rejection is itself a proof: "Those whom the Lord hath endued with knowledge shall find, in the very objections raised by the unbelievers, conclusive proofs to invalidate their claims and vindicate the truth of this manifest Light" (¶ 56)

14. The Maid addresses Bahá'u'lláh as Ancient Beauty, telling Him to pay no heed to unbelievers and "waft over all created things the sweet savours of the remembrance of Thy Beloved, the Exalted, the Great." (¶ 57) Tell them:

> 14.1. Those who desire to look upon God's countenance can behold Him; He has revealed Himself in this shining and luminous Beauty
>
> 14.2. Whosoever desireth to hearken unto His melodies, lo, hear them rising from His resplendent and wondrous lips
>
> 14.3. Whosoever desireth to be illumined by the splendours of His light, say: Seek the court of His presence

15. The Maid exhorts Bahá'u'lláh to put a question to the people and let God assay whose answer is correct (¶ 58):

> 15.1. "Is it God Who is potent to achieve His purpose, or is it ye who enjoy such authority?"
>
> > 15.1.1. Is it He Who is truly unconstrained—as implied by your statement that He doeth what He pleaseth and shall not be asked of His doings—or is it ye who wield such power, and make such assertions out of blind imitation, like your forebears at the appearance of every other Manifestation?
> >
> > 15.1.2. The proof of God's unconstrained power is that "He hath sent down the Manifestation of His Cause with verses which naught in the heavens or on the earth can withstand!" as ye yourselves "beheld and heard when once the Daystar of the world [Bahá'u'lláh] shone forth above the horizon of 'Iráq with manifest dominion" (¶ 59)
>
> 15.2. The Maid instructs Bahá'u'lláh to further say to the people that they should fear God, not contend with "Him Who representeth the Godhead," and believe in the Messengers of God. He is also to tell them that He believes in what was revealed to the Apostles of Old, in what was revealed to the Báb, and in what is now being revealed "from His Throne of glory" (¶ 60)

16. The Maid Returns to Addressing Various Faculties and Parts of the Temple

> 16.1. O Feet of this Temple! (¶ 61)
> > 16.1.1. We have wrought you of iron

16.1.2. Stand firm with such constancy as to cause the feet of every severed soul to be strengthened in the path of God; Be immovable in the Faith of God, and waver not

16.1.3. "Erelong shall We bring into being through you other feet, firm and steadfast, which shall walk unwaveringly in Our path, even should they be assailed by hosts as formidable as the combined forces of the former and latter generations"

16.2. O Temple of Holiness! (¶ 63)

16.2.1. We have cleansed Thy breast that the light of My beauty might be reflected therein and be reflected in the mirrors of the world

16.2.2. We have chosen Thee (for Our Own SelfThis is a "bounty which shall last until the Day that hath no end in this contingent world"

16.2.3. This is a "bounty which shall last until the Day that hath no end in this contingent world."Breast of the Temple, "We, verily, have caused all things to mirror forth thy reality, and made thee as a mirror of Our own Self"

16.3. O Breast of this Temple! (¶ 64)

16.3.1. "We, verily, have caused all things to mirror forth thy reality, and made thee as a mirror of Our own Self"

16.3.2. Through thee We have created other sanctified breasts; soon We shall bring into being through thee men who will testify to naught save My beauty, and be the mirrors of My Names amidst all created things

16.4. O Temple of Holiness [again]! (¶ 65)

16.4.1. We have made Thine inmost heart the treasury of all the knowledge of past and future ages

16.4.2. "In truth, that knowledge which belongeth unto Mine own Essence is such as none hath ever attained or will ever grasp, nor shall any heart be capable of bearing its weight."

16.4.3. "Within the treasury of Our Wisdom there lieth unrevealed a knowledge, one word of which, if We chose to divulge it to mankind, would cause every human being to recognize the Manifestation of God and to acknowledge His omniscience, would enable every one to discover the secrets of all the sciences and to attain so high a station as to find himself wholly independent of all past and future learning" (¶ 66)

16.5. O Inmost Heart of this Temple! (¶ 67)

    16.5.1. "We have made Thee the dawning-place of Our knowledge and the dayspring of Our wisdom unto all who are in heaven and on earth"

    16.5.2. "From Thee have We caused all sciences to appear, and unto Thee shall We cause them to return. And from Thee shall We bring them forth a second time"

    16.5.3. "Erelong shall We bring into being through Thee exponents of new and wondrous sciences, of potent and effective crafts, and shall make manifest through them that which the heart of none of Our servants hath yet conceived"

16.6. The Inmost Heart is instructed to Say: (¶ 68)

    16.6.1. "We are potent indeed to achieve Our purpose, and render no account for that which We bring to pass"

    16.6.2. Should We raise a soul to the station of Manifestation, it would still be subject to "Our Sovereignty" (¶ 69).

    16.6.3. No one knows the wisdom of "Our immutable method" but God

    16.6.4. People, do not dispute concerning My Cause, "for ye shall never fathom the manifold wisdom of your Lord, nor shall ye ever gauge the knowledge of Him . . . Whosoever layeth claim to have known His Essence is without doubt among the most ignorant of all people" (¶ 71)

    16.6.5. "Magnify My Cause and promulgate My teachings and commandments, for none other course beside this shall beseem you, and no other path shall ever lead unto Him"

17.　The Maid discusses the concept of a human temple being made the manifest (human) repository of all the attributes of the Holy Spirit: "O Living Temple! We have made Thee the Dayspring of each one of Our most excellent titles, the Dawning-Place of each one of Our most august attributes, and the Fountainhead of each one of Our manifold virtues unto the denizens of earth and heaven" (¶ 72)

18.　The Maid explains what Bahá'u'lláh as the Living Temple should tell the people. "Say:"

18.1. "We have made each one of Our Names a wellspring from which We have caused the streams of divine wisdom and understanding to gush forth and flow in the garden of Our Cause" (¶ 73)

18.2. "We have generated all Letters from the Point and have caused them to return unto It, and We have sent It down again in the form of a human temple"

18.3. "We have brought forth all Lights from the Orb of Our name, the True One, have caused them to return unto It, and have again made them manifest in the form of a human temple" (¶ 74)

18.4. "It is in Our power, should We wish it, to cause all created things to expire in an instant, and, with the next, to endue them again with life" (¶ 75)

18.5. "Naught is seen in My revelation but the Revelation of God, and in My might but His Might" (¶ 76)

18.6. Tell them that We use similitudes (metaphors and analogies) to explain these concepts t"for the sake of Our discerning servants" (¶ 77), and Say:

    18.6.1. "My creatures are even as the leaves of a tree. They proceed from the tree and depend upon it for their existence, yet remain oblivious of their root and origin"

    18.6.2. "My creatures are even as the fish of the deep. Their life dependeth upon the water, and yet they remain unaware of that which, by the grace of an omniscient and omnipotent Lord, sustaineth their very existence. Indeed, their heedlessness is such that were they asked concerning the water and its properties, they would prove entirely ignorant "(like Christ explaining why He uses parables in Matthew 13:10) (¶ 76)

18.7. Tell the people to fear God and beware lest they be accounted among those who allow the verses of their Lord to pass them by unheard and unrecognized (¶ 77)

18.8. Be not of those who either "ask the sun to expound the words of the shadow" [i.e. ask the Manifestation about the things they find important, rather than what the Manifestation speaks of] or "who inquired of the darkness about the light" [i.e. who ask the opponents of the Manifestation about Him] (¶ 79):

    18.8.1. Would you stand before the Báb and inquire about the Imams?

    18.8.2. Would you ask the Jews if Christ was the Messiah?

    18.8.3. Would you ask the Idols if Muḥammad was the Apostle of God?

18.8.4. Would you ask the people of the Qur'án if the Báb was "the Remembrance of God, the Most Exalted, the Most Great?"

18.9. Tell the people not to deal with the next Manifestation as they have dealt with You (¶ 80):

18.9.1. "By My Beauty! By those words which I have revealed, Myself is not intended, but rather He Who will come after Me"

18.9.2. "Do not object, when the verses of God are sent down unto you from the Court of My favour, saying, 'these do not proceed from an innate and untaught nature,' for that nature itself hath been created by My word and circleth round Me, if ye be of them that apprehend this truth"

19. The Maid explains the concept of a human temple being a mirror of the Holy Spirit

19.1. O Living Temple, We have (¶ 81):

19.1.1. Made Thee a mirror unto the Kingdom of names and a guide unto the straight and perspicuous path [cf. Christ's "I am the Way" (John 14:6)]

19.1.2. Imparted unto Thee Our Word

19.1.3. Endowed Thee with the "Staff of authority" and "the Writ of judgement" to "test the wisdom of every command."We have endowed Thee with the "Staff of authority" and "the Writ of judgement" to "test the wisdom of every command."

19.1.4. Caused Thy heart to be the repository of the "oceans of inner meaning and explanation

19.1.5. Appointed Thee as a Manifestation of Our own Self

19.2. Bring into being "resplendent mirrors and exalted letters that shall testify to Thy sovereignty and dominion, bear witness to Thy might and glory, and be the manifestations of Thy Names amidst mankind" (¶ 82)

19.2.1. We have caused Thee to be the creator of mirrors [i.e.: stalwart followers, believers, and teachers]

19.2.2. "And We shall cause Thee to return unto Mine own Self, even as We called Thee forth in the beginning" [likely an allusion to the Manifesation as pre-existent but called forth as Manifestation, afterward to return to Their station in spiritual realm].

19.2.3. Warn the mirrors not to fall prey to pride or "trappings of leadership" and to be submissive before God

19.2.4. Tell the mirrors: You were brought forth by My will and command. Become detached from all else but Your calling (¶ 83)

19.2.5. Temple, tell the mirrors that if You wish[493]

19.2.5.1.   You have the power instantly to transform all things into mirrors of the Names of God

19.2.5.2.   How much more would this be able by the power of God Himself

19.2.5.3.   Likewise, You have the power to transform the entire creation in an instant

19.2.5.4.   How much power lies in the Will of God, Your God, and the "Lord of all the Worlds"

19.3. Tell those who would be followers ("manifestations of My names"), fidelity in the Cause of God requires a subtle combination of belief, action, persistence, and sincerity (¶ 85)

19.3.1. Should you "offer up all ye possess," even your lives, in the path of God, and invoke Him as often as grains of sand, yet oppose the Manifestation when He appears, your works will be meritless in the eyes of God

19.3.2. Conversely, should you "neglect all righteous works and yet choose to believe in Him in these days, God perchance will put away your sins"

19.3.3. How many are those who purport to be religious but who end up being rebellious and froward (¶ 86)

19.3.3.1.   Those who fast, then reject the One who created the ordinance to fast

19.3.3.2.   Those who endure physical hardship but who then claim to be spiritually superior

19.3.3.3.   Those who live austere lives to acquire fame, though, in fact, "no mention shall remain of them"

19.3.4. Even if the names of these pretenders were to endure, what value would it have for them? (¶ 87)

19.3.4.1.   Was the idol 'Uzzá made any greater by this, that its name lived on amidst the worshipers of names?

19.3.4.2.   Conversely, if your name be forgotten by men but remembered by God, "ye will indeed be numbered among the treasures of His name"

19.3.5. It is for this reason that we have sent down the laws in "Our verses" to guide you

    19.3.5.1. Don't endure excessive hardships, but follow the revealed law

    19.3.5.2. Enjoy that which We have permitted and abstain only from that which We have forbidden

20. The Maid addresses the divines and the learned

20.1. O concourse of the Divines and the learned among men, your glory lies solely in your recognition of Him Who hath been sent by God (¶ 88)

20.2. Do not boast if you merely follow the laws of the Qur'án—that is to be expected from you; your reputation would be ruined were you to transgress the law

20.3. Your true glory lies in

    20.3.1. Submission to the Word of God

    20.3.2. Detachment from all else besides God

    20.3.3. Not allowing your learning to become a veil between yourself and the Manifestation when He appears

20.4. The divine or learned one who turns toward the Manifestation when He appears are

    20.4.1. The inmates of Paradise seek the blessing of his breath

    20.4.2. His lamp sheddeth its radiance over all who are in heaven and on earth

    20.4.3. Numbered with the inheritors of the Prophets

20.5. Further,

    20.5.1. He that beholdeth him [the divine / learned who turns toward the Manifestation] hath, verily, beheld the True One

    20.5.2. He that turneth toward him hath, verily, turned toward God, the Almighty, the All-Wise.

20.6. Don't become changed, because you are a source of guidance for others (¶ 89):

    20.6.1. Like a spring, if you be changed, so will those streams that branch out from you

    20.6.2. Like a tree, if the root becomes corrupted, "its branches, and its offshoots, and its leaves, and its fruits, will be corrupted"

    20.6.3. These analogies and "similitudes" We provide you for your instruction and steadfastness

21. It is only Our endowment of spiritual value that gives value to something (¶ 90)

21.1. We could adorn a handful of dust with "the vesture of Our Names," but this would be a token of Our favor, not a sign that the dust has any inherent value

21.2. Likewise, the Black Stone of the Kaaba is a point of adoration for Muslims, but not because the stone itself has "innate excellence," but because of its association with Revelations from God

21.3. Likewise consider places of pilgrimage and adoration, such as the Mosque of Aqsá: its worth is in its relationship to the Manifestations of God (¶ 91)

21.4. The wisdom in the honour bestowed on certain places through their association with the Manifestations of God is "inscrutable to all save God

22. Tell the people that when the promised Revelation occurs, they must strive to (¶ 92):

22.1. Sanctify their souls from all names

22.2. Cleanse their hearts from every trace of the love or hate of the peoples of the world

23. The Maid instructs Bahá'u'lláh what He should say to the Covenant Breakers [the people of the Bayán may be particularly intended – See ¶ 95]

23.1. "Lift up the veils and coverings that obscure your vision, and consider the testimonies of the Prophets and Messengers, that haply ye may recognize the Cause of God in these days" (¶ 93)

23.2. Fear God because it is you who benefit from recognition of the Manifestation

23.2.1. God is self-sufficient; "From everlasting was He alone; there was none else beside Him." Remember the ḥadíth of the Hidden Treasure

23.3. Behold those who, though His creation and who even recite prayers and Holy verses, war against God by breaking His Covenant (¶ 94)

23.3.1. When they unsheathe their swords against the Manifestation ("Luminary"), it is, in truth, against God, though they know it not

23.3.2. They remain dead and buried in the tombs of their

selfish desires

23.3.3. They, truly, are wrapt in a dense and grievous veil

23.3.4. It is as though they were devoid of all understanding or had never heard the Melody of God, the Most Exalted, the All-Knowing

23.4. If the Báb "had been someone else beside Me as you claim," and He had met Me, He would never have allowed Himself to be separated from Me, and We would have enjoyed each other's company (¶ 96)

23.4.1. As it was, He wept sorely in His [physical] remoteness from Me [note that this affirms that They never met in person]

23.4.2. He preceded Me solely to prepare people for My advent, as He says in His tablets

23.4.3. Would that you had ears to hear His lament in the Bayán

23.4.3.1. Lamenting the tribulations He foreknew would befall Me

23.4.3.2. Bemoaning His separation from Me

23.4.3.3. Giving voice to His longing to be united with Me

23.4.4. Indeed, the Báb beholds Me (and Him) at this very minute suffering at the hands of the very ones created to "attain His Day"

23.5. When We summoned you in the former Revelation, and the veils were rent asunder so that the Ancient Beauty came unto you "in the clouds," you (the people) repudiated Him (¶ 97)

23.5.1. Fear God and prostrate yourselves before God when the "luminary of divine verses dawneth upon you from the horizon of the Pen of the King of all names and attributes"

23.5.2. Better is this for you and more profitable than "whatsoever hath been created in the heavens and on the earth"

23.6. I admonish you (O people!) solely for the sake of God, and seek no reward from you, because My reward will come from God Who raised Me up and "made Me the Source of His remembrance amidst His creatures" (¶ 98).

23.6.1. Follow not the "Evil One"—the promptings of "your lusts and covetous desires, and hindereth you from treading the straight Path"

23.6.2. The Evil One has appeared "in such wise as the eye of creation hath never beheld" (¶ 99)[494]

23.6.3. However, "He Who is the Beauty of the All-Merciful hath likewise been made manifest with an adorning the like of which hath never been witnessed in the past"

23.6.4. Thus, the Call of God hath been raised, "and behind it the call of Satan"

23.6.5. Well is it with those who hear the one [and reject the other], "[f]or whoso cherisheth in his heart the love of anyone beside Me, be it to the extent of a grain of mustard seed, shall be unable to gain admittance into My Kingdom"

23.6.6. For whoso cherisheth in his heart the love of anyone beside Me, be it to the extent of a grain of mustard seed, shall be unable to gain admittance into My Kingdom.

23.6.7. This is the Day of Days, when "God's most great favour hath been made manifest" and "voice of all who are in the heavens above and on the earth below proclaimeth My Name, and singeth forth My praises"

24. The Maid exhorts Bahá'u'lláh to raise the Clarion Call of His Revelation

24.1. O Temple of Divine Revelation! Sound the trumpet in My Name! O Temple of Divine mysteries! Raise the clarion call of Thy Lord, the Unconditioned, the Unconstrained!

24.2. O Maid of Heaven! Step forth from the chambers of Paradise and announce unto the people of the world: By the righteousness of God! He Who is the Best-Beloved of the worlds—He Who hath ever been the Desire of every perceiving heart, the Object of the adoration of all that are in heaven and on earth, and the Cynosure of the former and the latter generations—is now come! (¶ 100)

24.3. "Take heed lest ye hesitate in recognizing this resplendent Beauty when once He hath appeared in the plenitude of His sovereign might and majesty. He, verily, is the True One, and all else besides Him is as naught before a single one of His servants, and paleth into nothingness when brought face to face with the revelation of His splendours."

Five Epistles to Kings and Rulers

To Pope Pius IX

1. Initial counsels to the Pope to recognize the new Revelation: "O Pope!" (¶ 102)

    1.1. Rend the veils because "He Who is the Lord of Lords is come overshadowed with clouds [a symbol explicated in the Kitáb-i-Íqán]" "even as He came down from it the first time

    1.2. Don't make the same mistake as the Pharisees by disputing with Him

    1.3. He brings both grace and justice

    1.4. Don't let a [new] name "debar thee from God"

    1.5. Don't let vain imaginings, nor the trappings of all you possess, veil you from the truth (¶ 103)

2. What the Pope should tell the "concourse of divines" [theologians and clerics]:

    2.1. Tell them to cease writing their treatises, for the Pen of Glory (Bahá'u'lláh) has appeared. The Hour only God foreknew has at last arrived (¶ 107)[495]

    2.2. All the atoms of the earth cry out: "The Ancient of Days is come in His great glory!"

    2.3. We, in truth, have given Ourself as a ransom for your own lives. Alas, when We came once again, We beheld you fleeing from Us, whereat the eye of My loving-kindness wept sore over My people[114]

    2.4. Think about how Christ was opposed when He appeared, how, when He revealed Himself, the very ones waiting to behold Him "turned aside from Him and disputed with Him" (¶ 108)

        2.4.1. At the time, only those destitute of any power recognized Him

        2.4.2. Today, every man vested with power "prideth himself on His Name!"

3. Discussion of the monks. Behold how the monks seclude themselves in devotion and "call upon Me at eventide and at dawn" clinging to My name, but when I appeared, they were veiled from My Self.[496]

    3.1. Don't let your devotions deter you from recognizing the object of all devotion, the Lord Almighty Who has come to "quicken" the world and unite its people (¶ 109)

    3.1.1.   How can you read and study the words of Christ and yet refuse to acknowledge God?

    3.1.2.   If you deny this Revelation, then in what sense do you believe in God? (¶ 110)

    3.1.3.   Don't let your deeds veil you from your own selves, and thus keep you back from drawing nigh unto God.

3.2.   "O concourse of monks!" Happy is he who sets aside his own desires and takes hold of guidance (¶ 111)

    3.2.1.   Come out of seclusion and bid the people enter the Kingdom of God, the Lord of the Day of Judgment (¶ 112)

    3.2.2.   [Teach them that] "[t]he Word which the Son concealed is made manifest... in the form of the human temple"[497]

    3.2.3.   "Blessed be the Lord Who is the Father! He, verily, is come unto the nations in His most great majesty

4.   Broadening the address: "O followers of all religions!" (¶ 113)

4.1.   We behold you wandering in error [even though what you need is right before you]:

    4.1.1.   "You are the fish of this Ocean; wherefore do ye withhold yourselves from that which sustaineth you?"

    4.1.2.   Today Peter ("the Rock") cries out: "Lo! The Father is come, and that which ye were promised in the Kingdom is fulfilled!"

4.2.   Bahá'u'lláh highlights His suffering [in terms that resonate for both Christians and Muslims] (¶ 114):

    4.2.1.   "My body hath borne imprisonment that your souls may be released from bondage"

    4.2.2.   We have consented to be abased that ye may be exalted

    4.2.3.   "My body longeth for the cross [like Christ], and Mine head awaiteth the thrust of the spear [like the Imám Husayn], in the path of the All-Merciful, that the world may be purged from its transgressions [cf. Christian understanding of Christ as a sacrifice for the sins of the world]."

    4.2.4.   The "people of the Qur'án" have risen against us and tormented Us with such a torment that the Holy Spirit lamented, and the thunder roared out, and the clouds wept over Us (¶ 115)

4.3.   He explains that calamities cannot deter Him (¶ 116):

4.3.1.   Should they cast Him into a fire kindled on the continent, He will assuredly rear His head in the midmost heart of the ocean and proclaim: "He is the Lord of all that are in heaven and all that are on earth!"

4.3.2.   And if they cast Him into a darksome pit, they will find Him seated on earth's loftiest heights calling aloud to all mankind: "Lo, the Desire of the World is come in His majesty, His sovereignty, His transcendent dominion!"

4.3.3.   And if He be buried beneath the depths of the earth, His Spirit soaring to the apex of heaven shall peal the summons: "Behold ye the coming of the Glory; witness ye the Kingdom of God, the Most Holy, the Gracious, the All-Powerful!"

4.3.4.   And if they shed His blood, every drop thereof shall cry out and invoke God in this Name through which the fragrance of His raiment hath been diffused in all directions

4.3.5.   Though threatened by the swords of Our enemies, We summon all mankind unto God" (¶ 117)

4.4.   Say: O peoples of the earth! Scatter the idols of your vain imaginings in the name of your Lord, the All-Glorious, the All-Knowing, and turn ye unto Him in this Day which God hath made the King of days.

5.   Further counsels for the Pope himself. O Supreme Pontiff, abandon thy physical possessions and speak forth the praises of God (¶ 118):

5.1.   Sell all the embellished ornaments thou dost possess, and expend them in the path of God

5.2.   Abandon thy kingdom unto the kings, and emerge from thy habitation, with thy face set toward the Kingdom

5.3.   Exhort thou the kings and say: "Deal equitably with men. Beware lest ye transgress the bounds fixed in the Book"

5.4.   Beware lest thou appropriate unto thyself the things of the world and the riches thereof

5.5.   Should anyone offer thee all the treasures of the earth, refuse to even glance upon them

5.6.   Be as thy Lord hath been [i.e., the simple life of Christ]

5.7.   Luxuries can be a veil to virtue (¶ 119)

5.7.1.   If a pearl "be covered in silk, its luster and beauty will be concealed

5.7.2.   Likewise, man's distinction lieth in the excellence of

> his conduct and in the pursuit of that which beseemeth his station, not in childish play and pastimes
>
> 5.7.3.   [T]hy true adornment consisteth in the love of God... not in the luxuries thou dost possess

6.   The new Revelation is not in the form of parables. Bahá'u'lláh explains to the Pope that while Christ spoke in parables, "He Who proclaimeth the Truh in this Day speaketh without them. [...] Should the inebriation of the wine of My verses seize thee, and thou determinest to present thyself before the throne of thy Lord:"

6.1.   Make My love your vesture

6.2.   Make remembrance of Me your shield

6.3.   Make reliance upon God your provision

7.   Explanation to Christians of the Báb's role: "O followers of the Son! [Christians]" Even as John was sent to prepare you for Christ, so the Báb cried out the following in the wilderness of the Bayán (¶ 121):

7.1.   O peoples of the world! Cleanse your eyes! The Day whereon ye can behold the Promised One and attain unto Him hath drawn nigh!

7.2.   O followers of the Gospel! Prepare the way! The Day of the advent of the Glorious Lord is at hand! Make ready to enter the Kingdom

8.   Further counsels for Christians, clarifying Bahá'u'lláh's station. The "Dove of Eternity" Who "warbleth upon the twigs of the Divine Lote-Tree" has further counsels for the "followers of the Son" (¶ 122):

8.1.   We sent forth him who was named John to baptize you with water, that your bodies might be cleansed for the appearance of the Messiah

8.2.   He [Christ], in turn, purified you with the fire of love and the water of the spirit in anticipation of these Days

8.3.   This is that peerless One foretold by Isaiah, and the Comforter concerning Whom the Spirit had covenanted with you

8.4.   Open your eyes, O concourse of bishops, that ye may behold your Lord seated upon the Throne of might and glory

9.   Speaking to a broader audience again—"Say: O peoples of all faiths!"—though in terms that will resonate with Christians in particular

9.1. Don't be like those who followed the Pharisees and were thereby prevented from recognizing the Spirit [Christ]. "The Ancient Beauty is come in His Most Great Name, and He wisheth to admit all mankind into His most holy Kingdom" (¶ 123).

9.2. He hath come again to redeem you.

9.3. "Should your eye be opposed thereto, pluck it out" (cf. Matthew 5:29; Mark 9:47)

9.4. "Will you again slay Him Who desireth to grant you eternal life?"Come forth from the darkness by the grace of the sun.

9.5. We, verily, have created you for the light, and desire not to abandon you unto the fire"; come forth from the darkness by the grace of this Sun (¶ 124)

9.6. Turn toward Him "with sanctified hearts and assured souls, with seeing eyes and beaming faces"

10. The rewards of the faithful

10.1. "Blessed the one who hath remained faithful to the Covenant of God... If ye follow Me (¶ 125):

    10.1.1. Ye shall behold that which you were promised

    10.1.2. You shall become "My companions in the dominion of My majesty"

    10.1.3. You shall become "the intimates of My beauty in the heaven of My power forevermore"

10.2. If you rebel against Me, I will in My clemency endure it patiently, that haply ye may awaken and rise from the couch of heedlessness

10.3. Fear God and follow not the ways of the hypocrites

11. The Day of "ingathering" has arrived, and "all things have been separated from each other" (¶ 126)

11.1. The desire of the Divine Sifter hath been to store up every good thing for Mine own Self

11.2. Naught hath He spoken save to acquaint you with My Cause and to guide you to the path of Him whose mention hath adorned all the sacred Books

12. A final appeal to the entire Christian community. "Say: O Concourse of Christians!" We have revealed Ourself to you on a previous occasion, and you "recognized Me not. This is yet another occasion you: (¶ 127)

12.1. This is the "Day of God" and He hath come down from heaven even as He did before

12.2. Again He desires to shelter you beneath the shade of His mercy.

12.3. He does not wish you to become to become consumed by the fire of your desires

    12.3.1. If you fail, the failure is of your own choosing, your own "waywardness and ignorance"

    12.3.2. You mention My name but know Me not

    12.3.3. You call upon me but fail to recognize My Revelation

    12.3.4. Rend asunder the veils that "ye may discover a path unto your Lord"

    12.3.5. Thus biddeth you He Who desireth for you everlasting life

12.4. O children of the Kingdom, We behold you in darkness, and this "beseemeth you not."

    12.4.1. If you are fearful that the light will shine upon your deeds

        12.4.1.1.   Then direct your steps toward the path Christ prophesied:

        12.4.1.2.   He said He would make you "fishers of men."

        12.4.1.3.   In this Day, We say "come ye after Me, that We may make you to become the quickeners of mankind"

13. Turning to other kings

13.1. O Pen of the Most High! Bestir Thyself in remembrance of other kings in this blessed and luminous Book, that perchance they may rise from the couch of heedlessness and give ear unto that which the Nightingale singeth upon the branches of the Divine Lote-Tree, and hasten toward God in this most wondrous and sublime Revelation" (¶ 130)

LETTER TO NAPOLEON III

1. Initial counsels to the "King of Paris" (¶ 131)

1.1. Tell the priests to ring the bells no longer

    1.1.1.   The "Most Mighty Bell," hath appeared, and "the mighty verses of Thy Lord" have been sent down again that you might remember God in these days when disorder and irreligion have enveloped everyone except those whom God was pleased to spare

1.2. "He Who is the Unconstrained is come" to unite the peoples of the world, "and gather all men around this Table which hath been sent down from heaven"

1.3. Deny not the favor of God:

    1.3.1. It is better for you than what you possess, all of which shall perish

1.4. The "breezes of forgiveness" have been wafted from God; "whoso turneth thereunto shall be":

    1.4.1. "cleansed of sins"

    1.4.2. cleansed of "all pain and sickness"

    1.4.3. "happy"

1.5. All creation celebrates the advent Him Who "is come in His great glory!" (¶ 132)

    1.5.1. "Some have known God and remember Him"

    1.5.2. "[O]thers remember Him, yet know Him not"

1.6. O King, hear the Voice of God calling to thee "from the Fire which burneth in this verdant Tree, on this Sinai... 'Verily, there is none other God but Me'" (¶ 133)

    1.6.1. We have sent Him Whose signs "have been revealed in the West"

    1.6.2. Turn toward Him on this, "the Day which God hath exalted above all other days"

    1.6.3. "Arise thou to serve God and help His Cause. He, verily, will... set thee king over all that whereon the sun riseth"

    1.6.4. We desire for thee "naught except that which is better for thee than what thou dost possess and all the treasures of the earth" (¶ 134)

    1.6.5. Arise [O King] and say to My servants that I am:

        1.6.5.1. "the Face of God amongst you"

        1.6.5.2. God's "Guide unto you"

2. The failure of the divines. The learned and divines who have thought to establish the truth of the Cause of God by "the things they possess" [i.e. their power or material wealth] have failed ("fallen"), even though they invoke God in My Name;[498] when I came unto them "in My glory, they turned aside" (¶ 135)

2.1. This is the same truth that Christ brought, and the same thing happened to Him

2.1.1.   The "Jewish doctors" [Pharisees] disputed with Him until they "perpetrated what hath made the Holy Spirit to lament"

2.1.2.   Strange that a Pharisee who had worshiped God for seventy years rejected the Son, while an adulterer was recognized and saved[499]

2.1.3.   We remind you of what happened in the past that you may be warned and be accounted in this Day among those who truly believe

3.   Counsel to the monks. "Say: O concourse of monks! Seclude not yourselves in your churches and cloisters;" come forth and busy yourselves "with what will profit you and others" (¶ 136)

3.1.   "Seclude yourselves in the stronghold of My love. This, truly, is the seclusion that befitteth you, could ye but know it"[500]

3.2.   "He that secludeth himself in his house is indeed as one dead"

3.3.   It is imperative for everyone to work toward the betterment of the human condition; whosoever "bringeth forth no fruit is fit for the fire"

3.4.   Enter into wedlock that you may bring forth progeny who will take your place in these beneficent endeavors

3.4.1.   We have forbidden lechery, "not that which is conducive to fidelity"

3.4.2.   Have ye clung unto the promptings of your nature, and cast behind your backs the statutes of God?

3.4.3.   But for humankind, who would remember Me and manifest My attributes on earth?

3.4.4.   Christ, Who married not, had no place to abide because of the treacherous acts perpetrated against Him

3.4.5.   His holiness consisted not in the things ye have believed and imagined [i.e. that He remained celibate and did not marry.], but rather in the things which belong unto Us

3.4.6.   Ask about these things [i.e. think for yourselves, don't rely on inherited dogma] that you may understand the true nature of His station, which transcends the "vain imaginings of all the peoples of the earth

4.   The King's involvement in the Crimean War, and his response to Bahá'u'lláh's first letter

4.1.   "O King!" We heard the words you said to the czar of Russia regarding the Crimean War—your Lord is omniscient—claiming that the reason for your attack was because you were awakened by the voices of the oppressed [Turks] drowned in the Black Sea,[501] when, in truth, it was but your own passions that prompted your attack, "for We tested thee, and found thee wanting" (¶ 137)[502]

4.2. While it is not our desire to address to you words of condemnation (out of regard for the station We have conferred upon you in this mortal life),[503] and courtesy is a divine attribute in all concerns, if you had been sincere, you would not have rejected and ignored the first tablet We sent you

4.3. While there is yet time, "[a]rise, and make amends for that which escaped thee" by setting aside the "dictates of thy desires," and by fearing My sighs and shielding Me from "such as act unjustly"[504]

4.4. Otherwise, "For what thou hast done, thy kingdom shall be thrown into confusion, and thine empire shall pass from thine hands, as a punishment for that which thou hast wrought" (¶ 138)[505]

4.5. "It behoveth thee when thou hearest His Voice calling from the seat of glory to cast away all that thou possessest, and cry out: 'Here am I, O Lord of all that is in heaven and all that is on earth!'"

5. What befell Bahá'u'lláh at the hands of the Ottoman authorities; response to the accusations against Him

5.1. "O King!" When We were in Iraq, We were summoned by Sulṭán 'Abdu'l-Azíz ["the King of Islám"] to proceed to Constantinople, where there befell Us "at the hands of the malicious that which the books of the world can never adequately recount" (¶ 139)

5.2. "Say," in response to those who "cavil at Him Who hath come unto you bearing the clear evidence of God and His proof," that "[t]hese things are not from Himself [note: this point is reiterated in the letter to the Sháh]; nay, rather they proceed from the One Who hath raised Him up, sent Him forth through the power of truth, and made Him to be a lamp unto all mankind"

5.3. From "day to day, nay, from hour to hour" our plight worsened until they took Us from our prison and "made Us, with glaring injustice, enter the Most Great Prison" (¶ 140)

5.4.   "And if anyone ask them: 'For what crime were they imprisoned?', they would answer and say: "They, verily, sought to supplant the Faith with a new religion!"

    5.4.1.   People, if you prefer that which is ancient, as opposed to this new Revelation, then why have you discarded the Torah and the New Testament?

    5.4.2.   If this be My crime, then Muhammad, the Apostle of God, committed it before Me, and before Him He Who was the Spirit of God [Christ], and yet earlier He Who conversed with God [Moses]

    5.4.3.   And if My sin be this, that I have exalted the Word of God and revealed His Cause, then indeed am I the greatest of sinners! Such a sin I will not barter for the kingdoms of earth and heaven

5.5.   Upon Our arrival at this Prison, We purposed to transmit to the kings the messages of their Lord, the Mighty, the All-Praised. Though We have transmitted to them, in several tablets, that which We were commanded, yet We do it once again as a token of God's grace. Perchance they may recognize the Lord, Who hath come down in the clouds with manifest sovereignty" (¶ 141)

5.6.   The more My tribulations increased, the greater became "My love for God and His Cause . . . in such wise that all that befell Me from the hosts of the wayward was powerless to deter Me from My purpose" (¶ 142)

    5.6.1.   I have "offered Myself up in the way of God"

    5.6.2.   "I yearn after tribulations in My love for Him, and for the sake of His good pleasure"

6.   The duty of the king to his people, and to the Cause of God

6.1.   As king, your subjects are "God's trust amongst you"; therefore, it is your job to watch over them as a good shepherd and not allow wolves to seize your flock "or pride and conceit to deter you from turning unto the poor and the desolate" (¶ 143)

6.2.   Were you to heed "the words of thy Lord," you would "be enabled to forsake all that thou dost possess and to proclaim My Name before all mankind"

6.3.   Therefore, cleanse your soul with "the waters of detachment"

6.4.   Bequeath your palaces to "the people of the graves," your empire to whoever desires it, and turn unto God, for this "is what

God hath chosen for thee."

6.5. Those who refuse to turn to the Countenance of God are as dead because they heed only their own "selfish desires"

6.6. Should you desire to shoulder the responsibilities of ruling your dominion, do it in order to aid the Cause of God, for whoever attains this station "hath attained unto all good that proceedeth from Him Who is the All-Knowing, the All-Wise"

6.7. Arise, therefore, in My name, and through the power of My sovereignty, stand before the peoples of the world and say (¶ 144):

6.7.1. "The Day is come, and the fragrances of God have been wafted over the whole of creation"

6.7.2. Whoso turns away from His Face is a victim of their own corrupt inclinations

6.7.3. Whoso turns away has gone astray

6.8. If you spread the news of My name and teach My Cause, God will exalt your name among all kings (¶ 145)[506]

6.8.1. Walk among men that you may "show forth His signs amidst the peoples of the earth"

6.8.2. Become inflamed with the undying "Fire" of this Cause that through you His love may be kindled within the hearts of His favored ones

6.8.3. "[E]nrapture the hearts of men through remembrance of Me"

7. The responsibility of all people to diffuse "the sweet savours of the rememberance of [God]," be detached from the world, act with justice and avoid hypocrisy

7.1. Anyone in this Day who does not do so is "unworthy of the station of man" and is of those who have acceded to their own desires and soon shall find themselves "in grievous loss" (¶ 146)

7.2. Does it behoove you to associate yourselves with the name of God yet commit "the things which the Evil One hath committed?"

7.2.1. Instead, "[p]urge your hearts from love of the world," defined as "that which turneth you aside from Him Who is the Dawning-Place of Revelation"

7.2.2. Eschew worldliness and "approach the Most Sublime Vision, this shining and resplendent Seat"

7.2.3. [However], you are welcome to partake of the benefits of this world "with justice"

7.3.   If your words differ from your deeds, how will you be distinguished from those who professed faith in God but rejected His Manifestation when He appeared? (¶ 147)

7.4.   Act with justice:

    7.4.1.   Shed not the blood of anyone

    7.4.2.   Judge not anyone unjustly

    7.4.3.   Wretched shall be the fate of those who sow discord in the land after the realm hath been well ordered

7.5.   "God hath prescribed unto everyone the duty of teaching His Cause" (¶ 148)

    7.5.1.   To do this, you must first adorn yourself with an upright character; otherwise, you will not influence the hearts of others

    7.5.2.   Do not exhort others to be just so long as you yourself are guilty of iniquity (¶ 149)

        7.5.2.1.   Do not commit acts that dishonor your name or the name of Our Cause

        7.5.2.2.   Be trustworthy and "[d]eal not treacherously with the substance of your neighbor" (¶ 149)

        7.5.2.3.   Don't withhold what you possess from the poor; God will double what ye possess

7.6.   When you teach, use the power of utterance [i.e. not the sword (coercion)] (¶ 150)

    7.6.1.   Don't argue or dispute with others

    7.6.2.   Whoso undertakes this endeavor with sincerity will be inspired and will inspire others

    7.6.3.   Win over the hearts with the "swords of wisdom and of utterance"

        7.6.3.1.   The sword of wisdom is hotter than summer heat

        7.6.3.2.   The sword of wisdom is sharper than blades of steel

        7.6.3.3.   Draw forth that sword in My name and through My might you will conquer the cities of the hearts

8.   Other laws and exhortations regarding conduct in this Day

8.1.   If you are aware of the sin of another, conceal it that God may conceal your own (¶ 151)

8.2.   Rich ones, if you encounter a poor one, treat him not disdainfully since everyone is created from the self-same substance

8.3. Truthfulness is a mighty virtue that will increase your stature among men and render you a "mighty recompense" from God

8.4. The laws from all previous Dispensations have attained consummation in the laws emanating from "this Most Great Ocean" (¶ 152)

8.5. The world is like the body that is "afflicted with divers ailments," the remedy for which is the "harmonizing of all its component elements." "Gather ye around that which we have prescribed unto you."

8.6. "All feasts have attained their consummation in the two Most Great Festivals [The Festival of Riḍván and the Declaration of the Báb], and in two other Festivals that fall on the twin days [The Birthdays of the Báb and Bahá'u'lláh]" (¶ 153)

    8.6.1. Other than these four days, do not withhold yourselves from your work or trade.

8.7. Priests and monks, shun not meat except during a "brief period" (¶ 154)

    8.7.1. "We have ordained a fast of nineteen days in the most temperate of the seasons, and have in this resplendent and luminous Dispensation relieved you from more than this"

8.8. Regard the whole human race "as one soul and one body"

9.   Final counsels to the King: reflect on the condition of the world, and how the people pursue things of no value

9.1. "Arise with the utmost steadfastness in the Cause of thy Lord, the All-Glorious" even as "thou [hast] been instructed in this wondrous Tablet," for "We, verily, have desired naught for thee save that which is better for thee than all that is on earth" (¶ 155)

9.2. "Meditate on the condition of the world and its people" (¶ 156):

    9.2.1. "He, for Whose sake the world was called into being," is imprisoned in 'Akká "by reason of that which the hands of the wayward have wrought," but from His imprisonment "He summoneth mankind unto the Dayspring of God"

    9.2.2. Meanwhile, you exult over what you possess even though you know all these things will perish

    9.2.3. You rejoice because you rule over "a span of earth" while in the estimation of "the people of Bahá" the material world in and of itself is worthless

9.2.3.1.   Abandon it to those who desire it

9.2.3.2.   Turn thou unto Him Who is the Desire of the world

9.2.3.3.   "Whither are gone the proud and their palaces? Gaze thou into their tombs, that thou mayest profit by this example, inasmuch as We made it a lesson unto every beholder"

9.2.3.4.   "Were the breezes of Revelation to seize thee, thou wouldst flee the world, and turn unto the Kingdom, and wouldst expend all thou possessest, that thou mayest draw nigh unto this sublime Vision"

9.2.3.5.   "We behold the generality of mankind worshipping names and exposing themselves, as thou dost witness, to dire perils in the mere hope of perpetuating their names" (¶ 157)

  9.2.3.5.a.   "[E]very perceiving soul testifieth that after death one's name shall avail him nothing except insofar as it beareth a relationship unto God, the Almighty, the All-Praised"

9.2.3.6.   "Consider the pettiness of men's minds":

  9.2.3.6.a.   "They seek with utmost exertion that which profiteth them not"

  9.2.3.6.b.   Were you to ask them if there is any advantage in that which they seek, they would be unable to respond with a reasonable answer

  9.2.3.6.c.   Whereas a "fair-minded" person would immediately answer, "Nay, by the Lord of the worlds!"

9.2.3.7.   "Such is the condition of the people and of that which they posses"

  9.2.3.7.a.   "Leave them in their folly"

  9.2.3.7.b.   "Turn thy sight unto God"

  9.2.3.7.c.   "Hearken then unto the counsel of thy Lord, and say: Lauded art Thou, O God of all who are in heaven and on earth!"

CZAR ALEXANDER II

1. Initial counsels to the Czar: his potential station, should he recognize Bahá'u'lláh

1.1. O Czar, listen to the voice of God and "[b]eware lest thy desire deter thee from turning towards the face of thy Lord, the Compassionate, the Most Merciful" (¶ 158)

1.2. Because We heard that for which you prayed to God, we mercifully answered thee

1.3. Because one of your ministers offered me assistance when I was imprisoned in the Síyáh-Chál, God hath ordained for you a station which you should be careful not to "barter away"

1.4. "Beware lest thy sovereignty withhold thee from Him Who is the Supreme Sovereign," who has come replete with signs, even as occurred in the past (¶ 159)

1.5. Arise among men "in the name of this all-compelling Cause" and summon the nations unto God (¶ 160)

1.6. Don't be confined to worshiping one of His names "when He Who is the Object of all names appeared"

1.7. Remember what happened when Herod condemned Christ; recall how God protected Christ and "sent Him down unto another land"

1.8. Blessed is the king "whom the veils of glory have not deterred from turning unto the Dayspring of beauty and who hath forsaken his all in his desire to obtain the things of God" (¶ 161)

2. Bahá'u'lláh alludes to His sufferings, His patience and joy, and the greatness of His message

2.1. "Hearken unto My voice that calleth from my prison" while I acquaint you with what has befallen Me, and My patience and forbearance, notwithstanding My power (¶ 162).

2.2. If you could perceive and understand the "treasuries of My Cause" and the "pearls of mysteries" that lie concealed in My words, you would "lay down your life in My path."

2.3. Know that although I am suffering physically at the hands of My foes, My spirit is filled with "a gladness with which all the joys of the earth can never compare."

2.4. My advent has caused (¶ 163):

2.4.1. The hearts of the Prophets and Messengers to rejoice

2.4.2.   The hands of the Messengers to be upraised in Their desire to meet Me

2.4.3.   Some to lament in their separation from Me (¶ 164)

2.4.4.   Others to endure hardships in My path

2.4.5.   And still others laid down their lives for the sake of My Beauty

3.   Bahá'u'lláh's fulfilment of scriptural prophecy

3.1.   My sole purpose is to extol God and not Myself

3.2.   "I am the One Whom the tongue of Isaiah hath extolled, the One with Whose name both the Torah and the Evangel were adorned"

3.3.   The scriptures have been revealed solely to presage My advent (¶ 165)

3.4.   Whosoever is receptive to the call of the scriptures "shall perceive therefrom the sweet fragrances of My name and My praise.

4.   Bahá'u'lláh counsels the Czar solely for the sake of God (¶ 166)

4.1.   The "malice and denial of all who dwell on earth" cannot harm Me

4.2.   "The allegiance of the entire creation" cannot profit Me

4.3.   We exhort you unto that which We were commanded

4.4.   We "desire naught from you except that ye draw nigh unto what shall profit you in both this world and the world to come"

4.5.   "Will ye slay Him Who summoneth you unto life everlasting?"

4.6.   "Fear ye God, and follow not every contumacious oppressor"

5.   Bahá'u'lláh counselfs the "proud ones of the earth" to renounce the things they possess and turn towards the Kingdom of God (¶ 167).

5.1.   "O proud ones of the earth! Do ye believe yourselves to be abiding in palaces whilst He Who is the King of Revelation resideth in the most desolate of abodes? Nay... In tombs do ye dwell, could ye but perceive it"

5.2.   To fail "to be stirred by the breeze of God" is to be "accounted among the dead in the sight of" God

5.3.   " Arise, then, from the tombs of self and desire and turn unto the Kingdom of God, the Possessor of the Throne on high and of earth below, that ye may behold that which ye were promised aforetime by your Lord, the All-Knowing"

5.4. The riches you have amassed shall not profit you or sustain you (¶ 168)

    5.4.1. Soon others will possess them after you return to the dust from which you came

    5.4.2. What value is there in

        5.4.2.1. "a life that can be overtaken by death"

        5.4.2.2. "an existence that is doomed to extinction"

        5.4.2.3. "a prosperity that is subject to change?"

5.5. Cast away these possessions and set your face toward "the favours of God which have been sent down in this wondrous Name."

6. Final counsels to the Czar

6.1. Once you have heard and recited these "melodies" from "the Pen of the Most High," say: "Praise be unto Thee, O Lord of all the worlds, inasmuch as Thou hast made mention of me through the tongue of Him Who is the Manifestation of Thy Self at a time when He was confined in the Most Great Prison, that the whole world might attain unto true liberty" (¶ 169)

6.2. Blessed is the king who turns his heart toward God and acts as bidden by God

    6.2.1. "Erelong will such a one find himself numbered with the monarchs of the realms of the Kingdom"

    6.2.2. "Thy Lord is, in truth, potent over all things"

QUEEN VICTORIA

1. Initial counsels to the Queen, to "[i]ncline thine ear unto the voice of thy Lord" (¶ 171)

1.1. "[A]ttire the head of thy kingdom with the crown of the remembrance of thy Lord, the All-Glorious"

1.2. He hath come in His most great glory, and

    1.2.1. "all that hath been mentioned in the Gospel hath been fulfilled"

    1.2.2. "[t]he land of Syria hath been honoured by the footsteps of its Lord"

    1.2.3. "[t]he Mosque of Aqsá vibrateth through the breezes of its Lord"

1.2.4.   "Bathá [Mecca] trembleth at the voice of God."

1.3.   "Lay aside thy desire, and set then thine heart towards thy Lord, the Ancient of Days. We make mention of thee for the sake of God, and the desire that thy name be exalted through thy remembrance of God" (¶ 172)

2.   Bahá'u'lláh's praise for the Queen

2.1.   "We have been informed that thou hast forbidden the trading in slaves;" this is "what God hath enjoined in this wondrous Revelation."

    2.1.1.   You will be rewarded for this even, as will all who follow what hath been enjoined

    2.1.2.   Those who turn aside from this Revelation, God shall bring their works to naught

    2.1.3.   Actions are acceptable after one recognizes the Manifestation

2.2.   "We have also heard that thou hast entrusted the reins of counsel into the hands of the representatives of the people" (¶ 173)

    2.2.1.   This is wise, for "thereby the foundations of the edifice of thine affairs will be strengthened"

    2.2.2.   However, it behooves these representatives

        2.2.2.1.   to be trustworthy

        2.2.2.2.   "to regard themselves as the representatives of all that dwell on earth"

        2.2.2.3.   to pray to God for guidance before entering the Assembly—"O my God! I ask Thee, by Thy most glorious Name, to aid me in that which will cause the affairs of Thy servants to prosper, and Thy cities to flourish"

        2.2.2.4.   to enter the Assembly for the sake of God

        2.2.2.5.   to judge between men "with pure justice"

3.   Bahá'u'lláh's counsels for "the elected representatives of the people in every land" (¶ 174), and the human body analogy

3.1.   Consult together, concerned only with what will profit humankind and improve its conditions

3.2.   "Regard the world as the human body which, though at its creation whole and perfect, hath been afflicted, through various causes, with grave disorders and maladies"

    3.2.1.   Its "sickness waxed more severe" at the hands of

"ignorant physicians, who gave full rein to their personal desires and have erred grievously"

3.2.2.   And if a member of the body was healed by an able physician, the rest of the body remained afflicted

3.2.3.   Unworthy motives—i.e. self-interest—limit the power of rulers to improve this body's condition, even when they strive to do so (¶ 175)

4.   Bahá'u'lláh presents the remedy for the "human body" that is the world, and explains the obstacles to this remedy taking effect

4.1.   The remedy which "the Lord hath ordained" is the "union of all [the world's] peoples in one universal Cause, one common Faith" (¶ 176), something that can be achieved only through the power of the Manifestation ("an all-powerful and inspired Physician")

4.2.   The Manifestation's remedy has historically been withheld by "ignorant physicians," like clouds that "interposed themselves between Him and the world"

4.3.   Consider these days when the "Ancient Beauty" hath come in "The Most Great Name" to "quicken the world and unite its peoples" (¶ 177)

4.3.1.   They arose against Him, and imprisoned Him, and separated Him from the faithful

4.3.2.   Were they told "The World Reformer is come," they would assert, "He is a fomenter of discord!" even though they have never met Him

4.3.3.   They banished Him, imprisoned Him, moved Him from land to land

4.4.   Those who thus "pronounced judgement" against the Physician are "among the most ignorant of [God's] creatures"

4.4.1.   "They cut off their own limbs and perceive it not"

4.4.2.   "They are even as a young child who can distinguish neither the mischief-maker from the reformer nor the wicked from the righteous"

4.4.3.   They are "wrapt in a palpable veil"

5.   Bahá'u'lláh's admonitions to the rulers of the earth to act with justice towards their people, to establish the Lesser Peace amongst themselves, and to treat Bahá'u'lláh Himself with justice

5.1.   "O ye rulers of the earth! Wherefore have ye clouded the radiance of the Sun, and caused it to cease from shining?" (¶ 178)

5.2.   "We beseech God to assist you in establishing peace"

5.3.   "We see you increasing every year your expenditures and laying the burden thereof on your subjects," which is "wholly and grossly unjust" (¶ 179)

    5.3.1.   You care only for yourselves when "[y]our people are your treasures"

    5.3.2.   It is only by them that you rule, subsist, and conquer

    5.3.3.   How strange, then, that you disdain them

5.4.   "Now that ye have refused the Most Great Peace, hold ye fast unto this, the Lesser Peace, that haply ye may in some degree better your own condition and that of your dependents" (¶ 180)

    5.4.1.   "Be reconciled among yourselves, that ye may need no more armaments save in a measure to safeguard your territories and dominions" (¶ 181)

    5.4.2.   "Be united, O kings of the earth, for thereby will the tempest of discord be stilled amongst you, and your peoples find rest" (¶ 182)

        5.4.2.1.   To ensure unity among you, agree that "should any one among you take up arms against another, rise ye all against him, for this is naught but manifest justice"

5.5.   "Should anyone seek refuge with you, extend unto him your protection and betray him not"

    5.5.1.   Beware not to do as did the Ottoman Sultan (the "King of Islám) did when we came to him at his bidding. "His ministers pronounced judgement against Us with such injustice that all creation lamented and the hearts of those who are nigh unto God were consumed" (¶ 183)

6.   Final counsels to the Queen

6.1.   "Rein in Thy pen, O Pen of the Ancient of Days, and leave them to themselves, for they are immersed in their idle fancies," but "Make Thou mention of the Queen, that she may turn with a pure heart unto the scene of transcendent glory, may withhold not her eyes from gazing toward her Lord, the Supreme Ordainer" (¶ 184)

6.2.   Queen, "[t]urn thou unto God" and recite this prayer (¶ 185):

    6.2.1.   "O my Sovereign Lord! I am but a vassal of Thine,

and Thou art, in truth, the King of kings. I have lifted my suppliant hands unto the heaven of Thy grace and Thy bounties. Send down, then, upon me from the clouds of Thy generosity that which will rid me of all save Thee, and draw me nigh unto Thyself"

6.2.2. "[R]end asunder the veils that have intervened between me and my recognition of [the Manifestation]"

6.2.3. "Deprive me not… of the fragrances of the Robe of Thy mercy in Thy days, and write down for me that which Thou hast written down for Thy handmaidens who have believed in Thee and in Thy signs, and have recognized Thee, and set their hearts towards the horizon of Thy Cause"

6.2.4. "Assist me… to remember Thee… and to aid Thy Cause in Thy lands"

6.2.5. Accept that "which hath escaped me when the light of Thy countenance shone forth"

NASÍRI'D-DÍN SHÁH

1. Bahá'u'lláh begins by explaining to the King that He is a "Vassal," a "Servant," Who has suffered for His servitude and love for God

1.1. "O King of the Earth! Hearken unto the call of this Vassal: Verily, I am a Servant Who hath believed in God and in His signs, and have sacrificed Myself in His path" (¶ 186)

1.2. "Unto this bear witness the woes which now beset Me, woes the like of which no man hath ever before sustained"

1.3. "I have summoned the people unto none save God… and have endured for love of Him such afflications as the eye of creation never beheld"

1.4. "To this testify those whom the veils of human fancy have not deterred from turning unto the Most Sublime Vision, and, beyond them, He with Whom is the knowledge of all things in the preserved Tablet"

1.5. "Whensoever the clouds of tribulation have rained down the darts of affliction in the path of God, the Lord of all names, I have hastened to meet them" (¶ 187)

1.6. "How many the nights which found the beasts of the field resting in their lairs, and the birds of the air lying in their nests, while this Youth languished in chains and fetters with none to aid or succor Him!"

2. Bahá'u'lláh is called upon to recall His initial imprisonment and exile, and then reminds the King that He is not seditious, that the King should treat all with justice, and that God is powerful to do "as He pleaseth"

2.1. "Call Thou to mind God's mercy unto Thee;" when Thou wert imprisoned, He delivered Thee and aided Thee with the hosts of the seen and the unseen (¶ 188)

2.2. Then "the king sent Thee to 'Iráq after We had disclosed unto him that Thou wert not of the sowers of sedition"

    2.2.1. "They that spread disorder in the land, shed the blood of men, and wrongfully consume the substance of others— We, verily, are clear of them, and We beseech God not to associate Us with them"

        2.2.1.1. But if they repent, God "is of, those who show mercy, the most merciful"

    2.2.2. Whosoever turns toward God should distinguish himself by his deeds and by following the laws of the Book (¶ 189).

    2.2.3. Whosoever ignores the commandments of God and follows his own desires is in grievous error.

2.3. "O King! I adjure thee by thy Lord, the All-Merciful, to look upon thy servants with the glances of the eye of thy favour, and to treat them with justice, that God may treat thee with mercy" (¶ 190)

2.4. The world with "its abasement and glory" will pass away, and the kingdom will remain in the hands of God

2.5. God has "kindled the lamp of utterance, and feedeth it with the oil of wisdom and understanding" (¶ 191)

    2.5.1. He reveals "what He pleaseth and protecteth it with a host of His well-favoured angels"

    2.5.2. "He is supreme over His servants and exerciseth undisputed dominion over His creation. He, verily, is the All-Knowing, the All-Wise"

3. Bahá'u'lláh proclaims that His knowledge is from God, Who has commanded Him to reveal His Cause

3.1. "O King! I was but a man like others, asleep upon My couch, when lo, the breezes of the All-Glorious were wafted over Me, and taught Me the knowledge of all that hath been" (¶ 192)

    3.1.1.   I am not a learned scholar; my knowledge does not come from some ordinary human source of learning, as you (the King) can yourself ascertain

    3.1.2.   This inspiration does not come from Me, but from God Himself Who commanded Me to reveal these teachings. I cannot do otherwise; I am "a leaf which the winds of the will of thy Lord... have stirred... They move it as they list."

    3.1.3.   The hand of God transformed Me

    3.1.4.   Only God could empower anyone to speak what I have spoken: "Can anyone speak forth of his own accord that for which all men, both high and low, will protest against him? Nay, by Him Who taught the Pen the eternal mysteries, save him whom the grace of the Almighty, the All-Powerful, hath strengthened"

  3.2.   God commands Me to speak to you (the King) now (¶ 193):

    3.2.1.   "The Pen of the Most High addresseth Me, saying: Fear not. Relate unto His Majesty the Sháh that which befell thee. His heart, verily, is between the fingers of thy Lord, the God of Mercy, that haply the sun of justice and bounty may shine forth above the horizon of his heart"

4.   The station of the King, his duty to be just, Bahá'u'lláh's disinterested love for the King, and what he can achieve by heeding the Voice of God

  4.1.   "God hath made thee His shadow amongst men and the sign of His power unto all that dwell on earth" (¶ 194)

  4.2.   How the King should appraise Bahá'u'lláh—with justice:

    4.2.1.   "Look upon this Youth, O King, with the eyes of justice"

    4.2.2.   "judge thou, then, with truth concerning what hath befallen Him"

    4.2.3.   "Judge thou between Us and them that have wronged Us without proof and without an enlightening Book"

  4.3.   The uniqueness of Bahá'u'lláh's love for the King

    4.3.1.   "They that surround thee love thee for their own sakes"

    4.3.2.   "this Youth loveth thee for thine own sake, and hath had no desire except"

      4.3.2.1.   "to draw thee nigh unto the seat of grace"

4.3.2.2.   "to turn thee toward the right hand of justice"

4.4.   If you "incline thine ear unto the shrill of the Pen of Glory and the cooing of the Dove of Eternity" then you would (¶ 195):

    4.4.1.   attain a station from which you would see nothing in the "world of being" except "the effulgence of the Adored One"

    4.4.2.   "regard thy sovereignty as the most contemptible of thy posessions"

        4.4.2.1.   abandon it to whoever desires it

    4.4.3.   turn your face toward "the Horizon aglow with the light of His countenance"

    4.4.4.   never be willing to bear the burden of kingship except to help thy Lord

    4.4.5.   be blessed by the Concourse on high

5.   Bahá'u'lláh rehearses the charges made against Him, and refutes them

5.1.   Some assert that I seek to perpetrate My own fame or acquire the vanities of this world—this is disproven ("this, notwithstanding that...") by the facts (¶ 196):

    5.1.1.   Never have I found a place of safety

    5.1.2.   I have always been immersed in a sea of tribulations

    5.1.3.   How many days and nights have My loved ones been "sorely shaken by reason of My afflictions" and My kindred wept in their fear for My life?

    5.1.4.   "Is it conceivable that He who expecteth to lose His life at any moment should seek after worldly vanities?"

    5.1.5.   The source of such accusations: "How very strange the imaginings of those who speak as prompted by their own caprices, and who wander distractedly in the wilderness of self and passion!"

        5.1.5.1.   "Erelong shall they be called upon to account for their words, and on that day they shall find none to befriend or help them"

5.2.   Others claim that We have disbelieved in God; and yet "every member of My body testifieth" (¶ 197):

    5.2.1.   "that there is none other God but Him;

    5.2.2.   that those Whom He hath raised up in truth and sent forth with His guidance are

        5.2.2.1.   the Manifestations of His most excellent names

        5.2.2.2.   the Revealers of His most exalted attributes

        5.2.2.3.   and the Repositories of His Revelation in the kingdom of creation"

     5.2.3.   "That through them [the Manifestations]

        5.2.3.1.   the Proof of God hath been perfected unto all else but Him

        5.2.3.2.   the standard of Divine Unity hath been raised

        5.2.3.3.   and the sign of sanctity hath been made manifest

        5.2.3.4.   and . . . every soul hath found a path unto the Lord of the Throne on high"

  5.3.   In refutation of the claim of disbelief in God, Bahá'u'lláh further testifies:

     5.3.1.   that there is none other God but Him

     5.3.2.   that from everlasting He was alone with none else besides Him

     5.3.3.   and that He shall be unto everlasting what He hath ever been

     5.3.4.   That God is too high for any to apprehend His true nature or fathom His essence

     5.3.5.   He verily is

        5.3.5.1.   exalted above the understanding of anyone besides Himself

        5.3.5.2.   and sanctified beyond the comprehension of all else save Him

     5.3.6.   that "[f]rom all eternity He hath been independent of the entire creation"

6.   Bahá'u'lláh reminds the King of the treatment of Muḥammad by the learned, and of a king who recognized the truth of the Prophet's Reveleation, before reiterating the station the can achieve if he heeds the "Nightingale"

  6.1.   Remember the days of Muḥammad, so that you can in this day understand what is presently "concealed behind the veils of glory" (¶ 198)

     6.1.1.   "[T]he divines of that age turned away from Him, and the learned contended with Him"

     6.1.2.   He thus commanded His disciples to disperse to different lands

     6.1.3.   When one group appeared before the king of Ethiopia and recited a verse from the Qur'án, He instantly recognized these verses as being "revealed by One Who is All-Knowing and All-Wise," and as embodying the same truth as the teachings of Christ

6.2.   "O King! Wert thou [like that Ethiopian king] to incline thine ear to the melodies of that Nightingale which warbleth... as bidden by thy Lord . . . thou wouldst (¶ 199)

    6.2.1.   cast away thy sovereignty

    6.2.2.   and set thy face towards this Scene of transcendent glory . . .

    6.2.3.   expend all that thou possessest in thine eagerness to obtain the things of God

    6.2.4.   Then wouldst thou find thyself raised up to the summit of exaltation and glory, and elevated to the pinnacle of majesty and independence"

6.3.   The nature of the choice before the king is crystallized:

    6.3.1.   "Of what avail are the things which are yours today and which tomorrow others shall possess?"

    6.3.2.   " Choose for thyself that which God hath chosen for His elect, and God shall grant thee a mighty sovereignty in His Kingdom"

    6.3.3.   We beseech God to help you hearken unto "that Word whose radiance hath enveloped the whole world"

7.   The first of four prayers[507] in the Tablet—for the peoples of the world to recognize the Manifestation

7.1.   The prayer begins with a recital of the suffering endured for the Cause of God (¶ 200). How many:

    7.1.1.   "the heads which were raised aloft on spears in Thy path"

    7.1.2.   "the breasts which were made the target of arrows for the sake of Thy good pleasure"

    7.1.3.   "the hearts that have been lacerated for the exaltation of Thy Word and the promotion of Thy Cause"

    7.1.4.   "the eyes that have wept sore for love of Thee!"

7.2.   Bahá'u'lláh implores God to:

    7.2.1.   "remove the veils that have come in between Thee and Thy creatures and debarred them from turning unto the horizon of Thy Revelation"

    7.2.2.   "[c]ause them [Thy creatures] . . . by Thy most exalted Word, to turn... unto the right hand of knowledge and certitude" so that they "may set their faces toward Him Who is the Manifestation of Thy Cause and the Revealer of Thy signs"

8. **Second prayer**—for God to be bountiful to humanity

8.1. "[w]ithhold not Thy servants" from the ocean of Revelation that contains the pearls of "Thy knowledge and Thy wisdom" (¶ 201)

8.2. "turn them not away from Thy gate, which Thou hast opened wide before all who are in Thy heaven and all who are on Thy earth"

8.3. "[l]eave them not to themselves" because they don't understand and flee from that which is better for them "than all that Thou hast created upon Thine earth"

8.4. be bountiful to them and "deliver them from self and passion" that they may

8.4.1. "draw nigh unto Thy most exalted Horizon,

8.4.2. taste the sweetness of Thy remembrance,

8.4.3. and delight in that bread which Thou hast sent down from the heaven of Thy Will and the firmament of Thy grace"

9. **Third prayer**—calling God to witness the purity of Bahá'u'lláh's motive, including in what He wishes for the king

9.1. "Thou well knowest" that My blood cries out to be spilt for love of Thee (¶ 202)

9.2. "Thou knowest, O My God," that I have only ever sought to obey You, to praise You, to win Your good pleasure, and to reveal what You have commanded Me to reveal (¶ 203)

9.3. "Thou beholdest Me, O My God, as one bewildered in Thy land." The people cavil at Me when I speak as You have commanded, but were I to neglect my duty in this, I would deserve Thine anger. I choose "Thy good pleasure" (¶ 204)

9.3.1. "With Thy love in My heart nothing can ever alarm Me, and in the path of Thy good pleasure all the world's afflications can in no wise dismay Me"

9.4. "This is an Epistle, O My God, which I have purposed to send unto the King." You know that I wish nothing from him "but that he should show forth justice to Thy servants and extend his favours unto the people of Thy kingdom" (¶ 205)

9.5.   "For Myself I have desired only what Thou didst desire":

    9.5.1.   "Perish the soul that seekest from Thee aught save Thyself!"

    9.5.2.   "Have mercy, O My God, upon this poor creature Who hath clung to the hem of Thy riches"

9.6.   "Assist Thou, O My God, his majesty the Sh<u>á</u>h to keep Thy statutes amidst Thy servants and to manifest Thy justice amongst Thy creatures, that he may treat this people as he treateth others"

10.   Bahá'u'lláh explains to the <u>Sh</u>áh the events that followed His exile to Iráq, demonstrating His unfailing loyalty to the government, and His utter repudiation in word and deed of sedition and disorder

   10.1.   Events in Iráq

      10.1.1.   "[T]his Servant" dwelt in Iráq for twelve years (¶ 206)

      10.1.2.   We asked for nothing from those in power during this time: "no account of Our condition was submitted to the court of thy presence, and no representation ever made to foreign powers.

      10.1.3.   Then a Persian official [the Persian Consul-General in Iráq] arrived and began to harass the Bábís ["this poor company of exiles"] though "they had at no time committed any act detrimental to the state and its people or contrary to the rules and customs of the citizens of the realm"

      10.1.4.   Fearing " some outcome [from these unjust actions] at variance with thy world-adorning judgement," I dispatched a brief account of the matter to Mírzá Sa'íd Khán [the Persian Foreign Minister] that he might convey it to you [the Sháh], and you could then take whatever action you thought appropriate

      10.1.5.   You issued no decree. Finally, tensions increased to the point of possible bloodshed, whereupon a few Bábís appealed to the governor of Iraq for the protection of Ottoman citizenship

      10.1.6.   If you were to examine these events fairly, you would agree that there was no alternative (¶ 208)

         10.1.6.1.   "His Majesty himself is witness that in whatever city a number of this people have resided, the hostility of certain functionaries hath enkindled the flame of conflict and contention"

      10.1.7.   "This evanescent Soul, however, hath, since His arrival in Iraq, forbidden all to engage in dissension and strife"

    10.1.7.1.   The deeds of this Servant bear witness to this fact

    10.1.7.2.   Although more Bábís lived in Iraq than any other land, none overstepped their limits or transgressed against their neighbors

    10.1.7.3.   For fifteen years now, all have dwelled in peace and "have shown forth patience and resigned themselves to God"

10.2. Events in Adrianople, and an explanation of the term "rendering assistance unto God"

    10.2.1. "After the arrival of this Servant in this, the city of Adrianople, some of the people of 'Iráq and elsewhere inquired about the meaning of the term "rendering assistance unto God" which hath been mentioned in the Holy Scriptures" (¶ 209)

    10.2.2. Here is one of the answers that were sent in reply, "that it may be clearly demonstrated in the court of thy presence that this Servant hath had no end in view but to promote the betterment and well-being of the world"

    10.2.3. "Rendering assistance unto God" does not mean "that any soul should fight or contend with another," for (¶ 210):

        10.2.3.1.   God is sanctified above the world and everything in it,

        10.2.3.2.   He has entrusted the kingdom of creation into the hands of kings because they manifest His divine power "each according to his degree,"

        10.2.3.3.   God desires for Himself the hearts of men, which are the repositories of His "love and remembrance" and "His knowledge and wisdom" (¶ 211)

            10.2.3.3.a. His goal in this is to cleanse the hearts of men from worldly desires that they might become "worthy recipients of the effulgent splendours of Him Who is the King of all names and attributes"

            10.2.3.3.b. Therefore, no stranger should be "allowed in the city of the heart, that the incomparable Friend may enter His abode"

    10.2.4. It follows, then, that "rendering assistance unto God" in this day implies not "contending or disputing with any soul," but (¶ 212):

    10.2.4.1.   Before all else, that the one who seeks to assist God should "conquer, with the sword of inner meaning and explanation, the city of his own heart"

        10.2.4.1.a. And "only then" setting out "to subdue the cities of the hearts of others," again with the "sword of utterance, of wisdom and of understanding"

10.2.5. Sedition or other foolish acts committed in the past "hath never been pleasing unto God" (¶ 213)

    10.2.5.1.   "[T]o be killed in the path of His good pleasure is better for you than to kill"

    10.2.5.2.   In this day, the beloved of God must act in such a manner that "their very deeds and actions guide all men unto the paradise of the All-Glorious"

10.2.6. "The friends of God have not, nor will they ever, set their hopes upon the world and its ephemeral possessions"

10.2.7. God's regarding men's hearts as His own is "but an expression of His all-surpassing mercy, that haply mortal souls may be purged and sanctified from all that pertaineth to the world of dust and gain admittance into the realms of eternity" (¶ 214)

    10.2.7.1.   God neither requires our love nor is hurt by our malice, for "that ideal King is, in Himself and by Himself, sufficient unto Himself and independent of all things"

10.2.8. Having concluded the explanation of "rendering assistance unto God," Bahá'u'lláh reminds the Sháh of his duty: "It behoveth the benevolence of the Sovereign, however, to examine all matters with the eye of justice and mercy, and not to content himself with the baseless claims of certain individuals" (¶ 215)

10.3. Events in Constantinople

    10.3.1. In Constantinople, with a company of exiles, We did not seek to meet with anyone " as We had no request to make and no aim in view but to demonstrate unto all that this Servant had no mischief in mind and had never associated with the sowers of sedition" (¶ 216)

10.3.2. Although it was difficult to "make application to any quarter, such steps were perforce taken to protect certain souls"

11. Bahá'u'lláh presents arguments as to why justice requires the Sháh to view the community of His followers favourably

11.1. He opens by explaining the station of a "just king" as "the shadow of God on earth, under whose justice "all should seek shelter" (¶ 217)

11.1.1. The king's favor should not be restricted to certain individuals and withheld from others, for "the shadow telleth of the One Who casteth it," i.e. God, who "nurtureth everyone"

11.2. He then explains that the character, nature, and motive of the followers of this Cause are plain to see and beyond reproach

11.3. First, independent of what one thinks of the rightness or wrongness of the Cause itself, its followers are obviously sincere and devoted (¶ 218):

11.3.1. "those who are associated with its name have accepted and embraced it as true and have forsaken their all in their eagerness to partake of the things of God"

11.3.2. "such renunciation in the path of the love of the All-Merciful is in itself a faithful witness and an eloquent testimony to the truth of their convictions"

11.3.3. no one of "sound judgement" would "sacrifice his life without cause or reason"

11.3.3.1. and any claim that "this people have taken leave of their senses" is "highly improbable" given that not "merely a soul or two" but "a vast multitude of every class . . . have hastened with heart and soul to the field of sacrifice in the way of the Beloved"

11.3.4. If the followers of this Cause who have renounced all else but God be "accounted as false," than by what proof "can the truth of what others assert be established" (¶ 219)?

11.3.4.1. Compare them to the late Hájí Siyyid Muḥammad—"one of the most learned divines . . . and one of the most devout and pious men of his time"— who ultimately he gave up the holy war he had declared against Russia after only "the inconvenience of a brief encounter"

11.3.5. For more than twenty years (1844–1870) this people has been subjected to the wrath of the king (¶ 220):

    11.3.5.1.   They have been scattered to different lands

    11.3.5.2.   Their children have been orphaned

    11.3.5.3.   Parents have lost their children

    11.3.5.4.   Mothers have been unable to mourn their offspring

    11.3.5.5.   Many have fallen in a single day from wealth and prosperity to "utter abasement and destitution!"

11.3.6. Through all this, they have not wavered; "even should their bodies be torn asunder they would not forsake their love of Him Who is the Best-Beloved of the worlds, but would welcome with heart and soul whatever might befall them in the path of God"

11.4. Next, consider the nature of the claims made against theses souls, and those who make such claims

11.4.1. Some "outwardly learned" have "troubled the heart" of the king regarding these innocent and dedicated souls (¶ 221)

    11.4.1.1.   Would that his majesty might decree that this Servant be brought before these "learned ones" and "produce proofs… in the presence of His Majesty the Sháh!"

    11.4.1.2.   This Servant is ready for such a gathering to clarify "the truth of the matter"

    11.4.1.3.   It is for the king to command such a gathering, through which he could "[d]ecide, then, for Me or against Me"

11.4.2. Recall that in the Qur'án the Prophet proclaims to the world: "Wish ye then for death, if ye be men of truth" (2:94) (¶ 222)

    11.4.2.1.   "He hath declared the yearning for death to be the touchstone of sincerity!" (¶ 222)

    11.4.2.2.   Surely it is obvious to you which people have chosen to lay down their lives in the path of God

    11.4.2.3.   Were books to be written, supporting the beliefs of these people, with the blood spilled in the path of God, countless volumes would already have appeared

11.4.3. How it is possible to impugn those "whose deeds are in conformity with their words," while accepting as truthful the assertions of those who have not sacrificed "one jot of their worldly authority in the path of Him Who is the Unconstrained?" (¶ 223)

11.4.4. Some divines who have declared Me an infidel have never even met Me nor have they become acquainted with My purpose

    11.4.4.1. "Yet every claim requireth a proof, not mere words and displays of outward piety"

11.5. "In this connection"—i.e. the discussion of those "learned" who accuse Bahá'u'lláh without having met Him or learned His purpose—Bahá'u'lláh cites several passages from the Hidden Words that address those who, "though outwardly known for learning and piety, are inwardly the slaves of self and passion" (¶ 224-228)

    11.5.1. "O ye that are foolish, yet have a name to be wise! Wherefore do ye wear the guise of the shepherd, when inwardly ye have become wolves, intent upon My flock?" (Persian Hidden Words #24)

    11.5.2. "O ye seeming fair yet inwardly foul! Ye are like clear but bitter water" (Persian Hidden Words #25)

    11.5.3. "O essence of desire! At many a dawn have I turned from the realms of the Placeless unto thine abode, and found thee on the bed of ease busied with others than Myself" (Persian Hidden Words #28)

    11.5.4. "O bondslave of the world! Many a dawn hath the breeze of My loving-kindness wafted over thee and found thee upon the bed of heedlessness fast asleep" (Persian Hidden Words #30)

11.6. "[R]oyal justice" requires that the Sháh not listen only to the words of the "claimant" [i.e. those who accuse Bahá'u'lláh and His followers] (¶ 229)

    11.6.1. The Qur'án supports this point: "O ye who believe! If a wicked man come to you with news, clear it up at once, lest through ignorance ye harm others, and afterward repent of what ye have done" (Qur'án 49:6)

    11.6.2. Among the ḥadíth is this admonition: "Believe not the tale-bearer"

11.6.3. Those who have never met Us have "misconceived the nature of Our Cause;" however, those who have met Us will testify that this Servant has

    11.6.3.1. "not spoken save in accordance with that which God hath commanded in the Book"

    11.6.3.2. called attention to the verse: "Do ye not disavow us only because we believe in God, and in what He hath sent down unto us, and in what He had sent down aforetime?" (Qur'án 5:59)

11.7. "[T]hese refugees" are confident that God's mercy will eventually end their tribulations. But for the king's own sake—his "highest good"—We nevertheless hope that the Sháh himself "will examine these matters and bring hope to the hearts" (¶ 230)

    11.7.1. A brief prayer to that effect: " Glorified art Thou, O Lord My God! I bear witness that the heart of the King is in truth between the fingers of Thy might. If it be Thy wish, do Thou incline it, O My God, in the direction of charity and mercy" (¶ 231)

12. Bahá'u'lláh sets out the prerequisites of the learned, and evaluates the divines of this age against that standard

12.1. The prerequisites of the learned [as set out in a Tradition attributed to the eleventh Imám] require that he (¶ 232):

    12.1.1. guardeth his self

    12.1.2. defendeth his faith

    12.1.3. opposeth his desires

    12.1.4. and obeyeth his Lord's command, it is incumbent upon the generality of the people to pattern themselves after him"

12.2. If the king will reflect on these verses, he will realize that those possessing these attributes are "scarcer than the philosopher's stone;" therefore, not everyone who lays claim to knowledge should be believed. Bahá'u'lláh cites a number of hadíth in support of this claim:

    12.2.1. "the divines of the Latter Days . . . 'shall be the most wicked of the divines beneath the shadow of heaven. Out of them hath mischief proceeded, and unto them it shall return'" (¶ 233)

    12.2.2. Another Tradition [attributed to the sixth Imám] states: "When the Standard of Truth is made manifest, the people of both the East and the West curse it"

12.2.3. Should anyone dispute the authenticity of these traditions, this Servant will gladly prove their validity

12.3. The learned who "have drunk of the cup of renunciation have never interfered with this Servant" (¶ 234)

    12.3.1. <u>Shaykh</u> Murtadá, for example, showed us kindness when We were in Iraq and never spoke ill of this Cause

13.   Bahá'u'lláh discusses specific dimensions of the injustice facing His followers:

13.1. People persecute them as a means to obtain royal favour (¶ 235)

    13.1.1. If you were to ask some of those who enjoy the <u>Sh</u>áh's favour what service they can render in return, they will simply "designate justly or falsely, a group of people before thy royal presence as Bábís, and forthwith to engage in massacre and pillage"

        13.1.1.1.   Examples given of such injustice in Tabríz and in the Egyptian town of Mansúríyyih, no account of which was given to the <u>Sh</u>áh

13.2. They are not given the basic protections that the State extends to other groups (¶ 236)

    13.2.1. This is why persecutors are emboldened to harass "this afflicted people"

    13.2.2. "Numerous confessions and divers creeds abide peacefully beneath the shadow of thy sovereignty. Let this people be also numbered with them"

        13.2.2.1.   Indeed, let all those who serve the king strive "to bring all religions beneath the shelter of his shadow, and to rule over them with perfect justice"

13.3. It is unjust for a whole community to be punished for the wrongdoing of an individual member (¶ 237)[508]

    13.3.1. "To enforce the laws of God is naught but justice, and is the source of universal content"

    13.3.2. However, to punish an entire group for the trespass of a single soul does not befit the <u>Sh</u>áh's justice

    13.3.3. In any group there are two sorts:

        13.3.3.1.   the "wise and reflecting soul" is unlikely to commit a heinous deed, because he either:

            13.3.3.1.a. Has forsaken the world, cares only for God, and will be restrained by the fear of God; or

13.3.3.1.b.   Seeks after the world, and will thus act in such a way as to earn the trust of the people and avoid deeds that would "alienate and alarm the people"

13.3.3.2.   "ignorant and foolish souls," who it is therefore evident are the ones from whom "reprehensible actions have always emanated, and will ever emanate"

13.3.4. A brief prayer for Naṣíri'd-Dín S͟háh, that he be guided and strengthened to "assist Thy Cause" (¶ 238)

13.3.4.1.   "Thou hearest the voice of My lamentation, and beholdest My condition, My distress and affliction!"

13.3.4.2.   Draw toward Thee the hearts of Thy creatures and the heart of the S͟háh

13.3.4.3.   Supply him [the S͟háh] with spiritual sustenance that he may forsake all else and turn toward "the court of Thy favor."

13.3.4.4.   Aid him "to assist Thy Cause and to exalt Thy Word amidst Thy creatures"

13.3.4.5.   "Strengthen him, then, with the hosts of the seen and the unseen, that he may subdue every city in Thy Name, and hold sway, through Thy sovereignty and might, over all that dwell on earth"

13.3.5. A continuation of the theme of the Cause/ the community / Bahá'u'lláh Himself being held responsible for every wrong act of any adherent (¶ 239):

13.3.5.1.   "So grossly hath Our Cause been misrepresented before thy royal presence that, if some unseemly act be committed by but one of this people, it is portrayed as being prompted by their beliefs. By Him besides Whom there is none other God! This Servant hath refused even to sanction the commission of reproved actions, how much less those which have been explicitly prohibited in the Book of God"

13.3.5.2.   God hath forbidden the drinking of wine, yet some still imbibe; the punishment for this act "applieth only to its heedless perpetrators," not to those "learned doctors of the age" who have "prohibited the people from such a wretched act"

14. Bahá'u'lláh presents the belief that Manifestations can appear after Muḥammad, and defends it through historical examples

14.1. "Yea, these servants regard the one true God as He Who 'doeth as He willeth' and 'ordaineth as He pleaseth'" (¶ 241)

14.2. Consequently, they do not view it impossible that God might send another Manifestation

    14.2.1. Otherwise, how would they be different from those who claim that the hand of God is "chained up" (Qur'án 5:54)

    14.2.2. And if God has revealed a new Cause, then naturally it should be embraced by all, for no refuge is there except the shelter of God's command

14.3. The "essential requirement" for one advancing a claim is "to support his assertions with clear proofs and testimonies," while the rejection of people, whether learned or not, has no bearing on the truth of the claim (¶ 242)

    14.3.1. Indeed, all the Prophets have been "the object of men's repudiation and denial" even as Muḥammad has noted:

        14.3.1.1. "Each nation hath plotted darkly against their Messenger" (Qur'án 40:5)

        14.3.1.2. "No Messenger cometh unto them but they laugh Him to scorn" (Qur'án 36:30)

14.4. Consider what happened to Muḥammad Himself (¶ 243):

    14.4.1. His enemies regarded injuries done to Him as "ranking among the greatest of all acts"

    14.4.2. The divines, both Christian and Jewish, rejected Him, whereupon "all people... bestirred themselves to extinguish the light of that Luminary"

    14.4.3. At last certain divines schemed to kill Him, but "God, verily, is the best of schemers" (Qur'án 8:30) (¶ 244)

14.5. Before Muḥammad, when Jesus revealed Himself, all the "divines charged that Quintessence of faith with impiety and rebellion" (¶ 245)

    14.5.1. In time He was convicted with the "sanction of Annas, the most learned of His day, and Caiaphas, the high priest"

    14.5.2. Christ was then made to suffer unspeakable torture until God "raised Him up to heaven"

14.6. While a "detailed account of all the Prophets... might lead to weariness," the basis of the persecution of the Manifestations by the divines is given:

14.6.1. "The doctors of the Torah" (Jewish divines) (¶ 246):

14.6.1.1.   Assert that no independent Prophet will come after Moses with a new Law

14.6.1.2.   Maintain that a "Scion of the House of David" will appear to promulgate the law of the Torah and "help establish and enforce its commandments throughout the East and the West" (¶ 246)

14.6.2. "The followers of the Gospel" likewise contend that God will never send another Revelation (¶ 247)

14.6.2.1.   They base this on the biblical statement that "the words of the Son of Man shall never pass away" (Matthew 24:35).

14.6.2.2.   They believe that neither the teachings nor the commandments of Christ will ever be altered.

14.6.2.3.   Yet in the Gospel itself, Jesus states (¶ 248):

14.6.2.3.a.   that He will go away but will come again

14.6.2.3.b.   that the Comforter shall come after Him

14.6.2.3.c.   that specific signs and portents will herald these events

14.6.2.4.   However, because certain Christian divines have interpreted these verses "after their own fancy," they failed to understand the true meaning

14.7. Bahá'u'lláh proclaims His ability to clarify other matters: "O would that thou wouldst permit Me, O Sháh, to send unto thee that which would cheer the eyes, and tranquillize the souls, and persuade every fair-minded person that with Him is the knowledge of the Book" (¶ 249):

14.7.1. " But for the repudiation of the foolish and the connivance of the divines, I would have uttered a discourse that would have thrilled and carried away the hearts"

14.7.2. However, the "wine of exposition" is sealed until such time as God pleases to unseal it; for now, "the season is not ripe"

15. A Fourth Prayer—for the protection of the Cause and of Bahá'u'lláh:

15.1. "O Lord My God! I ask Thee... to protect the lamp of Thy Cause within the globe of Thine omnipotence and Thy bountiful favor" from the "blasts of denial" from the heedless (¶ 250)

    15.1.1. "Increase, then, by the oil of Thy wisdom, the radiance of its light"

15.2. "I implore Thee... not to abandon Me amidst Thy creatures" (¶ 251)

    15.2.1. "Lift Me up, then, unto Thyself,

    15.2.2. cause Me to enter beneath the shadow of Thy mercy, and

    15.2.3. give Me to drink of the pure wine of Thy providence, that I may dwell within the tabernacle of Thy majesty and beneath the canopy of Thy favour"

16. Bahá'u'lláh draws a parallel between recent persecutions of His followers and the persecutions and interrogation of the Fourth Imam and his people

16.1. My people have been led as captives from Baghdad to Mosul, which should bring to mind what happened to the Fourth Imam when his followers were brought to Damascus (¶ 252)

    16.1.1. When asked if they were Kharijites ["Seceders," a faction opposed to both the Imams and the Umayyad state], they replied that they were faithful followers of Muḥammad and believers in His verses (¶ 253)

    16.1.2. When they were asked if they had disobeyed the laws of Islam, they replied that they "were the first to follow the divine commandments" and were "the sign of the Ancient of Days and the source of His remembrance amongst the nations" (¶ 254)

    16.1.3. When asked if they had "forsaken the Qur'án," the Imam answered that in his house it was revealed and that they are (¶ 255)

        16.1.3.1. "the streams that have branched out from the Most Great Ocean, through which God hath revived the earth" and will "revive it again after it hath died"

        16.1.3.2. the means through which "His signs have been diffused, His proofs revealed, and His tokens disclosed"

        16.1.3.3. those who possess "the knowledge of His hidden meanings and His untold mysteries"

    16.1.4. When asked for what crime they had been punished, the Imam answered, "For our love of God . . . and for our detachment from aught else save Him" (¶ 256)

16.2. We have not related the exact words of the Imam but have rather "imparted a sprinkling from that ocean of life eternal that lieth enshrined within them" (¶ 257)

    16.2.1. "[T]hose who hearken thereunto may be quickened and made aware of what hath befallen the trusted ones of God at the hands of a lost and wayward generation"

16.3. The irony of the actions of the persecutors: "We see the people in this day censuring the oppressors of bygone ages, whilst they themselves commit yet greater wrongs and know it not!"

17. Bahá'u'lláh concisely reiterates His purity of motive; His concern with the spiritual well-being of the people rather than with temporal matters; that God, "awoke" Him from His "slumber," and bade Him to speak; that "this thing is not from Me, but from God;" and that He embraces adversity in God's path (¶ 258)

18. The "*ubi sunt*" theme

    18.3.1. A man's wealth will not "endure forever, or protect him from the One Who shall, erelong, seize him by his forelock" (¶ 259)

    18.3.2. Behold those in the grave and try to distinguish between "the lord and the vassal"

    18.3.3. Every distinction hath been erased in death, "save only for those who upheld the right and who ruled with justice"

18.1. "Whither are gone the learned men, the divines and potentates of old?" (¶ 260)

    18.1.1. All have perished

    18.1.2. Their treasures are dispersed

    18.1.3. Their dwelling-places are deserted and crumbled

    18.1.4. Therefore, "[n]o man of insight will let wealth distract his gaze from his ultimate objective, and no man of understanding will allow riches to withhold him from turning unto Him Who is the All-Possessing, the Most High" (¶ 260)

18.2. Where are those who once "held dominion over all whereon the sun shineth" (¶ 261)?

    18.2.1. "Where is the commander of the swarthy legion and the upraiser of the golden standard?

    18.2.2. "Where is the ruler of Zawrá', and where the tyrant of

Fayhá' [references to the 'Abbásid and Umayyad dynasties respectively]? "

18.2.3. "Where are those before whose munificence the treasure-houses of the earth shrank in shame . . .?"

18.2.4. ""Where is he who stretched forth his arm in rebellion and who turned his hand against the All-Merciful?""

18.2.5. "Where are they who went in quest of earthly pleasures and the fruits of carnal desires?" (¶ 262)

    18.2.5.1. Their fair and comely women?

    18.2.5.2. Their paradisial gardens?

    18.2.5.3. Their "brightsome countenances wreathed in smiles?"

    18.2.5.4. "All have perished and are gone to rest beneath a canopy of dust"

18.3. How can anyone dispute the evidence to which they bear witness, and "deny that which they know to be true?"

18.3.1. "Do they not see that they are embarked upon a journey from which there is no return?" (¶ 263)

18.3.2. Blessed are they who

    18.3.2.1. Recognize this reality

    18.3.2.2. Detach themselves from all that hath been

    18.3.2.3. Deliver themselves entirely to "the Lord of all creation"

18.4. "And yet, what hope" is there that this world has "yet conceived" any who will not hindered by the "veils of glory" from this recognition (¶ 264)

18.4.1. "Is it yet within us to perform such deeds as will dispel our afflictions and draw us nigh unto Him Who is the Causer of causes?"

    18.4.1.1. [The implied answer would seem to be "no"; therefore:]

    18.4.1.2. "We beseech God to deal with us according to His bounty, and not His justice, and to grant that we may be of those who have turned their faces unto their Lord and severed themselves from all else"

19. Bahá'u'lláh highlights His suffering; predicts His upcoming exile to 'Akká, accepts His plight, and offers his imprisonment as a ransom for humanity

19.1. "I have seen, O <u>Sh</u>áh, in the path of God what eye hath not seen nor ear heard" (¶ 265)

      19.1.1. Acquaintances have repudiated Me

      19.1.2. My pathways have been straitened

      19.1.3. The fount of well-being hath run dry

      19.1.4. The bower of ease hath withered

19.2. However, I sorrow not for Myself (¶ 266):

      19.2.1. "I never passed a tree, but Mine heart addressed it saying: 'O would that thou wert cut down in My name, and My body crucified upon thee, in the path of My Lord!,' for I see the people wandering distraught and unconscious in their drunken stupor"

           19.2.1.1. "Methinks they have taken His Cause for a mockery and regard it as a play and pastime"

           19.2.1.2. They think they do well, but "[t]omorrow shall they behold that which today they are wont to deny!"

19.3. We shall soon be exiled from Adrianople to 'Akká, which is said to be (¶ 267):

      19.3.1. the most desolate of the cities of the world

      19.3.2. the most unsightly of them in appearance

      19.3.3. the most detestable in climate

      19.3.4. and the foulest in water

19.4. "Therein ['Akká] have they resolved to imprison this Youth, to shut against our faces the doors of ease and comfort, and to deprive us of every worldly benefit throughout the remainder of our days"

19.5. However, I will not complain no matter what befalls Me. I will "endure patiently as those endued with constancy and firmness have endured patiently, through the power of God" (¶ 268)

19.6. Bahá'u'lláh appeals to God to make His imprisonment the cause of freedom for humanity, and to protect the Cause:

      19.6.1. We pray God will release all from "chains and fetters" that they may turn their faces "towards His face, Who is the Mighty, the Bounteous"

      19.6.2. "We further beseech Him to make of this darksome tribulation a shield for the Temple of His Cause" and to protect it

      19.6.3. "Adversity hath ever given rise to the exaltation of His Cause and the glorification of His Name. Such hath been God's method carried into effect in centuries and ages past"

20. **Nothing people are attached to shall endure**

    20.1. People will soon discover what they "now fail to apprehend," on the day when they inevitably lose the things of the world to which they are attached

    20.2. "I know not how long they shall spur on the charger of self and passion and rove in the wilderness of error and negligence!" (¶ 269)

        20.2.1. The pomp of the powerful and the wretchedness of the abased shall not endure

        20.2.2. "All on earth shall pass away, and there remaineth alone the face of My Lord, the All-Glorious, the Most Bountiful"

        20.2.3. Every armour, fortress, throne, and palace has been destroyed in time (¶ 270)

    20.3. If the people could perceive what awaits them in the afterlife, they would "cease their censure, and seek only to win the good pleasure of this Youth" (¶ 270)

    20.4. "For now, however they have hidden Me behind a veil of darkness, whose fabric they have woven with the hands of idle fancy and vain imagination"

    20.5. Before long, the hand of God will "rend an opening through the darkness of this night and unlock a mighty portal unto His City. On that Day shall the people enter therein by troops"

    20.6. The people wish to tarry here [i.e. in this world] yet they "already have one foot in the stirrup" (¶ 271)

        20.6.1. "Look they to return, once they are gone? Nay, by Him Who is the Lord of Lords! save on the Day of Judgement, the Day whereon the people shall arise from their graves and be asked of their legacy"

        20.6.2. "Well is it with him who shall not be weighted down with his burdens on that Day . . . [when] all shall gather to be questioned in the presence of God"

21. **Bahá'u'lláh's concludes by beseeching God to purify the hearts of the divines**, to aid the people to come under His shadow, and to assist the Sháh to draw near to God, to aid His Faith, and to be just to the people

    21.1. "We beseech God to purge the hearts of certain divines from rancour and enmity, that they may look upon matters with an eye unbeclouded by contempt" (¶ 272)

21.1.1. May God raise them up to such a station that nothing will prevent them from "attaining that Day":

    21.1.1.1.   Not "the attractions of the world"

    21.1.1.2.   Not "the allurements of authority"

    21.1.1.3.   Not "wordly benefits"

    21.1.1.4.   Not "carnal desires"

21.2. "Though they [the divines] now rejoice in the adversity that hath befallen Us, soon shall come a day whereon they shall lament and weep"

21.3. Were I given the choice between "the wealth and opulence, the ease and comfort, the honour and glory which they enjoy" and My "adversities and trials... I would unhesitatingly choose My present condition"

21.3.1. Were it not for My suffering, My life would have no sweetness or profit for Me (¶ 273)

21.3.2. As anyone with discernment knows, I have spent most of my days "even as a slave, sitting under a sword hanging on a thread, knowing not whether it would fall soon or late upon him."

21.3.3. Yet "We render thanks unto God, the Lord of the worlds, and yield Him praise at all times and under all conditions"

21.4. "We beseech God to extend wide His shadow, that the true believers may hasten thereunto and that His sincere lovers may seek shelter therein" (¶ 274)

21.4.1. May He "bestow upon men blossoms from the bowers of His grace and stars from the horizon of His providence"

21.5. Moreover, We pray that God will assist the S͟háh

21.5.1. to do His will and pleasure

21.5.2. "to confirm him in that which shall draw him nigh unto the Dayspring of God's most excellent names"

21.5.3. not to condone "the injustice he witnesseth"

21.5.4. to "look upon his subjects with the eye of loving-kindness"

21.5.5. to "shield them from oppression"

21.6. "We further beseech God . . . to gather all mankind around the Gulf of the Most Great Ocean"

21.7. Finally, "We beseech God... to enable thee [the king] to aid His Faith and turn towards His justice, that thou mayest judge between the people even as thou wouldst judge between thine own kindred, and mayest choose for them that which thou choosest for thine own self" (¶ 275)

CONCLUSION SPOKEN BY THE MAIDEN

1.　　"Thus have We built the Temple with the hands of power and might, could ye but know it. This is the Temple promised unto you in the Book" (¶ 276)

    1.1.　Be fair, O peoples of the earth! Which is preferable, this, or a temple which is built of clay?"

    1.2.　"Follow ye His bidding, and praise ye God, your Lord, for that which He hath bestowed upon you. He, verily, is the Truth"

    1.3.　"No God is there but He. He revealeth what He pleaseth, through His words 'Be and it is'"

Notes

1. Bahá'u'lláh, "Lawh-i-Dunyá" (Tablet of the World), in *Tablets of Bahá'u'lláh Revealed After the Kitáb-i-Aqdas* (Wilmette, IL: US Bahá'í Publishing Trust, 1988), 94.
2. Ibid.
3. "The training institute has no parallel as an instrument for the systematic exposure of limitless numbers of souls to the life-giving waters of the Revelation and the inexhaustible meaning of the Word of God. But the friends' efforts to increase their understanding of the Faith and its teachings are of course not limited to participation in the institute process. Indeed, one strong indicator of an institute's effectiveness is the thirst it cultivates within those who engage with its materials to continue to study the Cause of Bahá'u'lláh—individually, but also collectively, whether in formal spaces created by the institutions or in more informal settings." The Universal House of Justice, letter dated 30 December 2021 to the Conference of the Continental Boards of Counsellors, accessed August 11, 2022, https://www.bahai.org/library/authoritative-texts/the-universal-house-of-justice/messages/20211230_001/1#758524470.
4. Shoghi Effendi, *God Passes By* (Wilmette, IL: US Bahá'í Publishing Trust, 1979), 212–13.
5. Shoghi Effendi, *The World Order of Bahá'u'lláh* (Wilmette, IL: US Bahá'í Publishing Trust, 1991), 109.
6. As will be explained, this term designates the fact that these Beings not only articulate divine guidance as Revelators and foretell future developments in social and spiritual evolution as Prophets, but also "manifest" perfectly in their actions and comportment the spiritual attributes and powers of Godliness itself.
7. For example, John E. Esslemont, *Bahá'u'lláh and the New Era*; William S. Hatcher and J. Douglas Martin, *The Bahá'í Faith: The Emerging Global Religion*; Kenneth Bowers, *God Speaks Again: An Introduction to the Bahá'í Faith*.
8. "Within a compass of two hundred pages it [the Kitáb-i-Íqán] proclaims unequivocally the existence and oneness of a personal God, unknowable,

inaccessible, the source of all Revelation, eternal, omniscient, omnipresent and almighty." Shoghi Effendi, *God Passes By*, 139.

9. John S. Hatcher, *The Purpose of Physical Reality* (Wilmette, IL: US Bahá'í Publishing Trust, 2005).

10. 'Abdu'l-Bahá. *The Promulgation of Universal Peace: Talks Delivered by 'Abdu'l-Bahá During His Visit in the United States and Canada in 1912*, comp. Howard McNutt (Wilmette, IL: US Bahá'í Publishing Trust, 1982), 4:2.

11. Bahá'u'lláh, Arabic Hidden Word #5, in *The Hidden Words of Bahá'u'lláh* (Wilmette, IL: US Bahá'í Publishing Trust, 1985).

12. Bahá'u'lláh, *Gleanings from the Writings of Bahá'u'lláh* (Wilmette, IL: US Bahá'í Publishing Trust, 1990), 184.

13. Ibid.

14. The Bahá'í writings assert that the essential reality of the human being is the rational soul, a spiritual essence from which derive all our distinctly human powers, such as conscious thought, reason, will, abstract thought, and conceptual memory. The Bahá'í teachings also assert that the relationship between the soul, or essential self, and the body is one of association, not incarnation. Included in this ontological conception of human reality is the belief that while the human soul has a beginning when it emanates from the spiritual realm during the process of conception, thus initiating its associative relationship with the body, it has no end, no demise. At the point when the body is no longer capable of serving as a physical "temple" through which the soul can express itself or relate to the physical realm, the soul—the self and all its attendant powers—ceases this associative relationship but continues to exist and develop in the realm of the spirit, where reality is no longer cloaked in the metaphorical guise of materiality.

15. Shoghi Effendi, *World Order*, 202.

16. "The Prophets, unlike us, are pre-existent." Shoghi Effendi, *High Endeavours: Messages to Alaska* (Alaska: National Spiritual Assembly of the Bahá'ís of Alaska, 1976), 71.

17. Shoghi Effendi, *Unfolding Destiny: The Messages from the Guardian of the Bahá'í Faith to the Bahá'í Community of the British Isles* (London: UK Bahá'í Publishing Trust, 1981), 448.

18. Shoghi Effendi quoted in *Lights of Guidance*, comp. Helen Bassett Hornby (New Delhi, India: Bahá'í Publishing Trust, 1994), 209.

19. John 1:14. This, and all further citations to the Bible, are from the King James Version.

20. John S. Hatcher, *The Face of God Among Us: How the Creator Educates Humanity* (Wilmette, IL: US Bahá'í Publishing Trust, 2010). See Part 3, "The Powers of the Prophet."

21. Bahá'u'lláh, *Gleanings*, 136.

22. Bahá'u'lláh, "Súriy-i-Haykal" (Súrih of the Temple), in *The Summons of the Lord of Hosts* (Haifa, Israel: Bahá'í World Centre, 2002), ¶ 144. All references to the Súriy-i-Haykal are from the same source, The Summons of the Lord of Hosts. Therefore, all the citations will be indicated by the paragraph number. The page numbers will not be included.

23. Bahá'u'lláh, *Gleanings*, 166.

24. Ibid., 2114.

25. Shoghi Effendi, *The Promised Day is Come* (Wilmette, IL: US Bahá'í Publishing Trust, 1980), 123.

26. Bahá'u'lláh, *Gleanings*, 176.

27. The Universal House of Justice which, in addition to being the central institution of the Bahá'í Faith today is envisaged, in the Bahá'í Writings to one day play a role in the overall administration of the global human family.

28. Bahá'u'lláh, Súriy-i-Haykal, ¶ 180.

29. 'Abdu'l-Bahá, *Foundations of World Unity* (Wilmette, IL: US Bahá'í Publishing Trust, 1979), 25.

30. Ibid.

31. Shoghi Effendi, *Promised Day*, 3.

32. Universal House of Justice, introduction to Bahá'u'lláh, *Proclamation of Bahá'u'lláh* (Wilmette, IL: US Bahá'í Publishing Trust, 1978), xiii.

33. Shoghi Effendi, *World Order*, 203.

34. Bahá'u'lláh, *The Kitáb-i-Íqán* (Wilmette, IL: US Bahá'í Publishing Trust, 1989), 255.

35. Ibid., 210.

36. The objective study of the work in regard to historical context or th various influences at work in the life and intent of the author. See part 2 of David H. Richter, ed., *The Critical Tradition*, 2nd ed. (New York: Bedford, 1997).

37. 'Abdu'l-Bahá, *Some Answered Questions*, newly revised ed. (Haifa, Israel: Bahá'í World Centre, 2014), 162.

38. Shoghi Effendi, *The Advent of Divine Justice* (Wilmette, IL: US Bahá'í Publishing Trust, 1990), 17.

39. Ibid.

40. Ibid.

41. 'Abdu'l-Bahá, *Some Answered Questions*, 95–96.

42. Ibid.

43. Ibid., 96.

44. This epithet was used by the Báb to designate the Manifestation for Whom He (as the Gate to that Prophet) had appeared to prepare the way.

45. This fact is indicated both indirectly by actions taken by the Báb

immediately prior to His execution when He mandated that His pen and seal rings be conveyed to Bahá'u'lláh and directly when, in his description of the Conference at Bada<u>sh</u>t, Shoghi Effendi observes that "Bahá'u'lláh, maintaining through continual correspondence close contact with the Báb, and Himself the directing force behind the manifold activities of His struggling fellow-disciples, unobtrusively yet effectually presided over that conference, and guided and controlled its proceedings" (*God Passes By* 31). In another passage from this same work, Shoghi Effendi, alluding to the Báb's awareness of what would unfold as a result of the Revelation of Bahá'u'lláh, states: "It should be noted, in this connection, that in the third Vahid of this Book there occurs a passage which, alike in its explicit reference to the name of the Promised One, and in its anticipation of the Order which, in a later age, was to be identified with His Revelation, deserves to rank as one of the most significant statements recorded in any of the Báb's writings. 'Well is it with him,' is His prophetic announcement, 'who fixeth his gaze upon the Order of Bahá'u'lláh, and rendereth thanks unto his Lord. For He will assuredly be made manifest. God hath indeed irrevocably ordained it in the Bayan'" (25).

46.   The Báb, *Selections from the Writings of the Báb* (Haifa, Israel: Bahá'í World Centre, 1982), 7.

47.   Siyyid Ká<u>z</u>im-i-Rashtí stated, "Verily I say, after the Qá'im [the Báb] the Qayyúm will be made manifest. For when the star of the Former has set, the sun of the beauty of Ḥusayn will rise." Nabíl-i-'Azam [Muhammad-i-Zarandí], *The Dawn-Breakers: Nabíl's Narrative of the Early Days of the Bahá'í Revelation*, trans. and ed. Shoghi Effendi (Wilmette, IL: US Bahá'í Publishing Trust, 1996), 41–42.

48.   Shoghi Effendi, *God Passes By*, 171.

49.   Nader Saiedi, "From Oppression to Empowerment," *Journal of Bahá'í Studies* 26, no. 1–2 (2016): 27–53.

50.   See Hasan Balyuzi, *Bahá'u'lláh: The King of Glory* (Oxford, UK: George Ronald Publisher, 1991), 227

51.   Shoghi Effendi, *God Passes By*, 163.

52.   Ibid., 166.

53.   Shoghi Effendi, *God Passes By*, 166.

54.   Ibid.

55.   The Báb, *Selections*, 155.

56.   Shoghi Effendi, *God Passes By*, 233.

57.   Balyuzi, *Bahá'u'lláh*, 206.

58.   Ibid.

59.   Shoghi Effendi, *God Passes By*, 160.

60.   Ibid.

61. Ibid., 171–72.
62. Alfred Tennyson, 1st Baron, "Ulysses," in *Poems by Alfred Lord Tennyson*, vol. 2 (London: Macmillan and Co., 1893).
63. Bahá'u'lláh, "Lawḥ-i-Ḥikmat (The Tablet of Wisdom)," in *Tablets of Bahá'u'lláh Revealed After the Kitáb-i-Aqdas* (Wilmette, IL: US Bahá'í Publishing Trust, 1988), 148–49.
64. Abbas Amanat, *Resurrection and Renewal: The Making of the Bábí Movement in Iran, 1844-1850* (Los Angeles: Kalimát Press, 2005), 173.
65. Ibid.
66. Ibid., 174.
67. Mullá Husayn quoted in Nabíl-i-'Azam, *Dawn-Breakers*, 62.
68. Amanat, *Resurrection and Renewal*, 149.
69. Ibid.
70. Shoghi Effendi, *God Passes By*, 24.
71. Research Department of the Universal House of Justice, *Scholarship* (Mona Vale, N.S.W. Australia: Bahá'í Publications Australia, 1995).
72. Ibid., 35.
73. Ibid., 36.
74. Ibid., 26.
75. Ibid., 37.
76. Universal House of Justice, *Issues Related to the Study of the Bahá'í Faith: Extracts from Letters Written on Behalf of the Universal House of Justice* (Wilmette, IL: US Bahá'í Publishing Trust, 1999), 19.
77. Ibid., 10.
78. Ibid.
79. Ibid.
80. Richter, ed., *Critical Tradition*.
81. John 6:35.
82. Bahá'u'lláh, *Kitáb-i-Íqán*, 3.
83. Ibid., 210.
84. Matthew 13:10–14.
85. Bahá'u'lláh, *Epistle to the Son of the Wolf* (Wilmette, IL: US Bahá'í Publishing Trust, 1988), 129.
86. Bahá'u'lláh, "Súriy-i-Haykal," ¶ 47.
87. Other Manifestations and Their religions are cited in the Qur'án and verified in the Bahá'í writings, but traces of these religions no longer exist.
88. Universal House of Justice, *Issues*, 20.
89. Bahá'u'lláh, "Súriy-i-Haykal," ¶ 44.
90. John 15:1; John 5:30.
91. This and other quotations from the Qur'án derive from *The Holy Qur'án*, trans. Abdullah Yusuf Ali (Elmhurst, NY: Tahrike Tarsile Qur'án, Inc., 2001), 4:171–72.

92. *Qur'án* 33:40.

93. Revelation 1:8; 1:10; 21:6; 23:13.

94. Bahá'u'lláh, *Kitáb-i-Íqán*, 162.

95. Ibid., 15–16.

96. 'Abdu'l-Bahá quoted in Shoghi Effendi, *World Order*, 76.

97. Words borrowed from another language. It is estimated by some that 42 percent of the English language is comprised of loanwords. See S. Kemmer, "Loanwords," accessed March 9, 2022, https://www.ruf.rice.edu/~kemmer/Words/loanwords.html.

98. In 2008, English was established as the official language for communication between pilots and air traffic control personnel by the International Civil Aviation Organization.

99. Adib Taherzadeh, *The Revelation of Bahá'u'lláh*, 4 vols (Oxford, UK: George Ronald Publisher, 1996–2001).

100. Bahá'u'lláh, *Kitáb-i-Íqán*, 255.

101. Clearly, it would be needless and quite difficult to list here all those attempts by individual Bahá'í scholars to explore the various levels of meaning in the works of Bahá'u'lláh, whether in talks, articles, or books. These days, with online resources, one of the simplest methods for exploring what research and creative exegesis have been done on a given work is to use a search engine, at least as a point of beginning. Of course, as has always been the case in research, even prior to computers and websites, inevitably one source leads to another until, over the course of time and effort, one achieves an expanding overview of the research that has been attempted. To cite but a handful of examples, if we look for research on the mystical writings of Bahá'u'lláh, such as *The Seven Valleys* (Wilmette, IL: US Bahá'í Publishing Trust, 1975), we will discover various articles, books, and chapters. On the commonly used site Wikipedia, for example, we find the following references regarding The Seven Valleys: John S. Hatcher, *The Ocean of His Words: A Reader's Guide to the Art of Bahá'u'lláh* (Wilmette, IL: US Bahá'í Publishing Trust, 1997); Moojan Momen, "'Abdu'l-Bahá's Commentary on the Qur'ánic Verses Concerning the Overthrow of the Byzantines: The Stages of the Soul," in *Lights of Irfan*, vol. 2 (Wilmette, IL: Irfan Colloquia, 2001), 99–118; Nader Saiedi, "Spiritual Journey in the Four Valleys and the Seven Valleys," in *Logos and Civilization: Spirit, History, and Order in the Writings of Bahá'u'lláh* (Ottawa, Canada: Association for Bahá'í Studies and University Press of Maryland, 2000), 79–110; Julio Savi, *Towards the Summit of Reality: An Introduction to Bahá'u'lláh's Seven Valleys and Four Valleys* (Oxford, UK: George Ronald Publisher, 2008). Similarly, by searching the same resource for exegesis and research on the Kitáb-i-Íqán, the reader will discover the following, among other

resources: Christopher Buck, *Symbol & Secret: Qur'án Commentary in Bahá'u'lláh's Kitáb-i-Íqán* (Los Angeles: Kalimát Press, 1995); Hooper C. Dunbar, *A Companion to the Study of the Kitáb-i-Íqán* (Oxford, UK: George Ronald Publisher, 1998); John S. Hatcher, *The Ocean of His Words: A Reader's Guide to the Art of Bahá'u'lláh* (Wilmette, IL: US Bahá'í Publishing Trust, 1997); Nader Saiedi, "The Kitáb-i-Íqán: Context and Order" and "The Kitáb-i-Íqán: Theology Revolutionized," in *Logos and Civilization* (Ottawa, Canada: Association for Bahá'í Studies and University Press of Maryland, 2000), 113–174. Perhaps the most accessible examples of scholarly exegesis of the Bahá'í writings can be surveyed in the three decades of articles that have gone through peer review prior to being published on the website for the Journal of Bahá'í Studies, the scholarly periodical published by the Association for Bahá'í Studies. Here, articles published through the years can be downloaded, and the various understandings of Bahá'í works can be evaluated, shared, and utilized for further study.

102. The "Rashh-i-'Ama" ("The Clouds of the Realms Above") is a poem of twenty lines revealed by Bahá'u'lláh in the Siyáh-Chál announcing the glad tidings of the advent of the Day of God. See Rashḥ-i-'Amá in Bahá'u'lláh, *The Call of the Divine Beloved: Selected Mystical Works of Bahá'u'lláh* (Haifa, Israel: Bahá'í World Centre, 2019), 3–7. "Although only nineteen lines long, this ode is indeed a mighty book revealing the character, the potentialities, the power and the glory of a Revelation identified with God Himself and destined to usher in that Day of Days so emphatically prophesied by the Báb and foretold by former Manifestations of God." Adib Taherzadeh, *The Covenant of Bahá'u'lláh* (Oxford, UK: George Ronald Publisher, 1992), 52.

103. Bahá'u'lláh, *Kitáb-i-Íqán*, 229.

104. Universal House of Justice, introduction to Bahá'u'lláh, *The Summons of the Lord of Hosts* (Haifa, Israel: Bahá'í World Centre, 2002), i.

105. Shoghi Effendi quoted in Universal House of Justice, introduction to *Summons*, ii.

106. Shoghi Effendi, *World Order*, 163.

107. Shoghi Effendi, *God Passes By*, 212.

108. Mohamad Ghasem Bayat, "An Introduction to the Súratu'l-Haykal (Discourse of The Temple)," in *Lights of Irfan*, bk 2 (Wilmette, IL: Irfan Colloquia, 2001), 13.

109. Shoghi Effendi, *God Passes By*, 94–95.

110. See chapter 4, pp. 126–31.

111. 'Abdu'l-Bahá, *Promulgation*, 432.

112. Shoghi Effendi, *Promised Day*, 65.

113. Photograph originally published in H. M Balyuzi, *Bahá'u'lláh, The King*

of Glory (Oxford, UK: George Ronald Publisher, 1980), 295.

114. https://bahaiwritings.wordpress.com/2012/02/25/picture-of-badi-the-pride-of-martyrs/

115. https://www.bl.uk/collection-items/star-tablet-of-the-bab.

116. Abu'l-Qasim Faizi, "Explanation of the Symbol of the Greatest Name," in *Conqueror of Hearts* (New Delhi, India: Bahá'í Publishing Trust, 1968).

117. Ibid.

118. Faizi goes on to explain that in regard to what Bahá'ís call "the Greatest Name." What he is referring to is the tradition in Islam that among the various "names" of God—words that allude to His powers and attributes—one is the most important, the greatest name. In Islam, it is a tradition that the identity of this particular name is hidden or concealed. But according to Bahá'í belief, that Greatest Name or attribute is "Bahá," denoting "Glory," and also "Light" or "Splendor." Thus, when in Adrianople the Islamic greeting or invocation "Alláh'u'Akbar" was changed to "Alláh'u'Abhá" after the "the most great separation," employing "Abhá," the superlative form of "Bahá," to signify "Most Glorious" or "Greatest Glory" or "All Glorious." The change of the greeting thus utilizes a form of the Greatest Name "Bahá" rather than "Akbar," even though the meaning is similar—"Akbar" also means "Most Great."

119. Bahá'u'lláh, *Gleanings*, 214.

120. Bahá'u'lláh, "Súriy-i-Haykal," n. 3, 237.

121. Henry Cornelius Agrippa of Nettesheim, *Three Books of Occult Philosophy. Translated out of the Latin into the English Tongue by J.F. Book II* (London: Gregory Moule, 1651), 266. https://archive.lib.msu.edu/DMC/Arts%20&%20Humanities/threebooksoccult.pdf.

122. Anonymous, "Sir Gawain and the Green Knight," in *The Norton Anthology of English Literature*, 6th ed., vol. 1, ed. M. H. Abrams (New York: W. W. Norton & Company, 1993).

123. 'Abdu'l-Bahá, *Some Answered Questions*, 273.

124. Bahá'u'lláh, *Summons*, 92.

125. See Shoghi Effendi, *God Passes By*, 221.

126. Bahá'u'lláh, "Súriy-i-Haykal," ¶ 5.

127. Ibid., ¶ 7.

128. Ibid.

129. Bahá'u'lláh, *Epistle*, 76.

130. Taherzadeh, *Revelation*, vol. 3, 133.

131. 'Abdu'l-Bahá, *Paris Talks: Addresses Given by 'Abdu'l-Bahá in 1911* (London: UK Bahá'í Publishing Trust, 1972), 175.

132. Shoghi Effendi, *God Passes By*, 163.

133. Inasmuch as there is no literal Satan, we can safely presume this narrative also represents an internal process in which Christ is demonstrating for us who read this account that the Manifestation purposefully denies Himself concerns for His personal well-being, physical comfort, or earthly powers, even though theoretically these are available to Him since He does possess free will. In short, the Manifestation exemplifies for us the sort of detachment to which we should aspire.

134. William Shakespeare, "Hamlet," in *The Complete Works of Shakespeare*, ed. Hardin Craig (Northbrook, IL: Scott, Foresman and Company, 1951), 3.1.1755–56.

135. Bahá'u'lláh, *Gleanings*, 214.

136. Bahá'u'lláh, "Súriy-i-Haykal," ¶ 44.

137. The Báb, *Selections*, 12.

138. Bahá'u'lláh, *Kitáb-i-Íqán*, 151.

139. Ibid., 154.

140. Ibid.

141. Shoghi Effendi, *Messages*, 155.

142. Shoghi Effendi, *Citadel of Faith*, 5. For more on the progressive stages of unfoldment of the World Order of Bahá'u'lláh see John S. Hatcher, *The Ascent of Society: The Social Imperative in Personal Salvation* (Wilmette, IL: Bahá'í Publishing, 2007).

143. Shoghi Effendi, *World Order*, 146.

144. See Bahá'u'lláh, *Kitáb-i-Íqán*, 176 and following.

145. Bahá'u'lláh, "Súriy-i-Haykal," ¶ 7.

146. Shoghi Effendi, *God Passes By*, 94.

147. Bahá'u'lláh, "Súriy-i-Haykal," ¶ 19.

148. Ibid., ¶ 20.

149. Ibid.

150. Ibid., ¶ 21.

151. Ibid.

152. Matthew 22:14.

153. Bahá'u'lláh, *Gems of Divine Mysteries* (Haifa, Israel: Bahá'í World Centre, 2002), ¶ 51.

154. Bahá'u'lláh, *Kitáb-i-Íqán*, 70.

155. Bahá'u'lláh, "Súriy-i-Haykal," ¶ 61.

156. Ibid.

157. Ibid.

158. Bahá'u'lláh, *Kitáb-i-Íqán*, 230.

159. Bahá'u'lláh, "Súriy-i-Haykal," ¶ 62.

160. Ibid., ¶ 63.

161. Bahá'u'lláh, *Kitáb-i-Íqán*, 198–221.

162. Ibid., 221.

163. For an elaboration on the nature of the literary device of the Maid of Heaven discussed earlier in this work, see also John S. Hatcher, Amrollah Hemmat and Ehsannollah Hemmat, "Bahá'u'lláh's Symbolic Use of the Veiled Ḥúríyyih," *Journal of Bahá'í Studies* 29, no. 3 (2019): 9–41.

164. Bahá'u'lláh, "Súriy-i-Haykal," ¶ 66.

165. Ibid., ¶ 67.

166. Ibid.

167. John 14:6–7.

168. Qur'án 33:40.

169. William Harmon and C. Hugh Holman, *A Handbook to Literature*, 8th edition, (New Jersey: Prince Hall, 2000, 356.

170. While this appellation the "Most Great Spirit" is not explicitly defined, its usage throughout the authoritative Bahá'í texts implies that spirit emanating directly from God that inspires and ordains the guidance and actions of the Manifestation. In some instances, it seems identical with the "Holy Spirit" that associates with the Manifestation as personified by the Maiden. For example, Shoghi Effendi, in discussing the Súriy-i-Haykal, observes, "In His Suratu'l-Haykal (the Súrih of the Temple) He thus describes those breathless moments when the Maiden, symbolizing the 'Most Great Spirit' proclaimed His mission to the entire creation." Shoghi Effendi, *God Passes By*, 101.

171. Bahá'u'lláh, "Súriy-i-Haykal," ¶ 50.

172. Ibid., ¶ 51.

173. Taherzadeh, *Revelation*, vol. 1, 42.

174. Shoghi Effendi qtd. in *Lights of Guidance*, 414.

175. The word *Haykal* (Temple) is composed in Arabic of the four letters *Há'*, *Yá'*, *Káf* and *Lám* (HYKL). Its first letter is taken to symbolize the word *Huvíyyah* (Essence of Divinity); its second letter, the word *Qadír* (Almighty), of which *Yá'* is the third letter; its third letter, the word *Karím* (All-Bountiful); and its fourth letter, the word *Faḍl* (Grace), of which *Lám* is the third letter.

176. Bahá'u'lláh, "Súriy-i-Haykal," ¶ 48.

177. Ibid., ¶52.

178. The second of the proofs in the Kitáb-i-Íqán mentioned in the previous note.

179. Bahá'u'lláh, "Súriy-i-Haykal," ¶ 81.

180. Ibid., ¶ 82.

181. Ibid.

182. Ibid.

183. Ibid., ¶ 83.

184. Ibid.

185. Ibid., ¶ 84.

186. Ibid.
187. Ibid., ¶ 192.
188. Bahá'u'lláh, *Hidden Words*, 3.
189. Bahá'u'lláh, *Epistle*, 14–15.
190. Bahá'u'lláh, "Súriy-i-Haykal," ¶ 6.
191. Bahá'u'lláh, *The Kitáb-i-Aqdas* (Wilmette, IL: US Bahá'í Publishing Trust, 1993), 32.
192. Shoghi Effendi, *God Passes By*, 101.
193. Bahá'u'lláh, "Súriy-i-Haykal," ¶ 85.
194. Ibid., ¶ 86.
195. Ibid., ¶ 87.
196. Ibid.
197. Ibid., ¶ 91.
198. Shoghi Effendi, *World Order*, 117.
199. Unsheathing the sword is used as a metaphor by Bahá'u'lláh for speaking—the sword representing the tongue. Specifically, we find Bahá'u'lláh exhorting men to withhold use of the sword as a means of coercion in matters of religion but, instead, to unsheathe the sword of the tongue: "Aid ye your Lord with the sword of wisdom and of utterance" and "Know thou that We have annulled the rule of the sword, as an aid to Our Cause, and substituted for it the power born of the utterance of men." Bahá'u'lláh, *Gleanings* 296, 303.
200. Bahá'u'lláh, "Súriy-i-Haykal," ¶ 95.
201. Ibid., ¶ 96.
202. Ibid., ¶ 98.
203. While this epithet traditionally alludes to the "self" or the "insistent self," in the context of what happens to Bahá'u'lláh in Adrianople, it might also here represent Mírzá Yaḥyá and Siyyid Muḥammad Iṣfáhání and their attempts to refute and undermine the claims of Bahá'u'lláh.
204. Bahá'u'lláh, "Súriy-i-Haykal," ¶ 99.
205. Ibid., ¶ 100.
206. Qur'án 39:68; Bahá'u'lláh, *Kitáb-i-Íqán*, 229.
207. Bahá'u'lláh, "Súriy-i-Haykal," ¶ 100.
208. Ibid., ¶ 101.
209. Bahá'u'lláh, *Hidden Words*, 28.
210. Ibid.
211. Ibid.
212. The entire Súriy-i-Haykal (including the letters) is approximately 36,600 words long. The word count of the five letters combined is about 22,600 words, with the letter to Naṣíri'd-Dín Sháh being 11,200 words long.
213. Bahá'u'lláh, "Súriy-i-Haykal," ¶ 106.
214. Ibid.

215. Ibid., ¶ 112.

216. Ibid.

217. Ibid., ¶ 113.

218. Ibid., ¶ 114.

219. Ibid., ¶ 115.

220. Ibid., ¶ 117.

221. Ibid., ¶118.

222. Ibid.

223. Ibid., ¶ 119.

224. Ibid., ¶ 118.

225. Ibid., ¶ 120.

226. Ibid., ¶ 121.

227. In John 14:16–17, Christ promises, "And I will pray the Father, and he shall give you another Comforter, that he may abide with you forever; Even the Spirit of truth; whom the world cannot receive, because it seeth him not, neither knoweth him: but ye know him; for he dwelleth with you, and shall be in you." The reader should note that the Comforter referred to in John appears to be able to operate as a reference both to Bahá'u'lláh and to Muḥammad. The word Comforter is a translation of the Latin paracletus ("Paraclete") which is defined in part as "one who consoles." For the connection to Muḥammad—also made by Muslim scholars— see Shoghi Effendi, *Lights of Guidance*, 494: "References in the Bible to 'Mt. Paran' and 'Paraclete' refer to Muḥammad's Revelation." The Guardian elsewhere makes clear that Bahá'u'lláh employs the term as a reference to Himself when addressing Christians; see for instance *God Passes By*, 210 ("And finally, in several passages addressed to the entire body of the followers of Jesus Christ He identifies Himself with the '*Father*' spoken of by Isaiah, with the 'Comforter' Whose Covenant He Who is the Spirit [Jesus] had Himself established, and with the '*Spirit of Truth*' Who will guide them '*into all truth*'[. . .]") and 95 ("To Him Jesus Christ had referred as the '*Prince of this world*,' as the 'Comforter' Who will 'reprove the world of sin, and of righteousness, and of judgment'[…]"), as well as T*he World Order of Bahá'u'lláh*, 104–5. Any difficulty posed by the idea that a single term can refer to two different historical Figures is, of course, resolved by Bahá'u'lláh's revelatory explanation of the two stations of the Manifestations of God in the Kitáb-i-Iqán: viewed from their station of "pure abstraction and essential unity" it is accurate to call them "all by one name" (152), as attested by Muḥammad's own declarations, cited by Bahá'u'lláh in that work—"I am all the Prophets"; "I am Adam, Noah, Moses, and Jesus" (182).

228. Bahá'u'lláh, "Súriy-i-Haykal," ¶ 122.

229. Ibid., ¶ 124.

230. Discussed first in Exodus 23:14–16 and then in the Qur'án 6:141, this term designates literally the time in the fall when the fruits of the harvest are gathered together. Figuratively, it symbolizes a time when the results of previous endeavors (the fruits of their labors) of prior Manifestations and their followers will be assembled under the banner of the Revelation of Bahá'u'lláh to bring about global peace and global governance.

231. Bahá'u'lláh, "Súriy-i-Haykal," ¶ 126.

232. Ibid., ¶ 127.

233. Ibid.

234. Ibid., ¶ 129.

235. Ibid., ¶ 130.

236. Shoghi Effendi, *Promised Day*, 30–32

237. Ibid., 50.

238. Ibid., 53.

239. Shoghi Effendi, *Promised Day*, 52.

240. Ibid. 53.

241. Ibid.

242. Pius IX, *Ubi Primum* [Encyclical Letter on the Immaculate Conception]. Accessed August 31, 2022. https://www.papalencyclicals.net/Pius09/p9ubipr2.htm

243. Shoghi Effendi, *Promised Day*, 55.

244. Ibid., 50.

245. Ibid., 51–52.

246. Ibid., 52.

247. Ibid.

248. Bahá'u'lláh, "Súriy-i-Haykal," ¶ 133.

249. Ibid., ¶ 131.

250. Ibid., ¶ 133.

251. The Crimean War.

252. Bahá'u'lláh, "Súriy-i-Haykal," ¶ 137.

253. The word prove in this context takes on the meaning of "testing."

254. Bahá'u'lláh, "Súriy-i-Haykal," ¶ 137.

255. Ibid., ¶ 138.

256. Ibid., ¶ 137.

257. Ibid., ¶ 138.

258. Ibid., ¶ 140.

259. Ibid., ¶ 141.

260. Ibid., ¶ 142.

261. Ibid., ¶ 143.

262. Ibid.

263. Ibid.

264. Ibid., ¶ 144.

265. Ibid., ¶ 145.
266. Ibid.
267. Ibid., ¶ 146.
268. Ibid., ¶ 147.
269. Ibid., ¶ 150.
270. This is obviously an allusion to the Bahá'í Fast, not to any Christian commemoration, such as the Lenten Season.
271. Bahá'u'lláh, "Súriy-i-Haykal," ¶152.
272. Ibid., ¶ 153.
273. Ibid., ¶ 155.
274. Ibid., ¶ 156.
275. Ibid.
276. Ibid., ¶ 157.
277. Ibid.
278. Even the Shah's reign was not entirely devoid of attempts at modernization. Such reforms as were initiated, however, occurred at the initiative, not of the Shah, but of his prime minister, Mírzá Taqí Khán, titled Amír-Nizám, but best known to history as Amir Kabir. For a detailed treatment see, for example, Lorentz, John H. "Iran's Great Reformer of the Nineteenth Century: An Analysis of Amīr Kabīr's Reforms." *Iranian Studies* 4, no. 2/3 (1971): 85–103. While this prime minister initiated some reforms—in the areas of education, finance, and the judiciary, for example—his tenure was short (1848-51); after dismissing the Amír-Nizám (prior to ordering his murder the following year), Naṣíri'd-Dín Sháh essentially abandoned any pretext of reform for the rest of his long reign. It is, of course, the great tragedy of Amír-Nizám's life and career that, while he is still remembered today as one of Iran's first reform-minded public officials, he failed to understand the true significance of the greatest issue confronting the nation during his tenure: it was he who, seeing in the Bábí movement nothing but a threat to the public order, and regardless of his other qualities, proved himself "arbitrary, bloodthirsty, [and] reckless" (*God Passes By* 4) in his savage suppression of the beleaguered Bábí community, culminating in his order for the Báb's execution—"that fateful decision which was not only destined to leave its indelible imprint on the fortunes of his country, but was to be fraught with such incalculable consequences for the destinies of the whole of mankind" (*God Passes By* 51).
279. Serfdom, a feature of feudal systems, bound the individual to land owned by a king, a lord, or some other form of aristocratic gentry. While feudalism was generally associated with the Middle Ages in Europe, Russia remained essentially feudal for most of the 19th century; many of the larger antebellum Southern plantations in the United States also

operated along feudal lines, with the additional evil of chattel slavery.

280. Bahá'u'lláh, "Súriy-i-Haykal," ¶ 158.

281. Shoghi Effendi, *God Passes By*, 104.

282. His confession to the attempt on the assassination of Naṣíri'd-Dín <u>Sh</u>áh, the event that incited the massive persecution and imprisonment of Bábís throughout Persia.

283. Shoghi Effendi, *God Passes By*, 104.

284. Ibid., 105.

285. Ibid.

286. Bahá'u'lláh, "Súriy-i-Haykal," ¶ 160.

287. Ibid., ¶ 162.

288. Ibid., ¶ 164.

289. Ibid., ¶ 166.

290. "O King! We heard the words thou didst utter in answer to the Czar of Russia, concerning the decision made regarding the war. Thy Lord, verily, knoweth, is informed of all." Bahá'u'lláh, "Súriy-i-Haykal," ¶ 137.

291. Bahá'u'lláh, "Súriy-i-Haykal," ¶ 158.

292. Bahá'u'lláh, *Epistle*, 33.

293. Bahá'u'lláh, "Súriy-i-Haykal," ¶ 160.

294. William Sears in his book *Thief in the Night* does an excellent job of examining how people might react now were a story reported in the news that Christ had returned. See William Sears, *Thief in the Night: or The Strange Case of the Missing Millennium* (Oxford, UK: George Ronald Publisher, 1961).

295. Shoghi Effendi, *God Passes By*, 217.

296. Bahá'u'lláh, "Súriy-i-Haykal," ¶ 180.

297. Ibid., ¶ 166.

298. Ibid.

299. Ibid., ¶ 168.

300. Ibid., ¶ 170.

301. Ibid., ¶ 180.

302. Bahá'u'lláh, "Súriy-i-Haykal," ¶ 172.

303. Ibid., ¶ 173.

304. Ibid.

305. Ibid.

306. Bahá'u'lláh, "Súriy-i-Haykal," ¶ 174.

307. Curiously, even though Queen Victoria herself may in her own rule have modeled some of these principles, her view of the unjust behavior of other rulers was complex, as especially shown in her interesting relationship with Napoleon III. After his visit to England, the queen, in a memorandum dated May 2, 1855, made the following assessment of the emperor's motives and character:

That he is a very extraordinary man, with great qualities there can be no doubt—I might almost say a mysterious man. He is evidently possessed of indomitable courage, unflinching firmness of purpose, self-reliance, perseverance, and great secrecy; to this should be added, a great reliance on what he calls his Star, and a belief in omens and incidents as connected with his future destiny, which is almost romantic—and at the same time he is endowed with wonderful self-control, great calmness, even gentleness, and with a power of fascination, the effect of which upon all those who become more intimately acquainted with him is most sensibly felt.

She goes on to observe, "How far he is actuated by a strong moral sense of right and wrong is difficult to say." The Queen alludes to various questionable actions he had taken and observes, "My impression is, that in all these apparently inexcusable acts, he has invariably been guided by the belief that he is fulfilling a destiny which God has imposed upon him, and that, though cruel or harsh in themselves, they were necessary to obtain the result which he considered himself as chosen to carry out, and not acts of wanton cruelty or injustice; for it is impossible to know him and not to see that there is much that is truly amiable, kind, and honest in his character." "Queen Victoria's Impressions of Napoleon III (Memorandum Dated 2nd May 1855)," Napoleon.org, accessed February 7, 2022, https://www.napoleon.org/en/history-of-the-two-empires/articles/queen-victorias-impressions-of-napoleon-iii-memorandum-dated-2nd-may-1855/.

308. Bahá'u'lláh, "Súriy-i-Haykal," ¶ 182.

309. Shoghi Effendi, *Promised Day*, 3.

310. Bahá'u'lláh, "Súriy-i-Haykal," ¶ 172.

311. Ibid., ¶ 175.

312. Ibid., ¶ 176.

313. Ibid., ¶ 178.

314. Ibid., ¶ 179.

315. Ibid.

316. Ibid., ¶ 180.

317. Ibid., ¶ 182.

318. Bahá'u'lláh, *Proclamation* (Wilmette, IL: US Bahá'í Publishing Trust, 1978), 39. "In one of His Tablets written before the First World War (1914–1918), 'Abdu'l-Bahá explained that Bahá'u'lláh's reference to having seen the banks of the Rhine 'covered with gore' related to the Franco-Prussian War (1870–1871), and that there was more suffering to come. In God Passes By Shoghi Effendi states that the 'oppressively severe treaty' that was imposed on Germany following its defeat in the First World War 'provoked the lamentations' of Berlin 'which half a century before, had been ominously prophesied.'" Quoted in Bahá'u'lláh, *Kitáb-i-Aqdas*, 217–18.

319. Ibid., ¶ 184.

320. Ibid., ¶ 185.
321. Queen Victoria, quoted in Shoghi Effendi, *Promised Day*, 65.
322. Acts 5:38–39: "And now I say unto you, Refrain from these men, and let them alone: for if this counsel or this work be of men, it will come to nought: But if it be of God, ye cannot overthrow it; lest haply ye be found even to fight against God." For Queen Victoria's response, see Shoghi Effendi, *Promised Day*, 65.
323. Shoghi Effendi, *Citadel of Faith: Messages to America, 1847-1957* (Wilmette, IL: US Bahá'í Publishing Trust, 1980) 6.
324. Áqá Buzurg-i-Níshápúrí, who, after hearing verses by Nabíl in which Bahá'u'lláh describes His sufferings, traveled on foot from Mosul to 'Akká to attain the presence of Bahá'u'lláh. See Shoghi Effendi, *Promised Day*, 65–69.
325. Shoghi Effendi, *Promised Day*.
326. Shoghi Effendi quoted in *Unfolding Destiny*, 449. Also, as previously noted, in the Súriy-i-Haykal, Bahá'u'lláh notes, "Within the treasury of Our Wisdom there lieth unrevealed a knowledge, one word of which, if we chose to divulge it to mankind, would cause every human being to recognize the Manifestation of God and to acknowledge His omniscience." Bahá'u'lláh, "Súriy-i-Haykal," ¶ 35.
327. Shoghi Effendi, *God Passes By*, 199.
328. Ibid.
329. Ibid.
330. Ibid., ¶ 186.
331. Bahá'u'lláh, *Tablets*, 173
332. Bahá'u'lláh, "Súriy-i-Haykal," ¶ 184.
333. *Kitáb-i-Aqdas*, 86.
334. Ibid., 87.
335. Siyyid Muḥammad Iṣfáhání was killed by seven Bábís, much to the displeasure and anguish of Bahá'u'lláh, who had specifically cautioned against any such action. As a result of this action, Bahá'u'lláh was interrogated by the city officials and the reputation of the Bahá'ís in 'Akká suffered for some time.
336. Bahá'u'lláh, "Súriy-i-Haykal," ¶ 184.
337. Ibid., ¶ 192.
338. Ibid.
339. 'Abdu'l-Bahá, *Some Answered Questions*, 95.
340. Ibid.
341. Ibid.
342. Ibid., ¶ 188.
343. Ibid., ¶ 189.
344. Ibid., ¶ 190.

345. Ibid., ¶ 191.
346. W. B. Yeats, "The Second Coming," in Ferguson, Salter, and Stallworthy, *The Norton Anthology of Poetry*, 5th edition (New York: W. W. Norton & Company, 2005), 1196, l. 15.
347. Bahá'u'lláh, "Súriy-i-Haykal," ¶ 193
348. Ibid., ¶ 194.
349. Ibid.
350. Ibid., ¶ 206.
351. Ibid., ¶ 216.
352. Ibid., ¶ 217.
353. Ibid., ¶ 267.
354. Ibid.
355. Bahá'u'lláh, "Súriy-i-Haykal," ¶ 199.
356. Ibid., ¶ 201.
357. Ibid., ¶ 205.
358. Ibid., ¶ 200.
359. Ibid., ¶ 201.
360. Ibid., ¶ 220.
361. Ibid., ¶ 204.
362. Ibid., ¶ 205.
363. Ibid.
364. Ibid., ¶ 250.
365. Ibid.
366. Ibid., ¶ 251.
367. Bahá'u'lláh, *Prayers and Meditations by Bahá'u'lláh* (Wilmette, IL: US Bahá'í Publishing Trust, 1987), 313.
368. Bahá'u'lláh, *Gleanings*, 215.
369. Shoghi Effendi, *God Passes By*, 244.
370. Shoghi Effendi, *Advent*, 18.
371. 'Abdu'l-Bahá, *Light of the World: Selected Tablets of 'Abdu'l-Bahá* (Haifa, Israel: Bahá'í World Centre, 2021), 112–13.
372. The papacy, of course, had not been directly impacted by the evolution of parliamentary government over the previous centuries, nor had its authority ever rested on the same set of political concepts as did that of the European monarchies; however, as a temporal as well as religious leader at the time when he received Bahá'u'lláh's letter, the pope had more in common with these monarchs than is the case for his successor today.
373. Bahá'u'lláh, "Súriy-i-Haykal," ¶ 194.
374. Ibid., ¶ 195.
375. Ibid., ¶ 196.
376. Ibid.
377. Ibid., ¶ 197.

378. Ibid., ¶ 198.
379. Ibid., ¶ 199.
380. Ibid., ¶ 223.
381. Ibid., ¶ 214.
382. Ibid., ¶ 217.
383. Ibid., ¶ 218.
384. Ibid.
385. Ibid.
386. Ibid., ¶ 220.
387. Ibid.
388. Ibid.
389. Ibid., ¶ 225.
390. Ibid., ¶ 226.
391. Ibid., ¶ 227.
392. Ibid., ¶ 228.
393. Ibid., ¶ 230.
394. Ibid., ¶ 233.
395. Ibid., ¶ 234.
396. Ibid., ¶ 235.
397. Ibid., ¶ 236.
398. Bahá'u'lláh, "Súriy-i-Haykal," ¶ 237.
399. Shoghi Effendi, *God Passes By*, Chapter V.
400. Bahá'u'lláh, "Súriy-i-Haykal," ¶ 241
401. Qur'án 3:40.
402. Qur'án 5:1.
403. Bahá'u'lláh, "Súriy-i-Haykal," ¶ 242.
404. Ibid., ¶ 243.
405. Qur'án 8:30. This delightfully ironic observation is well known by most Muslims.
406. Bahá'u'lláh, "Súriy-i-Haykal," ¶ 245.
407. Ibid., ¶ 249.
408. Ibid.
409. Bahá'u'lláh, *Kitáb-i-Aqdas*, 21.
410. Bahá'u'lláh, "Súriy-i-Haykal," ¶ 254.
411. As a lineal descendant of Muḥammad, the Imam is alluding to the revelation of the Qur'án.
412. Bahá'u'lláh, "Súriy-i-Haykal," ¶ 255.
413. Ibid., ¶ 256.
414. Similarly, as we noted earlier, most of the Jews at the time of Christ had also had failed to recognize in Him the fulfilment of their own scripture, which—in Psalm 22—even foreshadowed His dying words and the circumstances of His crucifiction.

415. Bahá'u'lláh, "Súriy-i-Haykal," ¶ 258.

416. Ibid.

417. Ibid.

418. Ibid., ¶ 259.

419. Ibid., ¶ 260.

420. Ibid., ¶ 262.

421. Ibid., ¶ 263.

422. Ibid., ¶ 264.

423. Ibid.

424. Ibid., ¶ 265.

425. Ibid., ¶ 266.

426. Ibid., ¶ 268.

427. Ibid.

428. A reference to the story of Joseph in the Qur'án. Bought as a slave by an Egyptian official, Joseph resists the attempts of his master's wife to seduce him. When other women blame her for her "evidently going astray" (Qur'án 12:30), she invites them to a feast and gives them each a knife. When Joseph appears, these "blamers" are so distracted by his beauty that they cut themselves, uttering: "Allah preserve us! no mortal is this! This is none other than a noble angel!" (Ibid., 12:31). In the context of those who will enter "by troops", the allusion speaks to the sudden recognition of the Manifestation's station by those from whom it has hitherto been veiled.

429. Bahá'u'lláh, "Súriy-i-Haykal," ¶ 270.

430. Ibid., ¶ 272.

431. Ibid., ¶ 273.

432. Ibid., ¶ 274.

433. Ibid., ¶ 275.

434. Ibid., ¶ 276.

435. Ibid., ¶ 44.

436. Bahá'u'lláh, *Gleanings*, 166.

437. Shoghi Effendi, *Lights of Guidance*, 519.

438. Bahá'u'lláh, "Súriy-i-Haykal," ¶ 276.

439. Ibid.

440. Bahá'u'lláh, *Kitáb-i-Aqdas*, n. 188.

441. 'Abdu'l-Bahá, *Some Answered Questions*, 284–85.

442. John 6:38.

443. John 14:7.

444. John 14:9.

445. Qur'án 5:73–75.

446. The "Lord's Prayer," Matthew 6:10.

447. John Milton, "Paradise Lost," in *The Complete Works of John Milton*,

ed. Douglas Bush (Boston: Houghton Mifflin Company, 1965), 1.25–26.

448. Quoted in Bahá'u'lláh, *Kitáb-i-Aqdas*, n. 23, 174.

449. Bahá'u'lláh, Hidden Words, no. 4.

450. Ibid., 175.

451. Bahá'u'lláh, *Prayers and Meditations*, 49.

452. John 14:6: "Jesus saith unto him, I am the way, the truth, and the life: no man cometh unto the Father, but by me."

453. See, for example, 'Abdu'l-Bahá Promulgation 29; Bahá'u'lláh, *Call of the Divine Beloved* ¶70, and *Gleanings* CLXII. Note that while the "lesser" and "greater" worlds refer generally to the human being and to the entirety of creation respectively, these apparently hierarchical designations are, in places reversed. *Gleanings* CLXII provides us with a breathtaking nuance to our earlier discussion of the role of the entirety of physical creation as a representation of God. Here, Bahá'u'lláh writes: "Some have described [the human being] as the 'lesser world,' when, in reality, he should be regarded as the 'greater world.'"

454. 'Abdu'l-Bahá. *The Promulgation of Universal Peace*, 4:2.

455. Bahá'u'lláh, *Kitáb-i-Aqdas*, n. 23, 174.

456. Ibid.

457. Ibid.

458. Ibid.

459. Ibid.

460. Ibid.

461. My own grandfather, Dr. William Benjamin Hardman, a surgeon in the town of Commerce, Georgia, died in 1918 after contracting the flu when he ventured out on a cold, rainy night to treat a young boy with a broken leg.

462. Mikhail Gorbachev, "When the Pandemic Is Over, the World Must Come Together," *TIME*, last updated April 15, 2020, https://time.com/5820669/mikhail-gorbachev-coronavirus-human-security/.

463. Ibid.

464. Ibid.

465. "Compose your differences, and reduce your armaments, that the burden of your expenditures may be lightened, and that your minds and hearts may be tranquillized. Heal the dissensions that divide you, and ye will no longer be in need of any armaments except what the protection of your cities and territories demandeth." Bahá'u'lláh, *Summons*, 188.

466. Gorbachev, "When the Pandemic Is Over."

467. Ibid.

468. Ibid.

469. This annexation, though not internationally recognized, has not been contested.

470. Bahá'u'lláh, *Kitáb-i-Aqdas*, n. 174, 241; quoting Shoghi Effendi, World Order 204 and 203.

471. Bahá'u'lláh, *Tablets*, 26.

472. Ibid., 159.

473. In particular, the reader would do well to examine the Guardian's statements in the section "American Bahá'ís in the Time of World Peril" (p. 122 and following), where he observes that World War II was but "a foretaste of the devastation which this consuming fire will wreak upon the world" (125). See Shoghi Effendi, *Citadel of Faith* (Wilmette, IL: US Bahá'í Publishing Trust, 1980).

474. Universal House of Justice, *Wider Horizon*, 135.

475. Bahá'u'lláh, *Gleanings*, 136.

476. Bahá'u'lláh, *Summons*, 168.

477. "The Other 9/11: George H. W. Bush's 1990 New World Order Speech," The *Dallas Morning News*, last updated September 8, 2017, https://www.dallasnews.com/opinion/commentary/2017/09/08/the-other-9-11-george-h-w-bush-s-1990-new-world-order-speech/.

478. Ibid.

479. Bahá'u'lláh quoted in Shoghi Effendi, *Promised Day*, 3.

480. John S. Hatcher, *God's Plan for Planet Earth and for Your Neighborhood* (Wilmette, IL: Bahá'í Publishing, 2018).

481. Quoted in *Unfolding Destiny* (London: Bahá'í Publishing, 1981) 454.

482. Bahá'u'lláh, "Súriy-i-Haykal," ¶61.

483. Ibid., ¶ 19.

484. Ibid., ¶ 20.

485. Ibid.

486. Ibid., ¶ 63.

487. Ibid., ¶ 67.

488. A very interesting way by which Bahá'u'lláh enables Himself to allude to the malfeasance of Mírzá Yahyá, hint that there is much more He could say, but allow the voice within (the Holy Spirit) to refocus Him on the hopeful future of the Cause.

489. Sense would seem to be that Bahá'u'lláh is the Holy Spirit expressed in the form of a living human being or "Temple" capable of manifesting divine attributes.

490. This concept of the power of God empowering Bahá'u'lláh through the Holy Spirit in terms of the phrase "'Be,' and it is!" is repeated throughout: in paragraphs 2, 8, 13, 36, 46.

491. This would seem to be an acknowledgment that the Súriy-i-Haykal is a complex work requiring intense study and reflection.

492. This calls to mind Bahá'u'lláh's observation that "The essence of belief in Divine unity consisteth in regarding Him Who is the Manifestation

of God and Him Who is the invisible, the inaccessible, the unknowable Essence as one and the same" (Bahá'u'lláh, Gleanings, 166), and the tradition "He is I and I am He except that He is He and I am I" (provisional translation of 'Abdu'l-Bahá's explication of the tradition "I was a Hidden Treasure").

493. Note the pronominal references here: She (the Maid of Heaven) is telling the Temple (Bahá'u'lláh) to inform the mirrors of the power that He (Bahá'u'lláh) has but notes that His power is subject to the power of the Will of God.

494. In the context of an address to the people of the Bayán, this is likely an allusion to Ṣubḥ-i-Azal (Mírzá Yaḥyá), indicating that he was "disguised" as never before in a previous Dispensation (being the nominee of the Báb Himself), has acted with greater perfidy than ever before, or both.

495. An allusion, we can presume, to the statement by Christ that the coming of the Son of Man was known by no one except God Himself: "But of that day and that hour knoweth no man, no, not the angels which are in heaven, neither the Son, but the Father" (Mark 13:32).

496. Important distinction here between the name and the essential reality of the Manifestation. Same sense in which Bahá'u'lláh says to leaders not to let a name debar thee.

497. Clearly this allusion to His own station ties in directly with the overall them of the Súriy-i-Haykal.

498. While this apply to both Christians and Muslims, here Bahá'u'lláh seems to be alluding to the pope and Christian divines.

499. See John 8:1–30. Christ interferes with the stoning of the woman, thus preventing the Pharisees from carrying out the law of Moses according to Leviticus 20:10—one of the several laws of Moses that the Pharisees accused Christ of breaking, thereby laying the basis for having Him put to death.

500. This sort of rhetorical phrase by Bahá'u'lláh is used frequently in His Writings to indicate that because we cannot understand the end in the beginning of things, the laws He brings that may seem strange or restrictive are the most felicitous and profitable path for us, even though at the time we may not see the ultimate benefit or outcome of His guidance.

501. See Shoghi Effendi, *Promised Day*, 51.

502. This is likely a reference to His first letter and Napoleon III's subsequent response.

503. This is pointedly related to the theme of delegation of authority throughout the Súriy-i-Haykal.

504. Possibly the Ottoman Turks who had imprisoned Bahá'u'lláh.

505. Within the year Napoleon III was defeated at the Battle of Sedan (1870) and sent into exile.

506. Notice the legacy of Queen Marie of Romania as opposed to Napoleon III and how her name will endure and become exalted by virtue of her recognition of Bahá'u'lláh and her defense of her beliefs as a Bahá'í.

507. As I explain in the text, while paragarphs 200 to 205 are all written in the form of a prayer, I have considered them as three distinct prayers for ease of analysis.

508. Note that the text here does not point to a specific example; it may be that Bahá'u'lláh is making a general point to forestall any argument that persecution is deserved because of this or that specific allegation of wrongdoing by one of His followers. However, this may also be a gentle remonstrance for the Sháh's horrific persecution of the Bábís in 1852, when thousands were put to death, tortured, and imprisoned in retaliation for the conspiracy of a handful of deluded Bábís to assassinate the Sháh.

Bibliography

'Abdu'l-Bahá. *Light of the World: Selected Tablets of 'Abdu'l-Bahá*. Haifa, Israel: Bahá'í World Centre, 2021.

———. *Paris Talks: Addresses Given by 'Abdu'l-Bahá in 1911*. London, United Kingdom: UK Bahá'í Publishing Trust, 1972.

———. *Some Answered Questions*. Newly revised ed. Haifa, Israel: Bahá'í World Center, 2014.

———. *Tafsír-i-Hadith-i-Kuntu Kanzan Makhfíyyan* ("Commentary on the Islamic Tradition 'I was a Hidden Treasure'"). n.p., n.d.

———. *The Promulgation of Universal Peace. Talks Delivered by 'Abdu'l-Bahá During His Visit in the United States and Canada in 1912*. Comp. Howard McNutt. Wilmette, IL: US Bahá'í Publishing Trust, 1982.

Agrippa, Henry Cornelius. *Three Books of Occult Philosophy*. Translated out of the Latin into the English Tongue by J.F. Book II. London: Gregory Moule, 1651.

Amanat, Abbas. *Resurrection and Renewal: The Making of the Bábí Movement in Iran, 1844-1850*.

Anonymous. *Sir Gawain and the Green Knight*. In *The Norton Anthology of English Literature*, 6th ed., vol. 1, ed. M. H. Abrams. New York: W. W. Norton & Company, 1993.

The Báb. *Selections From the Writings of the Báb*. Haifa, Israel: Bahá'í World Centre, 1982. Los Angeles: Kalimát Press, 2005.

Bahá'u'lláh. *The Call of the Divine Beloved: Selected Mystical Works of Bahá'u'lláh*. Haifa, Israel: Bahá'í World Centre, 2019.

———. *Epistle to the Son of the Wolf*. Wilmette, IL: US Bahá'í Publishing Trust, 1988.

————. *Gems of Divine Mysteries*. Haifa, Israel: Bahá'í World Centre, 2002.

————. *Gleanings from the Writings of Bahá'u'lláh*. Wilmette, IL: US Bahá'í Publishing Trust, 1990.

————. *The Summons of the Lord of Hosts*. Haifa, Israel: Bahá'í World Centre, 2002.

————. *Prayers and Meditations by Bahá'u'lláh*. Wilmette, IL: US Bahá'í Publishing Trust, 1987.

————. *Tablets of Bahá'u'lláh Revealed After the Kitáb-i-Aqdas*. Wilmette, IL: US Bahá'í Publishing Trust, 1988.

————. *The Hidden Words of Bahá'u'lláh*. Wilmette, IL: US Bahá'í Publishing Trust, 1985.

————. *The Kitáb-i-Aqdas*. Haifa, Israel: Bahá'í World Centre, 1992.

————. *The Kitáb-i-Íqán*. Wilmette, IL: US Bahá'í Publishing Trust, 1989.

————. *The Proclamation of Bahá'u'lláh to the Kings and Leaders of the World*. Wilmette, IL: US Bahá'í Publishing Trust, 1978.

Balyuzi, Hasan M. *Bahá'u'lláh, The King of Glory*. Oxford, UK: George Ronald Publisher, 1980.

Bush, George H. W. "The Other 9/11: George H. W. Bush's 1990 New World Order Speech." *The Dallas Morning News*.

Faizi, Abu'l-Qasim. "Explanation of the Symbol of the Greatest Name." In *Conqueror of Hearts*. New Delhi, India: Bahá'í Publishing Trust, 1968.

Ghasem Bayat, Mohamad. "An Introduction to the Súratu'l-Haykal (Discourse of The Temple)." In *Lights of Irfan*, bk 2. Wilmette, IL: Irfan Colloquia, 2001.

Gorbachev, Mikhail. "When the Pandemic Is Over, the World Must Come Together." *Time*. Apr. 15, 2009.

Harmon, William and C. Hugh Holman. *A Handbook to Literature*, 8th edition. New Jersey: Prince Hall, 2000.

Hatcher, John S. *God's Plan for Planet Earth and for Your Neighborhood*. Wilmette, IL: Bahá'í Publishing, 2018.

————. *The Ascent of Society: The Social Imperative in Personal Salvation*. Wilmette, IL: Bahá'í Publishing, 2007.

————. *The Face of God Among Us: How the Creator Educates Humanity*. Wilmette, IL: US Bahá'í Publishing Trust, 2010.

———. "The Metaphorical Nature of Physical Reality." *Bahá'í Studies*, vol. 3. Ottawa, Canada: Association for Bahá'í Studies, 1977.

———. *The Ocean of His Words: A Reader's Guide to the Art of Bahá'u'lláh*. Wilmette, IL: US Bahá'í Publishing Trust, 2002.

———. *The Purpose of Physical Reality*. Wilmette, IL: US Bahá'í Publishing Trust, 2005.

Hatcher, John S., Amrollah Hemmat and Ehsanollah Hemmat. "Bahá'u'lláh's Symbolic Use of the Veiled Ḥúríyyih," *Journal of Bahá'í Studies* 29, no. 3 (2019): 9–41.

The Holy Bible. Nashville, TN: Thomas Nelson Publishers, 1984.

The Holy Qur'án. Trans. Abdullah Yusuf Ali. Elmhurst, NY: Tahrike Tarsile Qur'án, Inc., 2001.

Hornby, Helen Bassett, comp. *Lights of Guidance: A Bahá'í Reference File*. New Delhi, India: Bahá'í Publishing Trust, 1994.

Milton, John. "Paradise Lost." In *The Complete Works of John Milton*. Ed. Douglas Bush. Boston, MA: Houghton Mifflin Company, 1965.

Nabíl-i-'Azam [Muhammad-i-Zarandí]. *The Dawn-Breakers: Nabíl's Narrative of the Early Days of the Bahá'í Revelation*. Trans. and ed. Shoghi Effendi. Wilmette, IL: US Bahá'í Publishing Trust, 1996.

Pius IX. *Ubi Primum* [Encyclical Letter on the Immaculate Conception].

Plato. "The Apology." In *The Dialogues of Plato*, volume 1. Trans. Benjamin Jowett. New York: Random House, 1937.

Richter, David H. *The Critical Tradition*, 2nd ed. New York: Bedford, 1997.

Saiedi, Nader. "From Oppression to Empowerment." *Journal of Bahá'í Studies* 26, no. 1–2 (2016): 27–53.

Scholarship. A compilation of extracts on scholarship from the Writings of Bahá'u'lláh, 'Abdu'l-Bahá, Shoghi Effendi, and the Universal House of Justice. Compiled by the Research Department of the Universal House of Justice. Mona Vale, Australia: Bahá'í Publications Australia, 1995.

Shakespeare, William. "The Tragedy of Hamlet, Prince of

Denmark." In *The Complete Works of Shakespeare*. Ed. Hardin Craig. Northbrook, IL: Scott, Foresman and Company, 1951.

Shoghi Effendi. *Citadel of Faith: Messages to America, 1847-1957.* Wilmette, IL: US Bahá'í Publishing Trust, 1980.

———. *God Passes By.* Wilmette, IL: US Bahá'í Publishing Trust, 1979.

———. *High Endeavours: Messages to Alaska.* Alaska: National Spiritual Assembly of the Bahá'ís of Alaska, 1976.

———. *Messages to the Bahá'í World: 1950-1957.* Wilmette, IL: US Bahá'í Publishing Trust, 1971.

———. *The Advent of Divine Justice.* Wilmette, IL: US Bahá'í Publishing Trust, 1990.

———. *The Promised Day is Come.* Wilmette, IL: US Bahá'í Publishing Trust, 1980.

———. *The World Order of Bahá'u'lláh.* Wilmette, IL: US Bahá'í Publishing Trust, 1991.

———. *Unfolding Destiny: The Messages from the Guardian of the Bahá'í Faith to the Bahá'í Community of the British Isles.* London, United Kingdom: UK Bahá'í Publishing Trust, 1981.

Taherzadeh, Adib. *The Revelation of Bahá'u'lláh.* 4 vols. Oxford, United Kingdom: George Ronald Publisher, 1996-2001.

Tennyson, Alfred. "Ulysses." In *Poems by Alfred Lord Tennyson*, vol. 2. London: Macmillan and Co., 1893.

The Universal House of Justice. *A Wider Horizon, Selected Letters 1983-1992.* Riviera Beach, FL: Palabra Publications, 1992.

———. *Issues Related to the Study of the Bahá'í Faith: Extracts from Letters Written on Behalf of the Universal House of Justice.* Wilmette, IL: US Bahá'í Publishing Trust, 1999.

Yeats, William Butler. "The Second Coming." In *Poems*. Ed. Richard J. Finneran. London, United Kingdom: Palgrave Macmillan UK, 1991.

Index

5 joys of Mary

the Annunciation
the Nativity
the Resurrection
the Ascension
the Assumption
(her ascent to heaven

CPSIA information can be obtained
at www.ICGtesting.com
Printed in the USA
BVHW051729191222
654561BV00004B/71